You Can Alway~ the Comp~

Read What These Enthusiastic People Are Saying:

"This is required reading for women of all ages and backgrounds who want to live the life they were meant to live—a life of creativity, fulfillment, passion and joy. Sage advice, indeed!"

Maureen McGovern
Recording Artist, *The Music Never Ends,*
With a Song in My Heart

"There are so many self-help books to choose from, it's bewildering. However, once in a while a classic comes along that stands out. *The Power of Focus for Women* is way above the crowd."

Patty Aubery
President, Chicken Soup for the Soul Enterprises

"This excellent book will give solace to women from all walks of life because of its practical, informative nature. It directly hits the mark—I especially liked the chapter on forgiveness."

Dr. Stephen R. Covey
Author, *The 7 Habits of Highly Effective People*

"One of women's greatest assets and liabilities is our ability to multi-task. We often take on too much and the end result is that many things don't have the power and punch that a concentrated focus would create. *The Power of Focus for Women* is a 'must-have' book for every woman."

Dr. Judith Briles
Author, *The Confidence Factor*

"Every once in a while you read a book that truly change your life. This is one of those books."

Kelly Courtne
Finance Manager, Crowfoot BMV

"If you're looking for a book that will get your attentio and challenge you to get your life on track—this is it!"

Carolyn Christiso
Author, *Wake Up, It's Later Than You Thin*

"*The Power of Focus for Women* helped me to trust mysel more, and in return, I discovered a great deal about mysel I am now taking greater risks, finding more balance an believing in my abilities to achieve a brighter future. I feel have a whole new perspective on my life, and that's exciting.'

Shirley MacInni
Trainer and Coordinator for At-Risk Adult Program

"Great book! Fran Hewitt is one of those rare individuals who can help people see where they are stuck, and then provide simple and practical solutions to set them free."

Jack Canfield
Co-founder, *Chicken Soup for the Soul* series

"I was such a people-pleaser before. This book taught m about integrity and the importance of being 'real'. I highl recommend *The Power of Focus for Women* to everyone who i ready for a change in their life."

Rae McCartne
Customer Service Agent, Air Canad

"Required reading for women of all ages and backgrounds This book shows you how to see yourself, be yourself an free yourself from everything that is holding you back!"

Kelly Bouchar
President, Bouchard Internationa

"Doing the Action Steps was a real eye-opener for me. I am now back on track and I have choices again!"

Sonja Gosteli
Vice President, Globi Web Solutions

"The Power of Focus for Women is a tremendous practical resource for women who want to be unstoppable. Lots of solid information with wonderful, inspiring stories."

Cynthia Kersey
Author, *Unstoppable*

"Living a real and balanced life is a challenge for all women. This book brings us face to face with the issues that have blinded us, and gives women permission to re-discover and re-write the script!"

Nola Peterson
Office Manager, Personal Health Planning Institute

"This book takes an up-close and personal approach to the issues we women face today and provides easy, effective solutions to help us create happier, healthier and more real lives. It's a must-read for all women."

Deborah Darling
Author, *Upsize Woman in a Downsize World*

"With humor and heart and using uncommon common sense, Fran Hewitt looks at the usual in unusual ways."

Rosita Perez
President, Creative Living Programs Inc.

"This book gets to the heart of matters, not only for women, but for mankind in general. It addresses the issues in an easy-to-read and understandable format—and provides meaningful answers for overcoming lifetime issues."

Patti Anderson
Account Executive, Shine FM

"So much common sense and so easy to read."

Sissy Grapes
Author, *Inspired Success*

"Let's hope every husband, brother, father or work associate who sees this book lying around will pick it up, because once they have read the first three pages they will be hooked. Even though this book is designed for women, it is equally valuable for their male counterparts."

Patricia Fripp
Sales Presentation Coach

"I am blown away by the caring and the intimacy that this book affords the reader. If you have ever longed for more but were unsure how to have it, this book is your roadmap!"

Barry Spilchuk
Author, *Let's Talk...About Relationships*

"This book has given me the tools to help me believe in myself. I've taken the courage to look inside, and I like what I see."

Debbie Henders
Home Business Owner

"It's so easy to get caught up in the rat race. *The Power of Focus for Women* has helped me to concentrate on what I want from my life. I am now more focused on who I am as a person, and on my most important relationships."

Susan Nicoll
Instructor, Early Childhood Training

"It's usually a struggle for me to sit down and read a book. I was a bit skeptical but gave the book a chance. I found it clear, concise, to the point, organized, easy and interesting to read. What I read I found to be real. Even better, the solutions were attainable. I am buying copies for my staff, friends and family."

Connie Quinton
Co-owner, Distinctive Catering Inc.

"This book will inspire you to discover your full potential as a woman."

Sharlene Massie
CEO, About Staffing Ltd.

"Buy this book now, put your name on it and don't lend it to anyone. You'll never get it back if you do!"

Erin Saxton
President, The Idea Network, Inc.

"Valuable advice and practical pointers for the demands of today's complicated life. This is a book that every woman needs to read."

Eileen McDargh
Author, *The Resilient Spirit*

"At last! A healthy dose of good old common sense. The eminently practical Action Steps that will help you create excellent balance. A must for women in business."

Irene Besse
President, Irene Besse Keyboards Ltd.

"Every woman should read this. And it wouldn't hurt if some men did, too!"

Nancy Mitchell Autio
Co-Author, *Chicken Soup for the Christian Woman's Soul*

"Congratulations, Fran! Your personal story and life lessons that are woven through the pages of this book will inspire readers to get up, move up, and stay up."

Earlene Vining
International Author and Speaker

"Revealing, probing and persuasive! This absorbing book has inspired me to challenge my self-sabotaging behaviors. One of the most rewarding and enlightening gifts for personal growth I have treated myself to in a long time."

Marie Wallace
President, Wallace Design and Space Planning Inc.

"*The Power of Focus for Women* clearly showed me that I alone am responsible for the quality of my life, and for teaching my children that attitude is everything."

Anna Alton
Single Parent

"Are you ready to be empowered? In this book, Fran's words of wisdom are delivered with passion along with down-to-earth techniques that will release your personal power."

Penny Kelly
Global Future Executive Senior Director, Mary Kay Cosmetics

"This book illustrates why and how 'laser focus' is the power that will set you free."

Dr. Denis Waitley
Author, *The Psychology of Winning*

The Power of FOCUS for Women

Fran Hewitt
Les Hewitt

Health Communications, Inc.
Deerfield Beach, Florida
www.hci-online.com

To preserve confidentiality, various names have been changed in this manuscript.

Library of Congress Cataloging-in-Publication Data

Hewitt, Fran, 1953-
　　Power of focus for women: how to live the life you really want / Fran Hewitt,
Les Hewitt.
　　　　p.　cm.
　　ISBN 0-7573-0114-2
　　1. Success—Psychological aspects.　II. Hewitt, Les.　III. Title.

BF637.S8 C2775 2000
158.1—dc21　　　　　　　　　　　　　　　　　　　　　　　　99-089886

Publisher:　Health Communications, Inc.
　　　　　　　3201 S.W. 15th Street
　　　　　　　Deerfield Beach, FL 33442-8190

Cover design and inside text design/layout by
Gail Pocock, Bulldog Communications, Inc. (403) 228-9861.

Fran

To Les, my wonderful husband, who
has always believed in me.
Thank you for giving me wings to fly.

To my magnificent children,
Jennifer and Andrew.
You are the treasure of my life.

Les

To Fran, an amazing partner, wife,
mother and role model.
Your ability to focus is awesome.

To Rosita Perez, and all of the other
courageous women who continue to
share their unique 'music' with
the rest of the world.

CONTENTS

ACKNOWLEDGMENTS

Some people say publishing a book is like giving birth for the first time. At the beginning you don't know for sure what the newborn will look like or whether it will receive all-around approval. Months before the due date there is anxiety, stress, uncertainty, and sometimes panic. When the delivery day is nigh, pressure increases and it seems the 'baby' will never arrive on time.

During this project, I went through all of these emotions. There were times when I was frustrated, unsure, and days when self-doubt was almost overwhelming. Having the support of a great team is the main reason *The Power of Focus for Women* is now a reality. I have many people to thank. First, to Les, my wonderful husband and co-author for his continued faith and incredible support from start to finish. I love you.

A very big thank you to Lynn Moerschbacher at the Achievers Canada office, for a wonderful job of typing, coordinating, and working the extra hours. How you deciphered Les' hand-written scrawl is a mystery! Thanks to Georgina Forrest who doubled up on typing, as well as the demanding job of obtaining permissions, sourcing the cartoons and ensuring feedback was on time. Thanks for keeping us organized, too. Our editors Elissa Collins Oman and Rod Chapman did an amazing job. Thank you, Rod, for being willing to burn the midnight oil during the last few weeks. A special word of thanks to Gail Pocock who did a fine job on the cover design and the inside text and layout. We both appreciate your patience, cooperation and commitment during the fifteen-hour days near the end. Thanks also to Sue Krawchuk for the initial work on the cover, and to Chris Smith for her muscle-testing expertise. A rousing cheer for our wonderful Readers Panel who diligently scrutinized every aspect of the manuscript and provided invaluable feedback: Anna Alton, Bonnie Elliot, Carolyn Christenson, Farhanna Dhalla, Georgina Forrest, Luise Kinsman, Verna Masuda and Susan Harris.

We appreciate our staff at Achievers, in particular Jean Romain who kept the administration department running smoothly. Thanks to Dave Harris for forging ahead with new projects in sales and marketing. Another key player we wish to acknowledge is our corporate consultant Glenn Huber, who implemented several new systems in our absence. Gratitude is also expended to Carol Stevens for ensuring our accounting was always in order.

Thanks to all of my team who have willingly given of their time and hearts in The Inner Circle Workshops: Eileen Head, my right-hand girl who has encouraged me so much over the years; Sally Adams who has kept me organized; Cyndy Watts for her warm heart and compassion; and all the others who have faithfully supported the work. To Peggy McGinn who keeps our light shining south of the border in Colorado—thank you for your faith and dedication.

Jennifer and Andrew, you make me proud to be your mother. Thank you for your patience and understanding during this project. Dad, I love you. So much of my life journey has involved finding that love—thank you. To my siblings, Catherine, Trish, Anna, Geraldine and Liam, and all of my extended family—I am blessed to have you in my life.

Over the years Les and I have also been blessed with many wonderful teachers and mentors, too numerous to mention here. However, a special word of gratitude goes to Jack Canfield, Barry Spilchuk, Mark Victor Hansen, Jim Rohn, Rosita Perez, Eileen McDargh; also George Addair, Valerie Morse, Peter Daniels, Ed Foreman, Earlene Vining, Glenna Salsbury and Patricia Fripp. Your encouragement and wisdom has played a major role in our growth. A very big thank you to the wonderful staff at Health Communications, Inc., for the opportunity to produce this book: Publisher Peter Vegso and his executive assistant Pat Holdsworth, Tom Sand, Terry Burke, Kim Weiss, Bret Witter, Lori Golden and Tom Galvin. A special word of praise to senior editor Allison Janse for your expert guidance, patience and understanding.

Finally, Les and I extend our heartfelt gratitude to all of those courageous women who shared their stories, provided inspiration and the indisputable evidence that proves—when you take a leap of faith you *can* live the life you really want.

How To Get The Most Out Of This Book

As you read, have a pen or highlighter beside you, and a notepad, Capture your best ideas immediately. You can read the book in it's entirety and complete the Action Steps later, or, if you prefer, complete one chapter at a time along with the Action Steps.

Use *The Power of Focus for Women* as a permanent resource to guide you in the weeks, months and years ahead.

Here's another tip. Consider setting up a book club with friends who are interested in personal development. Read one chapter every week and then get together for lunch or a coffee to discuss what you read. You can be sure the conversation will be stimulating!

I pulled the seatbelt across his frail body and buckled him in. The long illness had taken its toll. He looked half his normal size. The hospital had granted my father a day pass so I could take him home for a few hours. Looking at his shrunken, eighty-two-year-old frame, I was moved to tears. I wondered how I could ever have been afraid of this man. Yet for many years that had been my truth.

The illness had robbed him of his strength and power. However, two wonderful gifts had gradually taken root in his heart—humility and gratitude. The hard edges were gone. In his lucid moments at the hospital, my siblings and I would sit around his bed like hungry chicks, waiting to be fed a few words of love. Now here was my Dad sitting obediently beside me. Like a child on a field trip, he was delighting in every little thing—music on the radio, warm sun on his face, flowers in the gardens—missing nothing. Then it happened! I wish I could have captured the moment on video to replay over and over. I had waited my entire life for this. He turned to me and said, "Fran, I want you to know how proud I am of you. I love you." Those elusive words hung sweetly in the air between us, until I quickly grabbed them and tucked them into my heart.

> *In a moment a wound can be healed, in a*
> *moment a heart can be opened.*

> —Teresa Huggins/Ken Johnston
> (From the song, *In a Moment*)

I WAS FORTUNATE TO HEAR MY FATHER say those words. Many people never get to enjoy that privilege. In my work as a facilitator, I meet women from all walks of life who know the pain of this lack of validation. Many feel unloved and unworthy and therefore have difficulty sustaining relationships and living a joy-filled life.

This book is about validation, and the many other issues that are important to women. It's about the courage, joy, pain and burdens that will move you ahead—or hold you back—from living the life you really want. It's also about the power of focus. You'll learn how to set new boundaries and exciting goals that will boost your confidence, enrich your most important relationships and significantly free up your time.

This book is for all women. It will meet you wherever you are in life. No matter what circumstances you are facing, you will find value here. I say that with all sincerity, because the focusing strategies you are about to learn have dramatically changed my own life for the better. The ideas in this book evolved over time, as I successfully overcame significant personal challenges and heard the stories of many remarkable women who have done the same. I have been honored to meet some of these heroes in the course of my work during the last twenty years. You will be introduced to several of them as we go along.

Before we start, let me give you a little background. I was born and raised in Northern Ireland. Growing up in a family of six children, it was difficult to feel special and loved. Everyone was vying for center stage. My mother was a country woman and understood the demands of hard work. With six children, she never stopped. My father was the breadwinner. He was short on patience and frequently exploded in outbursts of anger. I feared him and his temper throughout most of my growing years.

In the late fifties and sixties punishing children at home and school, especially with the cane, was normal practice. In my early schooling I lived a five-year nightmare, putting up with regular caning and humiliation at the whim of my teachers. Perhaps I suffered more because of my sensitive disposition. Nevertheless, these experiences traumatized me for many years. Fighting low self-esteem became one of my major battles.

At the age of eleven I was sexually abused by a family friend, someone I trusted. I couldn't tell anyone. With nowhere to turn, I stuffed the pain inside and covered my shame with silence.

The war in Northern Ireland, or The Troubles as they were called, started when I was thirteen. Tension built up at home. A new layer of fear hovered over our family life. I would hear the bombs exploding at night. My father started carrying a gun. A knock at the door would send the family into panic, and I was convinced that my father would be shot.

Despite all this, my parents sacrificed financially to send me to a good school. With a fresh start and new teachers, I eventually found an academic footing. I went on to college and my first career, radiology. I worked at the Royal Victoria Hospital, located in the heart of one of the most troubled areas in Belfast. It was a danger zone, and more than once I was caught in gunfire as I left work. Luckily, I survived. On one occasion I found myself looking down the barrel of a shotgun in the hands of a cocky teenager who was hijacking the bus I was on. During this time I was lonely, and found the attention of the British soldiers flattering when they came in with the ambulances. I risked my life going to dances at the barracks. It was foolish, but I was a typical teenager who thought nothing bad could ever happen to her.

At the hospital, I saw first-hand what war could do to the human body. I witnessed a depth of suffering and anguish beyond comprehension—people hating people with their narrow-mindedness, neighbors turning on neighbors. After I lost a friend in a devastating explosion I realized how numb I had become to the pain around me. It was time to get out.

I met Les, my husband-to-be, on a blind date. After our engagement we decided to emigrate to Canada. My life was to start over at twenty-one. We were married two years later in picturesque Banff, Alberta, and I was happy.

By the age of twenty-nine I had two beautiful children, Jennifer and Andrew. Les had started his own seminar business, and I was exposed to self-development training every month. I relished the positive environment and the opportunity to learn. During that time I was concerned about my children's future. I wanted to be the best mother I could be, so I read every book on the subject and enrolled in every parenting course. After that I attended university and was soon facilitating my own parenting courses.

Teaching parenting to groups of young mothers was very rewarding. It surprised me how quickly these women opened up, wanting to talk about some of the more personal issues they were facing. This gave me the first taste of my current vocation—but it took many years to unfold.

A few years later, life threw me a curve ball. At thirty-three I developed breast cancer. Like many women before me, this was the biggest challenge I had ever faced. The cancer was in the advanced stages and the prognosis was serious. I was told my life expectancy was no more than five years. Once again, I was plunged into a pit of fear. This time, however, I felt there was no escape. In retrospect, my battle with cancer provided the impetus I needed to change, to begin living life to its fullest extent. Hidden beneath the fear and the pain was a fire waiting to be ignited, a passion waiting to be released.

Today, having lived long after my supposed expiry date, I am passionate about my work. For more than twenty years I have been involved in personal growth and the study of human behavior. During that time I've participated in more than 500 programs and facilitated numerous workshops for women.

Writing books, teaching seminars and facilitating workshops now provides me with a strong sense of purpose and gives my life meaning and joy. My programs are highly interactive and experiential. In each workshop I have the opportunity to spend three full days with fifteen to twenty women from all walks of life. It's incredibly rewarding to help these women become aware of their stumbling blocks, to facilitate healing, and to open their hearts to the possibilities of a passionate, joyful life. I feel privileged to do this work. In these workshops many of the same issues come up repeatedly—challenges with an unhealed past, limiting beliefs, abuse, feelings of low self-worth. Working with these hurting and courageous women gave me the inspiration to write this book.

They say teachers learn the most. Over the years I've gradually learned to embrace—and overcome—my own painful past. Without this learning I would not feel qualified, or have the audacity to teach others about life. I do not pretend to know anything I have not experienced myself.

My own journey has given me empathy, understanding and compassion for others. These are the foundation of my work today. I have written this book with every woman in mind, and the many challenges we all face in this increasingly complex world.

We'll start by looking at change. Many people fear change, yet it is essential if you want to see improvements in your life. Together we'll look at all the ways fear can hold us back, and how to get past it. Fear was one of my earliest challenges. I discovered that stepping into the fear was the best way to overcome it.

Is there something you'd like to change? Are you reluctant to take the risk? Later in this book I'll share a little-known formula called Three Steps No Failure. It will make the change process easier for you.

We'll build on this foundation by tackling some big issues. Authenticity is one of the biggest. In my experience the more authentic you can be, the more powerful you will feel. You'll learn about being real, about removing the masks behind which you hide. Being your real self can be so freeing.

Self-esteem, another major issue for many women, affects every aspect of your life. You'll discover how to build healthy self-esteem, from the inside out. I've also discovered that there are four deadly burdens that will drain your energy:

perfectionism, guilt, worry and resentment. You'll learn how to release all of these negative forces. No matter what life throws your way, you'll have the confidence and ability to bounce back quickly.

Time pressures and the sheer busyness of life today are making many women desperate to find some measure of balance for themselves. Do you ever feel stressed trying to juggle everything on your to-do list? Chapter Four is all about balance. Reading it will solve this issue for you, and help restore your sanity.

Another area in which almost all women need help is setting boundaries. Learning to say no is essential, especially when we are facing so many commitments and responsibilities. I used to struggle with this. Now I am a strong advocate of setting boundaries—they provide freedom. When you consciously set healthy boundaries, you will have more time for you. Giving up the need to please others is a way to reclaim your life. This book will show you how to do this, guilt-free. As a bonus, you will have much better communication and openness with your family and co-workers.

Personal image, health issues and concerns about money can create even more stress. You'll learn how to disengage from media pressure and get back to good, common sense basics. Chapter Seven will help you gain a healthy lifestyle and financial strength. To conclude, we'll explore the subjects of happiness and living on purpose. Would you like more love and joy in your life? Are you looking for more meaning and fulfillment? These powerful topics will inspire you.

I've asked Les, my husband and co-author who wrote the first book in this series, *The Power of Focus*, to offer a man's perspective about these issues. Women sometimes have difficulty figuring out why men think the way they do, and vice versa. By the time we are finished, you'll have a better understanding. You can use this inside information to enhance your communication with the men in your life, at home and in the workplace.

Women often feel they need permission to focus on themselves. We think that it's selfish, or self-centered, to put ourselves first. Let me assure you that it's okay to work on your own life, to improve, to learn, to become all you can be. When you feel good about yourself, all of your other relationships have a better chance of reaching their full potential.

This book is about you. It's for you, but it will also be up to you. The rewards you receive from implementing these ideas are your responsibility. Use *The Power of Focus for Women* as a resource. You can tap into it over and over again. Whether you are looking to heal a relationship with an aging parent like I was, or to venture into a new business opportunity, or simply to enjoy each day to the fullest, make a commitment now to follow through. The Action Steps at the end of each chapter will facilitate your progress.

Give yourself permission to dream. As you step into the future with faith and new hope, allow me to be your guide and walk by your side. My wish is that you will be truly enriched in the weeks, months and years ahead. Let's get started!

Sincerely,

Fran Hewitt

Climb Out
of Your Box!

*When we are no longer able to change
a situation, we are challenged
to change ourselves.*

—Viktor E. Frankl

I felt hopeless. I was miserable.
Fear and the consequences of not making a decision were
crippling my life. I had known for more than a year that I
needed to move on. But every day, bored and reluctant,
I would drag myself to the office. Somehow the familiar
routine was easier to cope with than exploring the unknown.
I rationalized the situation by telling myself that being
an administrative assistant wasn't a bad job. That was true—
it just wasn't the best job for me. What I wanted was to be
challenged more, to use my creativity and my teaching skills.
The daily routine of pushing paper and sitting at a computer
most of the day was draining the life out of me. I felt boxed
in and needed to climb out of the box. I stayed because I had
convinced myself that I was indispensable. I justified how
leaving was not an option because I would be letting my
husband Les down. It was his company and the business was
at a critical stage in its growth.

Unknown to him, however, I was falling apart. I was good at covering up my true feelings. Then one day I hit rock bottom—my Day of Desperation. I was so overwhelmed that all I could do was lock myself in our bedroom. Next to a window that overlooks our backyard sits a comfy, overstuffed chair. When our children were young I would read to them in this chair and cradle them in a soft blanket. I call it my 'quiet place'. This is where I retreat to think, read, pray, and on this day of depression, to cry. It seemed that I had everything—a wonderful husband, great kids, financial success, health—and yet, I had never been so frustrated and miserable. In desperation, I begged God to help me. The tears flowed freely. Isolated from the rest of the world and weary from months of anxiety, I sank into the depths of sorrow and fell asleep.

The words, "Call Marie!" woke me with a start. "What was that?" I thought.

"Call Marie!" The message was clear, front and center in my mind, but I still didn't understand.

Marie was a friend, a single mom who had been widowed a few years earlier. She had two young children as well as a thriving interior design business. The demands of work and home life were challenging for her to say the least. I had no idea why I was to call Marie, nor what I was to say to her. I only knew that I had to call her. Before I lost courage I picked up the phone.

"Marie, you need me and I can help. I want to offer my time free of charge for a month, in return for learning all I can about your business. If after a month you feel I can be of value to you, then we can talk."

Did I say that? Where did that voice come from? As I set the phone down I was shaking, aghast at my audacity. This was so out of character for me.

HAPPILY, I DID CHANGE CAREERS. Amazingly, my husband's business didn't suffer when I left. The four years that I worked with Marie were the most challenging and rewarding years

I had ever experienced. I knew nothing about the business and Marie was a demanding employer. And because of that I learned new skills, discovered hidden talents and developed strength of character. I became more confident and outspoken. Looking back, my career change had nothing to do with interior design and everything to do with faith. You see, I had listened to my spirit in faith. I made the phone call even though I didn't know what was happening at the time. Now I believe it was all part of a much bigger master plan because it helped prepare me for the work I do today.

Change is something we all struggle with.
In this chapter we are going to uncover the major reasons why we don't like to change. We'll see clearly what holds us back, even when we know we need to step out in a different direction.

- What is it that holds us back?
- Why can some people adapt to change more easily?
- Why is it that we are able to make changes in one area of our life and not in other areas?

You'll learn all of this and more in the pages ahead.

Making changes provides an opportunity to dramatically better our lives. We can improve our health, relationships, career, income, level of happiness and our hopes for a more optimistic future. Making changes requires a conviction that we are making the right choices.

There are five major barriers that will stop you from moving forward. The first step is to become aware of the barriers that are holding you back. When you take the time to observe what is really going on, you will be in a better position to make wise decisions.

> *You cannot change your destination overnight,*
> *but you can change your direction.*

—Jim Rohn

3

The Five
BARRIERS

1. Coasting In Your Comfort Zone

We all love comfort but unfortunately it is one of the culprits that keeps us stuck. Even when we know we need to make changes, we often choose what feels safe and familiar instead of what we really want. We're great at making excuses, living in denial and justifying why we choose to stay stuck.

For years I was using a very old version of database software. I could manipulate that program to do everything I wanted. My familiarity with it helped me to move and update files with speed and accuracy. Then as my business grew, I realized I needed to upgrade. That meant learning a whole new software program. I started making excuses to avoid making the change. Now isn't a good time, I would need to take classes in the evening. The thought of leaving my comfort zone was very threatening. I'm sure you can relate.

It's not only computer software we hang on to in our desire to stay close to the familiar. We do it in other areas too; we take the same route to work every day, we shop at the same stores, we order the same items from the menu instead of selecting something different. Too many routines stop you from challenging yourself. It's pretty much the same thing day in day out. Choosing to stay in a comfort zone eventually restricts your capacity for life. Is that what you really want?

- How about requiring more of yourself so you can create better options?

- How about no longer waiting for someone else, or your life circumstances to change, before making a move?

Everything truly rewarding lies outside your comfort zone. The more you can stretch your capacity to experience a fuller life, the more rewarding life becomes. Constantly challenging your comfort levels will help you feel more alive, more passionate, and more confident about getting what you want. Understand, there are no reassurances, guarantees or parachutes to help you when you take the leap. But go ahead, leap anyway!

2. Beware Of Apathy and Indifference

Realizing your life is on hold because you are stuck in the comfort zone trap is quite different from another obstacle to change: apathy. Indifference and a lack of passion rob many women from taking calculated risks that will improve their circumstances. For some it's their life-load that's holding them back. They are burdened enough already.

Change for these women is just another thing to do. Many are shut down emotionally—life feels flat and joyless. They go about the motions of living, but they are dead inside. I call them the living dead. It's sad—dead at forty but not buried until they're eighty.

Perhaps you are thinking, there's no way I can get excited about my job. I challenge you to change that. Feeling indifferent or bored is not a good return on the many precious hours you invest at work. Our jobs need to be more fulfilling than just picking up a paycheck. Even the most menial work can become stimulating with the right attitude. What could you do to build on your enthusiasm and boost your energy?

Reignite the life inside you.
Banish indifference to sulk in the shadows.
Don't dare settle for a life of survival.
When you are worth so much more.

—*Fran Hewitt*

It saddens me to see so many women living this way. Helping them to reconnect with their emotions is inspiring, and it's a joy for me to witness their awakening in my workshops. They allow themselves to tap into their emotions and their whole demeanor changes. They sense there is new hope, that life can be different.

It's not only people who are overburdened that end up feeling apathetic and indifferent. Many working women would like to change their situation but they've stayed too long at the same job and eventually indifference sets in. This robs them of any remaining desire. They don't care anymore, they don't like their work, they become tired and numb. It's just a job. Be careful—when you are apathetic in one area of your life, it can soon spill into others.

I have noticed a huge shift in the business world away from human connectedness. Due to the amount of time spent in front of computers and using other technology, we no longer take the time to build relationships, especially at work. It's easy for many women to slip into apathy when no one cares or notices them anymore. In large organizations you can become a faceless entity. Many co-workers don't even know your name or what you do.

Why not care enough about yourself to make a change?

No matter how bad your situation is, know this—you can change it. Have faith and believe that things can be different. Then start taking the necessary action.

NEW LIFE BEGINS WHEN YOU WELCOME CHANGE

3. Fear

Fear usually appears when you are about to take a risk. The level of fear is proportional to the size of the risk. If you are making small changes you may not feel too fearful. However, if you are planning major life changes, your fear is likely to be much greater.

> Christy was ready for change. At twenty-nine, she was lonely and painfully stuck in her shyness. She was chastised regularly at an early age. "If you can't say anything intelligent, don't say anything at all," was the message she grew up with. She was also taunted at school for her speech impediment. "The other kids were so cruel they would imitate my lisp and call me Clispy."
>
> Now Christy was ready to stand up and speak out. She set a goal to speak to someone new every day. This may not seem like a huge risk, but for Christy it meant facing her biggest fear. She practiced by chatting to the teller at the bank and the clerk at the grocery store. She would sit on a park bench and talk to people passing by. She discovered that a smile gave her control over her anxiety, and she usually got one in return. Diligently, she kept to her plan and within a few weeks she felt like a different person. "I feel so brave! If I can do this, I can do anything. I still fight the anxiety but it no longer overwhelms me."

I used to think I was the only person who felt fear. For me it was fear of rejection and humiliation. I would watch other women excelling in their lives, going back to school, competing for a job position, doing public speaking, and think, "If only I wasn't so fearful, I could be just like them." Then after attending a seminar one day, I approached a wonderful speaker who had earned one of the highest awards in the professional speaking industry, the Council of Peers Award of Excellence (CPAE), and asked her if she ever felt fear. She blew me away with her reply: "All the time."

All the time? And she still did it? Then I repeated the same question to all those other "fearless" women who were doing so well. "Of course," they all replied. I finally got the message. They felt the fear and did what they wanted to do anyway. I knew then that I needed to confront my fear if I wanted to accomplish my goals.

What do you fear?

- REJECTION
- HUMILIATION
- FAILURE
- ABANDONMENT
- BEING JUDGED
- SUCCESS

What's at the top of your list?

The twin seductions of comfort and apathy can cheat you out of your life, and the fear factor can stop you dead in your tracks. However, I believe there are two other reasons why women do not embrace the power of change in their lives. First, deep down many do not have confidence in themselves or in their abilities. Second, they do not care enough about themselves to take a chance, to dream and to invest time in pursuing those dreams. These destructive patterns keep many women stuck forever. Sadly, they die with their music still locked inside them.

If you lack self-confidence, know that you are not alone. Nearly half of the women I meet say they feel the same way. The good news is that you can avoid making this a life sentence. We will be fully exploring these issues and many others in the chapters that follow. So have faith—soon you will have the answers.

*Everything you want is on the
other side of fear.*

—George Addair

4. Justifying Your Actions

Sometimes we don't want to open our eyes to reality because the truth is too painful. It's easier to justify and rationalize being stuck instead of making changes.

Have you ever known someone who could not manage her money? Her bills were never paid on time plus the credit cards were overused and abused. Yet she can justify spending the money she doesn't have because she's addicted to shopping. Just like fun-loving Nancy, a comic book character who's always in debt but can't seem to stay away from the stores.

"Girls, don't you just love to shop? Shop until you drop is my motto," says Nancy. "I can't get enough. The stores close before I have a chance to drop. I get an electric buzz just stepping inside the changing room with my selections. Excitement overwhelms me, my heart races with anticipation. I have a system of selection of course. It wouldn't do to buy on emotion or overspend. A girl needs to be a sensible shopper these days and that means keeping an eye on her wallet. Here is my selection system:

If the item looks absolutely darling on me—it's a yes.

If it's on sale—of course I choose it—I'm actually saving 30 to 50 percent and saving is good.

If the outfit goes with something else in my wardrobe— it's a yes because I get two outfits for the price of one.

If I look slimmer, younger, more vivacious—need I even say it… yes.

If the outfit is something I could wear to work; you know a girl can't have enough work clothes, they help advance you—move you up the ladder—which of course guarantees more money—yes!

See, I really am a sensible shopper!"

Nancy lives in a fantasy world. This habit of justifying compulsive shopping will eventually catch up with her. She may end up with lots of clothes in her closet but nothing in the bank. Obviously most women don't share Nancy's compulsiveness. Justification usually shows up in more practical situations. Take for instance my friend Eleanor. She's a successful litigation lawyer who's been in practice for twenty years. One day she told me she was bored and wanted out. She had lost all desire for her work. "I was so passionate after I passed the Bar, I want that back again." She shared how the work had become routine and she'd lost her competitive edge. Eleanor had a dream to leave the law firm and start her own business. Eleanor never left. When I met her six months later, she justified why she felt she couldn't make the change. "The money is so good and my family is used to the lifestyle. Both kids will need braces soon and John just bought that new SUV. It would be too hard on them if I was to change my career."

Don't allow your justification to get in the way of making the changes you want or need to make. Change is a process. It may take longer than you want but at least start with a plan.

5. Putting Things Off
If you hadn't already noticed, procrastination is another major roadblock to change. Do you ever put things off?

Just about everybody does, to some degree or another. Here's the crash course to discovering why we play this stressful game. Check the list and see where you show up on it.

- You're bored
- You are overwhelmed with work
- Your confidence has slipped
- You have low self-worth
- You are doing work you don't really enjoy
- You are easily distracted
- You are just downright lazy

Piers Steel knows a lot about procrastination.
An assistant professor at the University of Calgary's Faculty of Management, Steel, thirty-six, has spent more than three years conducting a "meta-analysis" of practically everything ever written on procrastination. He's pored over nearly 700 professional papers from the fields of psychology, economics, philosophy and sociology, and examined historical documents dating back 3,000 years. His conclusion? "Procrastination is our normal state of being," says Steel. "It's not procrastinating that requires effort."

How often have you put off some unpleasant or unrewarding task until it is nearly too late, or worse? The deadline looms, the pressure mounts, and finally you swing into action. In the end, more often than not, the deed gets done. But the stress is draining. You swear you'll never put yourself through that again, but the vow is soon broken. Why, oh why, do we keep doing this to ourselves?

We know that we should act, and that failing to do so will bring us grief. And yet we do nothing. "When we procrastinate, it's almost always about long-term objectives," says Steel. "Instead of attending to those, we go with what is more pleasurable or less painful right now."

Men are slightly more likely to procrastinate than women. Young people are far more likely to do so than their elders (high school and university students are among the worst offenders). Impulsive people are especially vulnerable, because they are so easily diverted. Different people procrastinate about different things. Workaholics, for example, almost always meet their job-related deadlines. But many of them will put off going to a doctor, doing their taxes or seeking counseling for a troubled marriage. Typically, people feel bad about their inaction. "Often they are struggling against it, much like an addiction," says Steel. "People will say, 'No matter what I do, I can't seem to stop putting things off.'"

So if you are saddled with the curse of procrastination, what can be done about it? There are, says Steel, several possible remedies. It helps to understand the link between energy levels and delay: the more tired you are, the more likely you are to dither. So get plenty of sleep and exercise and deal with particularly aversive tasks in the morning, when energy levels tend to be higher. Another tip is to break down large projects into several staggered goals; as you complete each one, you are motivated to tackle the others. Personal routines are also good. By establishing a set of steps for doing things automatically, there's less chance for diversion. Steel offers the example of brushing teeth: children have to be constantly reminded to do it, but by adulthood it's become an ingrained behavior.

Some very successful and creative people have been notorious procrastinators, says Steel. For example, Agatha Christie (1890–1976). Still the bestselling author of all time, Christie wrote some eighty books, which have sold an estimated two billion copies. She did so despite repeatedly putting off each new work. At the outset of a novel, Christie would be paralyzed with self-doubt and convinced she would never write again. Eventually, Christie recalled that she had endured, and overcome, such phases before. Procrastination would give way to her prolific pen.[1]

Changing Other
PEOPLE

Shortly after I got married, there was one thing I wished I could change about my husband—his propensity to procrastinate.

I rarely put things off because I dislike the burden of incompletion. It creates unnecessary pressure and zaps my joy for living. From my 'got it all together' superior perch, I would watch

---

[1] Source: *Maclean's* magazine

as my poor husband struggled with his piles of unfinished projects, only to see him get distracted and delay the inevitable once again.

"I can change this," I thought, "I'll help him clean up the backlog and he won't feel so overwhelmed. Then he'll discover the joy and lightness of being an ex-procrastinator. He'll never be the same!"

After many exhausting weeks of tidying up his office files and keeping correspondence up to date, I discovered that new procrastinations were showing up. Now it was travel schedules, car registration and magazine subscriptions. The more holes I would plug in the dyke, the more new holes would appear.

One day I had a revelation. He would never change! Well, why would he? After all, he had the luxury of his own live-in Molly Maid mopping up and cleaning after him. He had his own Rescue Rhonda keeping him happy and irresponsible. So I quit trying to change him.

Instead, I worked on me. Molly Maid and Rescue Rhonda were fired. I learned to say no, and released my guilt for not helping with his self-imposed prison. I even learned to close the door to his messy office. Did he immediately change? Of course not! But my life is just great, thank you.

> *The only time a woman succeeds in*
> *changing a man is when he's a baby.*
>
> —Natalie Wood

Perhaps you're thinking, if only my husband would change then I'd be happy, or if only my boss would change his ways, then work would become bearable. For years, I attempted to change my Dad. I thought if I could teach him to be more positive he would change his critical attitude. That way we'd both be happier. After years of encouragement and cajoling I finally came to this conclusion: You cannot change another person unless they are willing. Recently a woman approached me excitedly, saying, "My husband changed since I attended your workshop." His change of course was due to the changes she had made. When you make a shift, in all likelihood your partnership will be affected.

I meet women who are desperate to change their partners. They leave self-help books in the bathroom, drag them to seminars, workshops and retreats hoping that their men will change. If you put the same focus and energy into changing yourself, you'll probably have more success.

The Common Denominator
Are you stuck in repeating patterns? It's impossible to change your life if you keep on doing the same old things over and over again. Some women just keep recycling the same old rubbish!

- Debbie keeps dating the wrong type of men
- Tammy runs from one financial mess to another
- Barbara gets fired from her job about every six months

"No, I don't want to change you Darryl. But it sure would be great if you were completely different."

Imagine if you always went to the store on Friday night to buy groceries for the week. Then the store decided to change its hours, closing early on Friday, but you still kept showing up every Friday night to buy your groceries. That's ridiculous, you say. Of course it is. But do you get the point?

For things to change you've got to change otherwise nothing much will change.

—Jim Rohn

If you keep repeating the same old patterns the common denominator is obvious. It's you. You're it! Instead of wasting enormous amounts of energy hoping to change everyone and everything, start with changing yourself. Next time you feel stuck in a familiar pattern, ask yourself: How have I set this up so I'm having this experience again?

Change is difficult. My mentor Jim Rohn, whose ideas were a catalyst for many of my own changes, makes a simple but profound observation: There are two fundamental reasons that cause people to change—desperation or inspiration.

The Day of
DESPERATION

Some wake-up calls—such as a diagnosis from your doctor—hit you hard. My cancer diagnosis was totally unnexpected. These wake-up calls are automatic precursors to change. There are also times when your desperation peaks; when you finally have had enough:

- I'm sick of being tired and resentful
- I'm fed up with my mediocre life
- I'm finished with this abusive behavior

When this happens, something has to change for you—now, today! This is your Day of Desperation, the day that can turn everything around. This is the day you take the pain of your discomfort, the frustration of your disgust, and the fuel of your anger and use them as an impetus for change. You arm yourself with an attitude of rigid determination. "No matter what it takes, no matter how difficult it is going to be, I will not accept another day of this. Nothing will stop me."

And the day came when the risk to remain
tight in a bud was more painful than
the risk it took to blossom.

—Anaïs Nin

What a wonderful day! This Day of Desperation allows you to mentally re-frame your discomfort, pain or helplessness to one of new possibilities, freedom and empowerment. So the next time you feel strongly that something is totally unacceptable, be conscious that this could be your big day, an opportunity to break free of the shackles that are holding you back.

Joan had been unhappy for thirteen long years.
She had endured endless emotional, psychological, and financial abuse at the hands of her husband.

Marrying the man of her dreams at the tender age of twenty-one had turned into her worst nightmare. "How could I have misjudged someone this much?" she would wonder as she cried herself to sleep. The feeling of shame was overwhelming, especially when she thought about her two children who were caught up in the same cycle of grief and pain.

The insults and putdowns had escalated over the years, first privately and then in public. There was nowhere to hide. Joan became zombie-like, losing her sense of self. Any sliver of confidence was long gone; self-respect was something from another world. Her new reality was an inability to feel anything but fear. At first she asked herself, "Why me?" It would be easier to deny responsibility. Was it her fault that the man she loved had surfaced as a cold, menacing figure hell-bent on erasing her last remnants of sanity?

The gun he had left on the desk at home one day, with two boxes of bullets placed strategically beside it, was not a figment of her imagination. This was a cruel mental game. The discovery of his lengthy suicide note did nothing to quell her anxiety. Joan clearly recalls her Day of Desperation. "It actually happened at night. I was in bed half asleep when I had this sensation that someone else was in the room. My husband was standing at the side of the bed, motionless, just staring at me with a vacant look that masked the evil intent in his heart. After a moment he left without saying a word. My heart was thumping so loud I thought I would faint. Was he planning to get rid of me tonight, murder me in my own bed?"

"Then it hit me. The kids! In a panic, I raced to their bedroom and flung the door open. They were both fast asleep. I collapsed on the floor, weeping. And then something snapped inside me. I heard myself say, 'No more, I've had enough!' Gradually a calmness came over me. The decision was made. My life was going to change."

The lawyer Joan hired started divorce proceedings immediately, but this only escalated the abuse. Now it came in the form of venomous letters, twenty-two in all. As a form of defense, Joan's counsel advised her to respond. However, at $250 an hour the legal bills were climbing rapidly. Finally Joan said, "Let's focus on the proceedings and stop these expensive games."

Despite winning a court-sanctioned separation, her children were legally bound to visit their father every other weekend. Invariably they returned in tears, begging not to be sent back again. Enough was enough! It was time for Joan to take charge.

First, she fired her lawyer. Next, she studied at the courthouse library, learning how to file documents, understanding what each document was for. She also read up on court procedure and learned the correct terminology. She even filed three written complaints against her husband's lawyer. One of them stuck. Momentum was building. Soon after, she filed her own case and won.

There was no stopping now: her confidence was getting stronger. She filed a suit against her own lawyer for incompetence and won again. In the process her legal bills were totally erased. All told, she has represented herself in court on eleven occasions, and won every single time!

JOAN WAS ONE OF MY GRADUATES at a recent three-day workshop. This courageous woman summarizes her experience as follows: "The real win was when I regained control. Little by little I became the person I used to be. I now take full responsibility for my life. Since then, I have never looked back. Life does not present problems, only challenges, and this is the rule I live by. In fact, sometimes I look forward to the challenges!

"For anyone who doubts their own ability, remember this. Before lawyers became lawyers, or doctors became doctors, they were students in the very same education system that most of us belonged to. If they can be successful, so can we. In fact, if they really want to, women can do anything they choose."

What a great story. It makes you want to jump up and shout "Hallelujah!" Desperation can become the springboard for inspiration. Knowing this creates confidence. If you are currently battling discouragement and uncertainty, the first step is making the decision to change—then you take action. No more procrastination, justifying, rationalizing or worrying about consequences. Desperation is your friend. Embrace it, be thankful for it, and use it to catapult you out of your present dilemma so you can be free to create the life you really want and deserve.

> *Those who live passionately*
> *teach us how to love.*
>
> —Sarah Ban Breathnach

The Joy of
INSPIRATION

Even if it's desperation that motivates you to make changes, there's usually a silver lining when the worst is over. If you take the time to reflect, valuable lessons can be learned. However, a much healthier way to make changes is through inspiration.

How do you become inspired?

There are many ways. We get inspired by watching others. Sometimes it's the underdog, the person least likely to win a talent contest, a championship medal, or become successful in business, who proves everyone wrong! We love to encourage the person who has been given no chance but has the courage and determination to give it their best shot. Often these surprise winners light a fire in us. We think, if she can do it, why can't I? This can give you a boost to make the changes you want to make.

Look for other ways to be inspired. It could be a great book, an epic movie, beautiful art, music that moves you to tears, or a dramatic production that has you on your feet cheering at the end. Looking up to someone, such as a mentor who you respect and admire, can inspire you to be successful too.

One of the best motivators is to make a list of compelling goals. Paint a vivid picture of what you want and visualize what it will feel like when it becomes a reality. Inspiration will ignite your creativity and passion. Just thinking about the possibilities can make it difficult to sleep at night.

Support and Environment

The people you surround yourself with do make a difference. If you were brought up in a happy household where love and joy were plentiful, chances are you had the opportunity to test your strengths and weaknesses without fear of reprisal. And if you made a wrong decision it wasn't the end of the world. People who have strong networks—a loving family or a solid group of friends—seem to handle the ups and downs of life better than those who feel alone or who are lacking encouragement. Most women enjoy the support of other women. We like being together. There are lots of opportunities for this, including book clubs, business networks, and social clubs. Having a 'buddy' or focusing partner who you connect with once a week is a great way to help you stay accountable as you strive to accomplish an important goal or make changes.

Keep building your support systems. They are vitally important. Now let me introduce Anna Jarmics.

The small oval-shaped metal container was intriguing.

It was different, not like a normal toy. And she had found it first. Her brothers and sisters would be so envious. Ten-year-old Anna Jarmics bent down and picked up her new prize off the rubble-strewn pavement. Seconds later a blinding explosion propelled her several feet down the street. The previously un-detonated grenade had lain there undetected, one of the souvenirs in war-torn Hungary. Both of her hands were mangled, her life dramatically altered in an instant. It was 1945.

Anna was rushed to an army hospital three blocks away. She remained conscious. The doctors immediately amputated both of her hands just below the wrist. Times were tough and supplies were meager. She endured the traumatic procedures without anesthetic. Recovery was painful and slow. There were no rehab facilities in those days. Altogether she spent six months in hospital.

Now sixty-eight, Anna has never been bitter or angry about her misfortune. In fact she wouldn't even use the word misfortune in her vocabulary. What do you do when you're ten years old with no hands? Well, you go to school and you eventually learn how to pick up a pencil. Then, despite having no fingers or thumbs, you somehow learn to write. It's hard, and it takes persistence, but Anna is not a quitter. Never has been.

In 1956 she moved to England, got a job cleaning offices, married, and had three children. Her travels continued in 1968 when she immigrated to Canada. Anna wanted to drive her own car. With no hands? Impossible!

Anna Jarmics doesn't use the word impossible in her vocabulary either. The day of her driving test she said the instructor looked more nervous than she was. All the staff at the driving school were glued to the windows as she stepped into her vehicle. They were cheering when she returned, having passed on her first attempt.

When pursuing a job at a local hospital, she said to the skeptical human resources person, "Let me show you what I can do. I'll work two weeks for nothing, then you can give me a paycheck." She got the job. Anna is always looking for new challenges. She relishes change and looks at life as a series of positive opportunities. Among her long list of victories are several trophies she's won for target shooting. She garnered first, second and third prizes for her exquisite watercolor paintings, and she is considering an exhibition in the near future. She's also an accomplished calligrapher. There have been other physical challenges along the way. While working as a security guard, Anna broke her back, requiring two major operations before she was on her feet again.

You can add persistence to her list of qualities. She'll be the first to tell you she has a very definite competitive streak. And she has a can-do attitude. "I don't find anything difficult. I can do anything I want," she says.

Perhaps her crowning achievement is her twenty-year love affair with the game of darts. It started innocently enough, watching a friend play at a local Legion hall. He said, "You should play." So she did. Her very first throw was a bulls-eye and she has been winning ever since. In fact, several men refuse to play with her because she always beats them. Her many championship wins include a gold medal in darts at the Senior Olympics.

When asked what advice she would offer other women, particularly those struggling with change, Anna said this: "It's important to think for yourself. Buy a journal. Take time to write down your thoughts. Ask yourself questions. What bothers you most? Why? What can you do about it? Go back and read over your notes. It will give you clarity and help you make decisions."

Anna has learned to overcome her physical pain using mental strength instead of pills. She practices meditation and believes greatly in the power of prayer. "I leave it up to God. I always say, what will be, will be. I'm just having fun." Inspiring words from a very inspiring woman.

Do you approach change in a positive way, or do you react negatively when something unexpected happens? Your answers have a lot to do with your future success or lack of it. Sometimes, like Anna, we are jolted into change. Life has a way of doing that—it often happens when we least expect it. Although it can be scary, as Anna Jarmics discovered, it usually works out for the better.

NO MATTER WHAT HAPPENS

Live Life Fully

Selling Other People
ON CHANGE

Let's say you've decided to take action to make a specific change. Here's an important consideration: *who will be affected by this new behavior?*

Julie has just turned thirty and is married with kids. Her children are three, four and six years old and they have all been blessed with non-stop energy.

Julie has a part-time bookkeeping job and works out of her home. At the end of the day she's usually exhausted, but the feeling of being trapped at home has become her biggest challenge.

George, her husband, is busy running a landscaping business. His work often takes him into the evening. Julie would love just one night a week where she can be free to do something she really enjoys, without worrying about preparing meals and all of the other household chores.

She used to enjoy art so she decides to check out the courses at the local community college. There's one for oil painting, perfect! It's one night a week and will take six months to complete.

If you were Julie, how would you handle this potential new change that will definitely affect the family schedule? Would you:

A) Just announce one night that you've already
   enrolled and that everyone will have to look
   after themselves.

B) Reconsider. Maybe this is not the best time. After all, the kids are still young and need support. In a couple of years things will be better.

C) Set up a family council. Talk about how you're really feeling and explain the benefits everyone will receive if you take the course.

If you choose Option A, you will certainly get a reaction. There could even be endless debate and gnashing of teeth. But George may feel bad because you didn't include him at the outset—he was just informed.

If Option B is your decision, you are really selling out by justifying and rationalizing. This is a classic case of backward thinking (I don't deserve to be a priority in my own life).

Of course, Option C is your best bet. Everyone is included, you express your feelings, you'll have more energy, appreciate your family more and not resent being stuck at home all the time. It's a real win-win. The point is that when you want to make a definite change, it will probably affect other people either at work, in your family, or with a primary relationship. Always announce the change in the form of a benefit.

EXAMPLES

At home: (Mom to teenage kids)
"In order for me to prepare supper early so you can get to the ballgame on time, I need you to tidy up the kitchen before I get home."

At work: (Supervisor to staff)
"In order for us all to enjoy Friday afternoons off every week, we're suggesting starting work forty-five minutes earlier each day."

At home: (Woman to partner)
"In order for us to have our date night once a week, I need help with the chores."

We'll explore this more thoroughly when we talk about setting boundaries in Chapter Five.

©THE NEW YORKER COLLECTION, 1995. BRUCE ERIC KAPLAN

"I need a change. Normally, I just wear the faint odor of vague discomfort and unhappiness."

The 'Now' Generation

Sometimes we rush headlong into change and it's not always helpful. Thanks to technology, we live in a super-fast world of modems, e-mails, the Internet, cell phones and handheld organizers. This has its advantages.

The downside is that when we want something, we want it instantly. Our pace of life is changing dramatically. Where have patience and the ability to wait gone? We are becoming frenetic and stressed out, always racing to the finish line. We expect everything faster as we gulp down another instant meal. Quick, buy it now; nothing down, pay later.

Why have we bought into all this? It's called instant gain. We can own it today and worry about going broke later. Many people consider delayed gratification to be an old-fashioned value. But at what cost?

Check your family first. What message are you sending your children by giving them everything they want immediately instead of having them work toward a goal or save up for it? It's little wonder our society is becoming more impatient, narcissistic and self-centered. A word of caution—as you decide to make changes, check that your values and standards are not being sabotaged at the same time.

Change takes time. Especially if you want to change some old habits and replace them with new ones. Don't be too pressured by our hurry-up society and impatience to see results. Give change a chance.

Daniel Goleman in his best-selling book, *Emotional Intelligence,* offers more proof. His research shows that adults who had resisted temptation as early as age four, were more socially competent, personally effective, self-assertive and better able to cope with the frustrations of life.

A Man's Perspective Les Hewitt

Over the years I've had a few challenges with change. Procrastination is a tough habit to break and I'm still not out of the woods yet on this one.

However, I have made significant progress. In the hope that this will help you understand men better, let me explain one of the dilemmas of the male entrepreneur. Maybe you work with someone who owns their own business or are married to him. If not, you may cross paths in the future. The dilemma is this. Generally, we are great starters but very poor finishers. I know some businesswomen have the same struggles, but I think men create much bigger messes. A few years ago I had a great idea to develop a new product for my coaching program. I also had two major deadlines coming up that could not be missed. Now I was juggling three balls in the air. Of course the new product idea, being fresh and exciting, was taking a lot of my time and energy.

Some wise person once said that there is no such thing as an unrealistic goal, there are only unrealistic timeframes. How true! The inevitable happened. Running out of time I started dumping mini-projects on everyone around me. This caused a lot of stress in the office with everyone working extra hours and me outsourcing furiously. Somehow we met the deadline. Back then I would bring extra work home to Fran, hoping that she would do it for me. However, she has since become wise to this, and has established firm boundaries that have forced me to change my ways.

What's the point? Don't become a dumping ground for men who leave everything to the last minute. Say no. By doing so you will be forcing us to reconsider the error of our ways.

CONCLUSION

A ship that is anchored in the harbor is sheltered from the wind and rough seas. But it was not built to stay in the harbor. The ship only makes progress when it heads out to sea and loses sight of the shore.

Don't let the lure of comfort and safety rob you of what you want. Set your sail, move into open waters and steer ahead with confidence as the shore fades into the distance. If you feel anxious at the start, that's okay. Feel the fear and do it anyway.

Don't wait until desperation becomes the only way out. Instead, inspire yourself to change. Find your passion and stamp out procrastination and apathy forever. Make change your friend. That decision will enable you to live a fuller life.

ACTION STEPS

**Commitment
to Change**

These action steps are designed to help you implement the key strategies from this chapter. Pick the best time for this, then focus and follow through.

1. If you could make three changes that would significantly improve your life immediately, what would they be?

a) _____

_____

b) _____

_____

c) _____

_____

2. What is preventing you from taking action?

_____

_____

_____

_____

3. How do you rationalize and justify not making the changes you know you need to make?

_____

_____

_____

4. What's your greatest fear about making changes?

_____

_____

_____

5. If there was one thing you could do that would force you out of your comfort zone, and you knew you couldn't fail, what would it be?

_____

_____

_____

_____

_____

6. If you implemented the three changes you listed in Question One, what specific benefits would you enjoy as a result?

_____

_____

_____

7. Name three things you can do to take the first step towards reaching your new goals.

a) _____

_____

b) _____

_____

c) _____

_____

8. Name someone you trust, respect and like who would be an excellent focusing partner to keep you accountable. Set up an appointment to discuss this. Then put it into practice.

_____

It's Time
to Get Real

Can I ever know you or you know me?

—Sara Teasdale

She is the genuine article, authentic, true to life, straightforward, honest and very much down to earth. She tells it like it is— pure, simple, undistorted.

What type of woman fits this description? This is a person with strong character. She knows where she stands; she is confident and outgoing. Every phrase describing this woman can be summed up in one word: real. The dictionary provided those keywords. They are in black and white, indisputable. As you can see, real is a very revealing word when used to describe people. What makes our hypothetical woman especially remarkable is that many people today are not real. They've lost their true identity.

This chapter will uncover the main reasons why this happens and what you can do about it. Being true to yourself is a major building block for living the life you really want. We'll focus on one of the most powerful elements that affects your ability to be real—the masks you wear. We'll also look at your roles and responsibilities, and the labels attached to you.

Are You a
MISSING PERSON?

Are you ready to be authentic in your life, or do you want to play it safe hiding behind your self-imposed limitations? Are you ready to become more real than you've ever been? That means giving up the superficial games you play, games that keep the real you hidden. Everyone plays these games, but most people don't even know what they are. In the next few pages you'll discover how you play some of these games.

In my experience this is a widespread ailment. I've certainly worn a few masks that were tough to remove. In this chapter I'm going to ask you to be bold and make a commitment—no more acting, pretending or playing charades. Strip any false images away. But first, a warning: in the process you may feel exposed, naked and fearful. You may ask yourself, "What if I don't like what I see?" Even worse: "What if other people don't like what they see?"

If it's any comfort, most people will ultimately prefer and respect the real you. Those who don't? Maybe those relationships are not in your best interest and should be terminated. That choice will be easier to make later, after you have read this chapter.

> *While an original is hard to find*
> *She is easy to recognize.*
>
> —Anonymous

I believe that everyone is born with unique gifts and talents. Often these talents remain hidden. A big part of life is figuring out what your gifts are and how you are supposed to use them. When this happens you can expect a positive surge of energy, like a butterfly shedding its cocoon and preparing to fly.

Outer Truth Versus
INNER ILLUSION

Many women feel a disparity between who they are and who they think they should be. This shows up in their behavior. They put on an act, trying to look like the person they imagine the world wants to see. This causes discomfort, a discomfort centered on this fraud. Often they think it's about being better—better educated, better looking, better dressed, better spoken. But really, it's a form of self-rejection.

How do you perceive yourself? Are you showing up all the time or are you playing the illusion game? The illusion occurs because we think that no one else can see our pretense. In fact, most people can see right through our act. But because we are unaware of our games, we end up fooling ourselves.

Many women are like walking billboards advertising their game. However, they are unconscious of the message being delivered. One may advertise, "I'm a doormat," but then can't understand why others use and abuse her. Another advertises "I'm inferior," and wonders why it's difficult to find friends.

> After her job interview Dianne said, "I felt confident I could do the job, but they just wouldn't hire me." What Dianne couldn't see was how she shifted nervously in her chair and kept her eyes lowered as she answered questions in a voice that was barely audible.

The real you is the person you were born to be, complete with strengths and weaknesses, talents and frustrations, your funny little habits and the wisdom at your core. The real you is the person you were before the dramas and traumas of life changed you. Being your real self is all you ever need to be. Stop attempting to be someone you're not.

For years I've worked hard on my own self-awareness. Now I have the privilege of teaching these principles, and yet I'm disappointed when I see myself falling back into old patterns.

My parents encouraged me to always tell the truth. However, one day when my father challenged me to be honest, I was punished for what I'd done. That day I learned that being truthful isn't safe. Even now, when I'm questioned directly, a little voice in the back of my head whispers that it's not safe to be truthful.

What fascinates me is that I'm most real in my workshops. There is no place to hide. I know the importance of being open and vulnerable in these group settings, so I've learned to be

Reprinted by permission from Adrian Raeside and Creators Syndicate, Inc.

comfortable sharing my essence, warts and all. Sometimes I feel like a sacrificial lamb when someone doesn't understand what I'm doing and totally rejects my opinion. It's painful.

Being vulnerable is one of the risks you take when you become more real. But the more you challenge yourself, the stronger you become. I enjoy being as real as I can be. I wouldn't have it any other way. Over time I've learned that the benefits far outweigh the risks. I'm more spontaneous, my relationships are cleaner, and when I make mistakes there is plenty of laughter.

I encourage you to do the same. But as you move into this new realm, be aware that some people are not ready to hear the truth. Often these people are family and friends, so be tactful. Pick the best time to have these delicate conversations and practice good communication skills. You'll learn some excellent techniques for this in Chapter Five.

Where Did The
REAL YOU GO?

As an adult you might think it's better to leave the past alone, believing, "The past is the past; I can't do anything about it now."

There's more to it than that. Your life is a journey influenced by parents, teachers, extended family and other significant relationships. These people have helped mold you into the person you are today. Unfortunately, some of their influences may have been negative. Those negative influences can actually sabotage the real you.

Let's go back to early childhood. What do all young children want and need? Mostly to feel loved, to feel safe, to get attention, and to feel significant. Children look to the significant people in their lives for guidance and for direction, and they often adopt their ways. Children learn to model whatever behavior is expected. "Be nice." "Be good." "Be brave." The world of children is dominated by big people upon whom their very lives depend. As children, we learned that if we behaved badly the big people might withdraw their love or even threaten to leave us. Gradually we suppressed those parts of our natural character that were judged as bad, shameful or lacking. By the time we reached our teen years, we may have discarded some of our natural talents altogether, because they were considered not good enough or not worthy of pursuit. "You'll never be a singer; you can't even carry a note." "Nobody in our family has ever started a business! Who do you think you are?"

The opposite happens when parents use undue pressure to force a teenager or college graduate to follow a specific career path because it runs in the family.

Have you ever observed someone who has been pushed into an inappropriate role? It's frustrating. Resentment sets in and the person experiences a feeling of being trapped. The real talent may be screaming to be set free.

In the award-winning movie *Billy Elliot*, the main character is a young boy who lives in a small mining town in Britain. The unemployment situation is bad and there is fear that the mine will close. Billy's father is a staunch trade union leader. Most of the men in the town are miners, including Billy's older brother. Like generations before him, Billy is expected to follow suit.

Almost by accident the young boy discovers he has a talent for dancing, particularly ballet. This goes down like a ton of bricks with his family, but Billy persists and ends up years later as a leading performer in the Royal Ballet. His talent was just too exceptional to be wasted, but it took a positive stand by the woman who coached him to create understanding and eventually admiration from his family.

I can relate to this. When I was seven a new girl joined our class. Her name was Catherine. She was a great artist. Catherine could draw anything, even animals. The life-like portraits she painted were absolutely amazing. I was in awe. I remember comparing my talent to hers and deciding, "I will never be good enough." I threw my art and talent away into the waste basket of my judgement. With that judgment, I threw away my potential.

Today I am in a remodeling phase of my life. I've retrieved what I threw into that wastebasket many years ago. Now I'm celebrating because I *can* paint, and I've discovered that I paint well. It's never too late to rekindle the flame of your personality, or to pursue a dream that you may have long ago discarded. Grandma Moses didn't start painting until she was well into her senior years, and she became world-famous.

What have you thrown away? Was it a unique talent? An ambition? Maybe it was an emotional need to feel loved, accepted or included. The thing you discarded—or buried deep inside—is still part of the real you.

Here's another thing: as children, we are told in many ways that it isn't okay to be ourselves. "Don't be selfish." "Don't cry." "Don't be scared." In fact, at that moment we are intensely experiencing those feelings, but our reality is being denied.

Children observe the world from a unique perspective. If a situation appears threatening they learn to cope, adapt or avoid. What seems traumatic to them may not even be noticed by a busy parent. Left to their own coping mechanisms, children use their imagination to handle traumatic situations. They can even develop new personalities. On the way to adulthood, young girls and boys often create a closet-full of personas to cover up the real person underneath. Those personas are called masks.

YOUR MASKS MAY DECEIVE THE OUTSIDE WORLD

But not your heart

I erased myself, recalls Patti, the third girl born into her family. I became what my Dad wanted me to be. He wanted a boy. I decided to become my Dad's buddy, to be his boy. I acted tough and pretended to be courageous. When it came to clothes I was a tomboy—tomboys don't wear dresses. I'd put on jeans and my Dad would laugh and say, "That's my boy." Later I became jealous of my sisters. Dad called them his princesses. At age sixteen I decided to stop the act. I wanted to find the real Patti.

Old patterns die hard. Sometimes my boyish aggression still comes to the surface in a most unladylike manner. It's taken years to uncover my natural personality and femininity. My Dad thinks I've become a weakling. However, I'm glad I stopped pretending. Awakening my true spirit has set me free.

Take Off
YOUR MASK

Part of discovering who you are is finding out who you are not. Some people's masks become so glued to their body that they have no idea who they really are. The mask becomes a comfortable substitute.

Shedding the façade can be scary. In essence, you need to ask yourself, "Who am I?" That's a big question. The sheer magnitude of this causes many women to hesitate in stripping off the mask. But before you contemplate leaving everything just the way it is, know this: all masks have something in common. Masks prevent you from sharing the most valuable gift you have. That gift is the real you. A distorted replica simply can't replace the real you.

To become emotionally healthy, to have a deeper connection with yourself and with others, the mask needs to come off. John Powell, author of *Why Am I Afraid to Tell You Who I Am?*

says this: "Most of us feel that others will not tolerate such emotional honesty in communication. We would rather defend our dishonesty on the grounds that it might hurt others, and, having rationalized our phoniness into nobility, we settle for superficial relationships."

The Five Most
COMMON MASKS

To be fully alive and enjoy all that this bountiful world can provide, you need to examine yourself by asking, "What specific mask am I wearing, and how is it holding me back?" Which of the five most common masks discussed below fits you?

1. Approval-Seeker Mask

Are you hyper-vigilant about what others think of you and how to please them? Do you seek approval about your figure, the clothes you wear, the size of your home, the car you drive and how much money you earn? Be honest—will you do almost anything to get the approval of others?

> "I've spent my whole life caring about what other people think of me," says Mary. "I know I'm a people pleaser. It's important that my friends see me as Merry Mary—always happy, outgoing and fun to be with. They compliment my upbeat attitude all the time. If only they knew how I really feel. My life is one big act. I often feel sad because I don't have a close relationship. I'm such a fraud!"

The cost to Mary's self-respect is enormous, yet many women feel just like her. Somewhere along life's path they bought into the idea that it wasn't okay to express their true thoughts. Instead of inner validation, they seek solace by attempting to please everyone else.

To you, is *appearing* more important than *being?*

The Approval-Seeker Mask is one of the most common. Behind this mask is a pleasing and agreeable woman. She has difficulty setting boundaries because the needs of everyone else appear to be more important than her own. Her unconscious stance is, "You count, I don't."

Almost everyone wants to be liked. When this desire over-rides everything else, however, the approval-seeker's life becomes focused on how other people react and respond to her. The approval-seeker will do whatever it takes to have peace at any price. She takes responsibility for how other people feel and act. The Approval-Seeker Mask is her way of getting attention. However, deep down she feels unlovable.

Do you see yourself here? Does this mask fit you?

Discarding the Approval-Seeker Mask is incredibly free-ing, but doing so requires a huge shift in focus. Instead of always paying attention to others, you need to turn your focus onto you. This is not being selfish. It's about finding a healthy equilibrium between meeting your own needs and genuinely serving others.

Before I give you some tips for removing this mask, first let me clarify something. It's important that you distinguish between approval-seeking behavior and being acknowledged for something that deserves recognition. If, for example, you organized a family reunion for one hundred people because you simply wanted to help, not for any self-serving reasons, then by all means take the applause and feel good about it.

IT'S HARD TO CELEBRATE YOU
WHEN YOU ARE ALWAYS WISHING YOU
WERE SOMEBODY ELSE

These tips will help you give up the Approval-Seeker Mask:

- Get in touch with your emotions. Respect your feelings—they belong to you and are real. You don't need to apologize for having them. Practice speaking openly and honestly. Let your behavior reflect this.

- Allow others to see you as you really are, not as you manipulate them to see you.

- Take care of yourself first. Only then will you be more available to others. This means setting new boundaries that permit you to do this consistently. (*Read Chapter Five for more about setting boundaries.*)

When you are absorbed by what others think of you, the reality is that you are making the situation all about you. "What do they think of me?" No wonder people perceive this behavior as being self-centered. Whether you like it or not, the universe does not revolve around you. People in your circle are not spending all day thinking about you unless you are seriously ill or in the middle of a crisis.

To put this into perspective, if your personal life story, including your deficiencies, became headline news in a national newspaper, how many people would care? Not many—most people are far too busy figuring out how to make their own lives work.

Give up the need for constant approval. It will take time and courage to eliminate this bad habit, but the real you will thank you profusely.

2. Victim Mask

This powerful mask can lead to a miserable existence. The woman behind this mask feels that life is unfair. She plays the martyr role. "If you knew my story, you'd understand and have pity on me." This woman likes to blame and complain instead of taking responsibility. Often she is stuck in backward thinking.

- It could have been so different if I'd had a better education.
- If only my banker had supported my idea.
- My husband should have made me happy, but now I'm all alone.

The woman who wears the Victim Mask believes she has no choices. She gives her power away and sees herself as less-than. This shows up in the powerless language she uses.

- I can't.
- I should.
- I have to.

She feels that her situation is hopeless and that she is helpless to change it. What sort of energy does this person give out? You're right—negative. In fact, if you spend too much time around someone like this, you will feel your own energy being drained away. It's exhausting.

Despite this, some women wearing the Victim Mask have the ability to attract rescuers and caregivers, some of whom are wearing the Approval-Seeker Mask. When these people are around, she loves to talk about her problems. It looks like she has the weight of the world on her shoulders.

The victim blames others for her unhappiness. She indulges in pity parties and often uses the guilt card as an ace to help her get what she wants. Aging parents often do this; it is a difficult situation for adult children to resolve.

> "I'm out of work again and can hardly make ends meet," mourns Val. "I can barely afford a pack of cigarettes. There are no good jobs anyway. Lousy pay, lousy hours, treating me like dirt—it's all the same, so I quit. That's the third time this year. You'd think my kids would help out after all the sacrifices I've made for them, but no, they'd rather see me suffer."

Val is mired in her own negativity because she isn't willing to consider any new options or practical solutions. But until she makes changes, she is bound to stay stuck.

Victims often feel that other people are taking advantage of them, so they have a low level of trust. This is a payoff for choosing to be a victim. They never need to take responsibility, and they can keep using their sad story to get attention. These crutches are difficult for victims to throw away. The mask also covers up a belief that says, "I am unlovable." Let's face it, bad things happen to everyone. We all feel victimized at times. However, the person who wears this mask is making a life-long career of being a victim. The good news is that you can remove the Victim Mask whenever you choose. Here's how:

- Start with a change of attitude. Dare to change your perspective on life. You have options—become creative. Make a list of ten options that will improve your situation. Force yourself to write down every one. The first few options may not be the best. The real gems often surface toward the end of your list. Then choose one and take the first step.

- Carefully monitor your language. Shut off all negative self-talk, those coulds, shoulds and can'ts. Instead, substitute affirming statements. I am worthy. I am loveable. I deserve a better life. You will not see radical change overnight. This is a process. It takes time to integrate these beliefs at an emotional level. At first they may sound false. Introduce them initially as thoughts, then verbalize them. Even better, use a 3 x 5 card and read them aloud every day with as much feeling as you can muster. By doing this repeatedly, you will plant a seed in your unconscious mind. Your mind doesn't know the difference between fact and fiction—it simply accepts the message.

- Look for inspiration. Get excited about designing a new plan for your life. Realize that other people have transformed their lives after enduring tough challenges. Look outward. Find one person who will not tolerate your victim attitude and ask for positive support. If you demonstrate that you are serious about changing your circumstances, the right people will respond. Be wary of other victims who don't want to change. Avoid them. You need positive energy to set you free.

3. Busy Bee Mask

More than any other, this mask gets the most use. The woman wearing it is constantly picking up, dropping off, making to-do lists, volunteering, being productive. She is always on the move.

I know what you're thinking: "This is my life right now. Am I really wearing this mask?" To help you differentiate, answer these two questions:

- Can you sit alone and do nothing?
- If you stopped *doing,* would you still feel worthy?

The thought of wasting time being unproductive is abhorrent to the Busy Bee. This woman never gives herself free time and fears having nothing to do. The Busy Bee Mask is a clever defense mechanism that helps her avoid facing her true feelings.

Have you noticed how feelings keep coming to the surface throughout this chapter? It's no accident. Feelings are at the core of every life-changing decision you make.

Now think about this: what if the sheer pace of your hectic schedule burns you out? What then? You'll be forced to stop. Life has a way of throwing little curve balls when you least expect it. These curve balls show up as a heart attack, divorce or business failure, to name a few.

When you are forced to stop and think, you have a great opportunity to face your underlying emotional pain. You can examine yourself by asking:

- Why am I living like this?
- What am I running from?
- What am I afraid of?

Whenever I was upset, I'd go to the kitchen and start cleaning. My family knew this was a warning sign to keep clear. I'd scrub furiously, washing and mopping everything in sight, all to avoid feeling. Now I take "me time" to experience my feelings and face the truth. I learn more about myself when I do this. My kitchen isn't getting nearly as much attention these days, but I'm a lot more relaxed.

Slow down and question your need to be so busy. There are three possibilities:

- You are passionate about what you do.
  You love your work and it energizes you.
  You also take breaks and you understand
  the importance of balance.

- You simply need more help and support.
  Your To-Do List is real and everything on it
  requires attention. The problem is that nobody
  else is sharing the load with you.

- You have an unhealthy compulsion to be busy.
  You drive people crazy when your busy motor
  is in overdrive.

The first two points above have nothing to do with the Busy Bee Mask. You're a busy person, and while you may need to do something about reducing your load, you don't need to figure out how to remove the Busy Bee Mask. But if you saw yourself in the third possibility, discovering what is behind the compulsion is critical. What pain are you seeking to avoid? What belief system did you adopt that said life was all work and no play?

BEING BUSY IS ONE THING, KNOWING
WHAT YOU ARE BUSY ABOUT IS
FAR MORE IMPORTANT

Here are a few steps you can take to remove the Busy Bee Mask:

- Every day, challenge your compulsion to be busy. The mask will gradually lose its power over you.

- Schedule some quiet time for yourself. Start with ten minutes and gradually increase it. Sit alone in complete privacy—no television or reading magazines. These are just subtle ways to keep you doing. Release any emotions that surface. Later, capture your thoughts in a journal or verbalize them. Yes, it's okay to talk to yourself!

- Remove unessential items from your to-do list.

4. Intellectual Mask

Have you ever been trapped at a party enduring a lengthy, overly cerebral discussion full of obscure facts and figures? Incredibly boring, the talk amounts to analysis to the point of paralysis. And throughout the entire episode, not one flicker of emotion escapes from this bland conversationalist. If you have, you just had an encounter with The Intellectual.

While I think men wear the Intellectual Mask more than women, some women are also over-the-top intellectuals who use their academic prowess as a smokescreen. The woman who hides behind this mask prefers thinking to feeling. She's rigid in her thinking, wrapped up in concepts and analysis. Because she lacks an emotional connection (here come those feelings again), she has difficulty relating to others at work, especially if she is in a supervisory role. As well, her emotional void often causes problems within her family, where she may be perceived as cold and detached. People who wear the Intellectual Mask are not generally big on hugging!

This woman likes to be super-objective, living a life that is structured by rules and regulations. She can rationalize any situation to make a point, and in the process ensures that associated feelings are kept hidden. Women who wear the Intellectual Mask may have developed the belief that showing emotion is a sign of weakness and therefore should be kept under control. The intellectual prefers the boardroom and the classroom to the social world of people and their problems.

What about you? Do you ever get feedback that you are "too much in your head," or overly analytical?

There is nothing wrong with thinking. We do it every day. It's an essential component for designing the type of life that gives you the most joy. However, thinking should not be at the expense of feeling. Any behavior that becomes too extreme is unhealthy. A big part of our lives involves interacting with people, and developing relationships with these people requires both a mental and emotional stimulus. The woman who wears the Intellectual Mask may feel fragmented by a deeper need to connect with others emotionally and the discomfort it creates for her. If you are struggling with this, here are a couple of suggestions:

- Identify your emotions in general conversation. Become familiar with the all-important feeling words. I feel happy. I'm bored. I'm feeling angry. Instead of saying, "The new promotion I received is recognition for my ability to conduct accurate research," you can say, "I feel honored by this promotion because it recognizes my ability to conduct accurate research."

- During conversation, use your mental acuity to discern what the other person is feeling. Make it a game, if that stirs your intellectual juices. Provide accurate feedback that shows you really understand what the other person is saying. And yes, that means taking a genuine interest, even if it is a new sensation for you.

Here are two examples of good "feelings" feedback:

- Sounds like you're pretty excited about buying this piece of property.

- That must have been really scary.

Practicing these simple techniques will create a healthy alignment between your heart and your head, and you will become a lot more real to the people who know you.

5. Rescuer Mask

Any time a cry for help goes out, the Rescuer will be first in line. This woman is perceived as a caregiver because she has a compulsive need to help others. The Rescuer looks for people to save. She believes they can't do without her, so she wants to take responsibility for them. Her mantra is, "They need me."

In the course of helping, however, the Rescuer can become overbearing. She doesn't realize that her own inherent need to be needed is helping to keep people stuck. This shows up in many simple, everyday situations.

"I've given up on John ever learning how to pack a nutritious lunch. It's easier for me to do it for him."

Do you play these games, too? Are you into judging what is best for others, instead of letting them have their own experiences? Rescuing mothers are overprotective of their children, a habit that often causes future rebellion. If you want to avoid the terrible teens, back off when they are young.

Most women are raised to be sensitive to the needs of others. Traditionally, we are considered nurturers, while men are seen as hunters and providers. If this is a touchy subject for you, just wait. We'll talk more about the true nature of roles and labels before the end of this chapter.

The danger of this women-as-nurturers premise is that our self-worth is based on our ability to care for other people. This makes us vulnerable to manipulation. Legions of women have been brought up this way. It is not a selfish act to nurture yourself first. The higher road is not being an approval-seeking martyr or a self-flagellating doormat. Rescuers fall into the same lose-lose trap—and they do it naively in the name of love and support.

Do you ever feel resentful doing so much for others? Remember, we're talking about extreme behavior here, not the normal, healthy, giving nature that well-balanced people demonstrate. Do you give beyond the point of love? Are you always putting the needs of others before your own needs? Many women answer these questions with a heartfelt yes! Here are some suggestions to help you remove this mask.

- Understand that every action you take is motivated by intention. All behavior has a purpose. Ask yourself: am I doing this to fulfill a personal need (to be loved), or am I doing it from unconditional love, expecting nothing in return? If you knew you would be loved anyway, would you still be a Rescuer?

- Next time you jump into rescue mode, slow down and ask yourself, "Does this person need to be rescued, and is it my responsibility?"

Uncover the real you; you'll be glad you did.

There is a fine line separating some of these masks, especially the Approval-Seeker, the Busy Bee and the Rescuer. I've worn these for years. They fulfilled my need to be loved. For a long time I didn't know what a boundary was, or what enabling behavior meant. I was raised to be a saint (I had high and holy ideals) but I could never live up to that vision. Knowing that caused me a lot of grief and guilt, until I learned how to overcome it.

My mother, God bless her, always said, "Give, give, give until you drop." I cloned that belief, and lived with it much of my adult life. Thankfully, today I'm wiser. That's one of the benefits of growing older, having the ability to choose a different perspective.

I often wish I could go back and fix parts of my life, but that's not helpful. I refuse to focus on pain and guilt. It's better to move on. The more I question my intentions, the easier it is for me to be real and eliminate the need for masks. Today I'm grateful that I know how to give joyfully, to serve and to love unconditionally, but it's still a struggle to avoid unhealthy extremes.

All masks are difficult to remove. Often our programming goes deep and may be intertwined with misunderstood negative or spiritual beliefs.

- It's selfish to think of yourself.
- Idle hands are the devil's workshop.

If we wear a mask it doesn't mean we need to mentally beat ourselves up. Wearing a mask is simply what we do to hide our pain. Primarily, it's a defense mechanism. There are also times when it is better to withhold our true feelings, when wearing a temporary mask is appropriate.

During dinner on a first date at an upscale restaurant, for example, you may notice that your potential new suitor snorts as he eats. It may be more tactful to don a smiling mask, while making a mental note that this will be a one and only event.

MY OUTER BEHAVIOR IS THE TRUTH

Whereas My Inner Perception Of That Behavior Is Often An Illusion

Being real is more relevant when you are really hurting or sad. Friends will be able to respond to this genuine need when you don't use a mask to hide your feelings. Masks create emotional avoidance. They will cause you to miss out on many opportunities for intimacy. Make a promise to yourself: from now on, *have the courage to be real.*

Don't Be Fooled by the Masks I Wear

Don't be fooled by me. Don't be fooled by the face I wear. I wear a mask. I wear a thousand masks—masks that I am afraid to take off; and none of them are me.

Pretending is an art that is second nature to me, but don't be fooled, I give the impression that I am secure, that all is sunny and unruffled within me as well as without; that confidence is my name and coolness is my game, that the water is calm and I am in command; that I need no one. But don't believe me, please. My surface may seem smooth, but my surface is my mask, my ever varying and ever concealing mask.

Beneath lays no smugness, no complacence. Beneath dwells the real me in confusion, in fear, in aloneness. But I hide that. I don't want anyone to know it. I panic at the thought of my weakness and fear being exposed. That is why I frantically create a mask to hide behind, a nonchalant, sophisticated façade to help me pretend, to help shield me from the glance that knows. But such a glance is precisely my salvation, my only salvation, and I know it. That is, if it's followed by acceptance; if it is followed by love.

It's the only thing that can liberate me from myself, from my own self-built prison walls, from the barriers I so painstakingly erect. It's the only thing that will assure me of what I can't assure myself, that I am really worth something. Who am I, you may wonder? I am someone you know very well. I am every man you meet and I am every woman you meet.

—Charles C. Finn
(From the poem, *Please Hear What I'm Not Saying*)

Roles and
RESPONSIBILITIES

Many women define themselves by the work they do or the role they play in the family. "I'm a teacher/doctor/computer programmer/mother/wife/widow." All of these words fall short of describing the multifaceted dimensions that make them complete human beings. Most people talk about what they do or who they serve, but they have little or no idea about the rest of their makeup.

In a workshop I facilitated recently I asked a young mother, Lynn, "Who are you, apart from your role at home?" There was silence, no response. Then her bottom lip started to quiver with emotion, tears ran down her cheeks and she admitted, "I don't know." Lynn's situation is not unusual. So many women are caught up in the busyness of their life at home or in the office that they don't realize their entire well-being is based on the success of these roles. To avoid this, see yourself as a whole person.

If you are an income earner, a portion of you carries out specific duties at work and at home. But where does the rest of you show up? Has the other portion been put on hold or buried somewhere? It's difficult to see yourself as anything but a Mom when you're at home with small children most of the day. If your hours are filled with looking after an elderly parent, your caretaking role is prominent; and if you are an entrepreneur investing fourteen hours a day living, eating and breathing your business, sleep may be the only other item on your agenda.

There are stages in your life when a particular role may be all-consuming. The danger is over-identifying with your role, holding on so tightly that you choke off the other parts of your life. Perhaps your saving grace is knowing that it won't last forever.

The Mother Hen

I wasn't happy and I knew it, but I didn't understand why. My family was wonderful and my husband Les loved and supported me. Yet there were many days when I couldn't keep myself up. I worked hard on my moods, and for the longest time put on a pretty good act.

Realizing I needed help, I consulted a psychologist. Her analysis was quick and accurate. She told me my symptoms were common. I was over-identifying with my role as a mother. I admitted that I had invested an incredible amount of time with my two children, all the way from preschool to high school graduation. But isn't that what a good mother is supposed to do, I argued?

After further questioning, the psychologist pointed out that the mothering hadn't stopped with my kids. She clearly demonstrated that I was even mothering my husband. In fact, it had become more of a parent-child relationship. I was horrified! I had no idea what the true role of a wife was or how it was different from the role I played with my children. My life was consumed with giving, giving, giving, but my spirit wanted something else. I was losing my identity and dying inside. On reflection, I realized I had a tendency to nurture anyone who had a need. My motto was: If it moved, feed it, burp it and mother it.

Gradually, I learned to handle my mother role more lightly. My children received an immediate reward. They became more accountable and were able to test their new freedom and flexibility. Mother Hen had stopped presiding over every detail in their lives. I also learned that being a wife could be a lot more fun.

I set new boundaries with my husband. He grumbled for a few days when I stopped making his lunches. I had to remind him (and myself) that I was not his mother.

For many years I had extended my excessive nurturing to my father and five siblings, jumping into the family fray every time a mini-crisis occurred. I now keep all of that in perspective.

My life is experienced at full capacity. I am enjoying all of who I am, not just my ability to nurture, although that will always be an important part of me.

I have talked to many mothers who are caught in the same trap. Bestselling author and talk show host Dr. Phil McGraw makes a crucially important comment about this. "As a mother, your primary relationship is with your husband." He's referring to a family that lives under the same roof. When a baby enters the world, it joins a relationship already in progress. Women who become mothers have a natural tendency to pour 100 percent of their attention and affection on the children. This is okay in the short term, but if it becomes excessive—all baby, no husband—a rift will develop in the primary relationship. Taken to extremes, this may permanently result in all baby, no husband. Many marriages fall apart because of this.

What Labels Are
YOU WEARING?

Roles represent only a part of your life, and the same goes for labels. Labels don't provide the total picture. However, wearing the wrong labels can change who you are at a core level, if you buy into them.

"Ever since I was little," Erin laments, "I labeled myself ugly. When I looked at my older sister I saw beauty. She had wonderful curly hair and a really pretty face. When I looked in the mirror I saw the ugly duckling. That was my self-imposed label. I hated having photographs taken with my sister because they just enhanced my ugliness. I was so jealous!"

Labels can be imposed from the inside (self-talk), or externally (by others). Have you been branded with any of these labels: fat, dummy, ugly, skinny, stupid, weirdo, daddy's girl, goody two shoes, worthless, bimbo, klutz, scattered, or good-for-nothing? That's only a small sampling—there's a lot more than that. Sometimes parents unwittingly pin these labels on us, and we retain them into maturity. Some of these old labels may need to be challenged and eliminated. Do you remember this rhyme?

> *Sticks and stones will break my bones*
> *But names will never hurt me.*

The line, "names will never hurt me" may sound good, but it's a lie. Names can, and do hurt. So be careful what you call people, even if your excuse is, "I was only joking."As a child, in Ireland, we added another verse:

> *And when you're dead and in your grave,*
> *You'll suffer what you called me.*

Nothing like a heavy dose of guilt to give your words impact! Sometimes, specific events cause us to place labels on ourselves.

- I failed the exam twice, therefore I must be dumb.
- I just went through a painful divorce; I'm a failure when it comes to marriage.

Labels can also be connected to our health. My friend Jill was totally attached to her cancer label. Whenever she sat in a group all she talked about was her illness. Surprisingly, she never lacked an audience. Even during recovery, the cancer label was still her main focus in conversation. I asked her what life would be like without cancer. "Who would you be without your label?"

"I would be a nobody," she replied. "People wouldn't pay any attention to me."

What labels are you carrying around? If there is a perceived payoff, they will be difficult to eliminate. Excavating the real you requires exploring, evaluating and eliminating your labels.

As Margaret Young says, "Often people attempt to live their lives backward: they try to have more things, or more money, to do more of what they want, so they will be happier. The way it actually works is the reverse. You must first be who you really are, then do what you need to do, in order to have what you want."

A Man's Perspective   Les Hewitt

Men wear masks too. You're probably not surprised by that. We have our macho image, superior, egotistical and controller masks that we flaunt regularly, and "old boys clubs" reign in many business arenas. We probably deny wearing our masks a lot more than women do.

One day I was doing a presentation for a young stockbroker who had expressed some interest in our coaching program. We sat in his company's impressive boardroom; rich cherry wood and marble everywhere. He was wearing an Armani suit, crisp white oxford shirt and a killer red silk tie. Shiny new brogues completed the outfit befitting a successful businessman. He told me he was married with two young children. I asked him about the balance between work and family, the amount of time he took off and how he coped with the stress of his job. We also talked about health and fitness and how his business was doing. He thought our coaching program sounded good but it wasn't for him right now as he had everything under control. He exercised regularly, took lots of time off and the brokerage industry was doing great.

Have you ever had a gut feeling during a conversation that something doesn't feel right, yet you just can't put your finger on what it is? I had that feeling. As I stood up to leave, something prompted me to ask one more question. I said, "By the way Frank, are you having any fun?"

I've never seen a man's demeanor change so fast. He paled, then beckoned me to sit down again and said, "You know something, I am *so* tired." Then the real story came out. He and his wife had separated recently, and the time spent with the kids was minimal. There was no exercise program and his marital problems were affecting his productivity at work. What a transformation! The macho image mask, the egotistical mask and the "everything's under control" front all evaporated in a matter of minutes, and underneath was a frightened, confused young man who didn't know where to turn for help.

Here are a couple of tips to help you find the real man underneath all of those disguises. First, develop the skill of asking good questions. Simple ones are often the most effective. Maybe you could even use, "Are you having any fun?" Second, suspend your own self-interest and really listen. Focus all of your attention on what he is saying. Men are hurting inside just as much as women are. They just don't like to show it.

CONCLUSION

Take a close look at the masks you are hiding behind and the labels you are wearing. Rip away all the unnecessary baggage and pretenses that are restricting your full participation in life. Knowing this has been a tremendous breakthrough for me. As I pushed myself to become more authentic, I became very conscious of when I was putting on a mask.

Before, I wasn't even aware when I had them on—I couldn't figure out why I wasn't feeling good about myself.

From now on, let the real you take center stage so you can share your unique talents with the world. You will begin to feel more congruent, more integral and more powerful. Other people will acknowledge and value your openness. Real people are much preferred to fake replicas.

ACTION STEPS

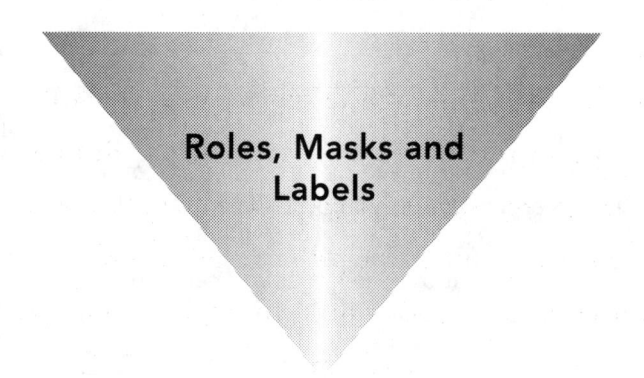

Roles, Masks and Labels

Use separate sheets or a journal to complete the following.

These Action Steps will help you uncover the roles you play and the amount of time you spend on each. To discover your authentic self, you need to strip away those things that are not serving you—your masks, labels and distorted self-image. Whatever you are identified with will control you. It is never who you are that holds you back in life, it's who you think you are.

1. Role Map

List the five major roles that occupy your time. These are the five most common hats that you wear. Consider what you do at home, with the family, at the office, in the community, at church, at play and in the business world. When you have completed your selection, take a large blank sheet of paper and draw five circles that represent each of your roles. Let the size of each circle reflect the amount of time and energy you spend in that role. Then label the circles. Now look at the largest and smallest circles. Is this what you want? Is one role consuming too much of you? Are you being controlled by any particular role? Is your life out of balance?

Make your comments below.

_____

_____

_____

_____

Now, inside each of the five circles make a detailed list of the responsibilities and activities you perform in that role.

How do you feel about this, now that you can see the bigger picture?

_____

_____

_____

Which of these roles are true expressions of your authentic self?

_____

_____

_____

What specifically would you like to change?

_____

_____

_____

_____

_____

Defining Your Responsibilities

Below make a list of what you are responsible for, and what you are not responsible for.

I AM responsible for:

  my own happiness

  my own feelings

_____

_____

_____

_____

I AM NOT responsible for:

  everyone else's happiness

  everyone else's feelings

_____

_____

_____

_____

2. Releasing Your Masks

Check the masks you wear.

MASK
- ❏ Approval-Seeker
- ❏ Victim
- ❏ Busy Bee
- ❏ Intellectual
- ❏ Rescuer
- ❏ Other

1. Why are you wearing this mask?

_____

_____

_____

_____

2. Who do you wear it with?

_____

_____

3. What is your biggest fear about discarding this mask?

_____

_____

_____

3. Lose Your Labels

Make a list of the names and labels you have attached to yourself. Consider those labels that have negatively influenced your self-worth and self-concept, or are a result of a particular event. For example: "I didn't complete my degree, therefore I'm a failure."

❏ _____ ❏ _____ ❏ _____

❏ _____ ❏ _____ ❏ _____

❏ _____ ❏ _____ ❏ _____

❏ _____ ❏ _____ ❏ _____

❏ _____ ❏ _____ ❏ _____

Make a list of the labels that other people have imposed on you. Write their names beside the label.

❏ _____ _____

❏ _____ _____

❏ _____ _____

Check off each of the above labels (self-imposed and imposed by others) that you are still wearing. What payoff do you get from this?

_____

_____

What is it costing you to keep these labels? If the cost appears too high, remove them from your mind and from your vocabulary.

_____

_____

Winning the Battle for Self-Esteem

Self-esteem isn't everything;
it's just that there's nothing without it.

—Gloria Steinem

THE TRUTH

I could hear a voice
Shouting to my left,
But the blow to my head
Had momentarily dazed me.
I could barely make out
The numbers on the blackboard any more.
They were fuzzy because
My tears were getting in the way.
The teacher hit me again.
"You're so stupid!" she yelled.
I didn't need her to remind me.
I was eight years old
And I already knew it was the truth.

—Fran Hewitt

When I was growing up, people in authority ruled.
They were never challenged—school teachers were given free rein to mold and shape the children in their care. To discipline, teachers often used humiliating tactics and heavy-handed punishments. Church and religion were huge influences. I remember having a real fear of God. The thought of going to hell was never far from my mind.

That was my reality. These day-to-day experiences, along with my sensitive nature, spelled disaster for any sense of self-esteem. What I didn't know was how the pain of my reality would stay with me for years.

I never would have guessed, either, that my spirit could survive and even thrive, eventually leading me to greater purpose and meaning.

TO SOME WOMEN THE TOPIC OF SELF-ESTEEM is extremely daunting. Others do not have the faintest idea what it means, or the significant role it plays in their life. They ask, "Has it got something to do with confidence?" or "Who has time for self-esteem, I'm just trying to raise my kids and pay off a mortgage."

For years I struggled to understand the concept of self-esteem. I used to think the way to get it was to be really good at something, like a job, to be the best in the field. Now I realize this approach was flawed. It was based on wanting other people to look up to me and show respect. This is the opposite of self-esteem, coming from a position of need and emptiness.

How we feel about ourselves affects every aspect of our experiences, from how we do our work, raise our children and interact in relationships. It affects how we let others treat us and how we treat others. All of our life circumstances are shaped by who and what we think we are. Self-esteem is essential for a fulfilling life; it is the key to success or failure.

The great bonus about self-esteem is that we have the ability to work on it. The stronger our self-esteem, the more likely we are to attract healthy relationships. The more resilient we are, the better we can cope with life's adversities. High self-esteem means we are more likely to be ambitious at work as well as in our personal lives—creatively, emotionally and spiritually.

> We are totally responsible for our own self-esteem.
> Nobody else can do the work for us.

I hope you are starting to see how the major topics in this book are coming together—accepting your reality, the desire to change, removing your masks. Each topic is like a link in a chain. Couple each link together and you begin to forge a powerful chain that will break down life's barriers.

The link we are discussing in this chapter, healthy self-esteem, is like attaching a wrecking ball to the end of the chain. Creating healthy self-esteem will obliterate almost every obstacle that gets in your way.

An Inside Job

Focus on building self-esteem, and it will sustain you for a lifetime. It doesn't matter how tough your journey has been, how old you are or how disadvantaged you perceive yourself to be, you can create this crucially important quality. To help you clearly understand how it works, we'll first distinguish between true self-esteem and the pseudo or false variety. Then we'll start putting the building blocks together that will make you more resilient, more confident and more powerful.

Another word for esteem is regard. To have high self-esteem is to have a high regard for yourself. In the same vein, self-acceptance is accepting who you are, and that means all of you, just as you are. Other terms are self-worth and self-concept. The basic premise is, no matter what others may think of you, no matter what situations occur, no matter what you do, you are able to love and value yourself. Of course this doesn't restrict you from continually improving your skills, your knowledge or your habits.

Self-improvement never ends—it is a life-long process. Above all else, you must understand that building healthy self-esteem is an inside job. You build yourself up from the inside out. Self-esteem is not determined by worldly success, physical appearance, popularity or any other external value. It is accomplished by taking personal responsibility, having integrity, demonstrating competence, feeling worthy and embracing self-acceptance.

I struggled with low self-esteem throughout most of my early life. When I became a Mom, I panicked. If there was one thing I wanted for my children it was for them to be confident, to love and value themselves, to have the ability to stand up and speak out, to be the best they could be. But how could I encourage them to create something that I didn't have myself?

This desire for my kids was so powerful that it started me on an incredible journey of self-discovery and recovery. I decided to learn everything I could about the subject. I read everything I could get my hands on. I took every opportunity to learn and eventually taught other parents how to build self-esteem in their kids. Today I'm grateful when I look with pride at my son and daughter—two confident young adults who have the ability to stand up and speak out. The bonus was that by raising them this way, I was able to heal myself.

Pseudo
SELF-ESTEEM

External Sources

Struggling with self-esteem is a daily reality for many women. When we don't have an inner sense of value, we often look elsewhere to create it. It's like having an empty space inside us, a void that needs to be filled up. The lower our level of self-esteem the bigger the void, and the greater the hunger to fill it. Many women attempt to satisfy this hunger through external sources.

They buy into lifestyle and image, whatever it takes to have the perfect look. Shopping for things becomes a substitute for inner harmony. It's pseudo self-esteem. What happens when these external trappings no longer give our self-esteem a boost? The emptiness returns.

> Jean likes to treat herself by shopping at exclusive boutiques, each with its own aroma of elegance. After making a purchase she feels a surge of pure joy. As she takes hold of the perfect store bag, crisp and lovely in itself, she can't wait to take ownership of the delicate tissue-wrapped object that it contains. For a time Jean feels energized and uplifted. But like any pleasure, whether it is a chocolate bar or a beautiful sunset, it doesn't last. Life has a way of taming our pleasure and reminding us of reality—like when the VISA bill arrives.

Loving Things

Do you like to shop? Does it give you a thrill to acquire new possessions? Most women would answer yes. How do you feel, for instance, when you buy a new outfit and receive a compliment? "Did you lose weight? That outfit looks stunning on you!"

You feel great, don't you? Your self-esteem button is pushed and you get a little boost. But how long does that last? Maybe until you're tired of the outfit, or you don't feel good wearing it any more. So off you go to buy something else.

In an effort to look better and feel better we buy new furniture, a new car, the latest gadget for our homes. The media does its bit, too. Every day we're bombarded by advertising messages to buy more, buy bigger, buy better, buy now pay later. Many women feel driven to buy. They think having possessions reflects on their self-worth. If they can't afford to buy the newest, greatest thing, they feel miserable.

Do you ever go shopping just because you're feeling low? When my kids were little I used to drag them to the mall. Not just to get out of the house, but to buy something so I could feel better. I'd fill my shopping cart with all sorts of items I didn't really need. Then I'd look forward to going home and unloading them. I'd get my "up" fix. However the up wouldn't last long, because I'd feel bad about the money I'd spent duplicating what I already had. I would rationalize this by looking at the savings on my bulk purchases of socks and pantyhose. After all, a girl can't have too many of those.

What I really needed was to learn how to feel better about myself without filling my home with unnecessary clutter. I still like to shop of course, but now I'm aware of my feelings and intentions. I first check how I feel. If I'm uneasy about a purchase, for whatever reason, I don't buy it. I let my intuition guide me. Practice this, it works. For some people shopping is a compulsion. Others use the fridge. They think that if they eat more, it will satisfy the inner hunger. The results show up on the outside, but the yearning within remains.

Using People
In the previous chapter we discussed the power of masks and why women wear them. It's all about manipulating others, with the illusion that in the process our self-esteem will be strengthened. Approval-Seekers manipulate people so they will be liked. Victims manipulate individuals in the hope they will be cared for—this gives them the illusion of power. Rescuers build the illusion of self-esteem by giving conditionally.

We play other games too. We criticize other people to bring them down and raise ourselves up, or we attempt to control others so that we are in charge. The bottom line is that we don't think we have value unless someone else confirms it. But using people never builds true self-worth. It only results in lose-lose relationships.

Using Things and Loving People
I think we have this backwards, especially in North America. We often attach more importance to the things we acquire, than to people. We want more and more, and even when we

get it we're not happy. Let's put this into perspective. Think about people who live in countries where poverty is rife and a lean-to shack is called home. Surveys have been conducted to gauge the level of happiness shown by these people. Surprisingly, many say they are very happy. Children can be seen playing contentedly even though they have little or no material possessions. These communities have a sense of caring and sharing that is often beyond anything seen in so-called civilized countries. The people are happy with so little, and yet we can be miserable with so much.

Are you getting caught up in the trap of materialism? Is it time to shift your perspective?

Our society today seems more focused on using things than loving people. The reverse would be much better—loving people instead of loving things. What a concept! But it isn't that simple. We still have a few hurdles to clear before starting on the positive building blocks.

Treadmill Women

The nagging void of inner emptiness is hard to fill. Women, however, are creative, and most can come up with interesting ways to conquer the situation. Treadmill women are absolutely driven to fill the void. They do it by setting and achieving endless goals, creating massive to-do lists and racking up awards and recognition at work. Applause and monetary gain are byproducts of this effort.

I can hear you saying, "Wait a minute, what's wrong with applause and monetary gain?" Let's make an important distinction here. Setting goals and focusing on a life of achievement is a healthy way to live provided you are doing it for healthy reasons. If you want to be at the top of your field and you acquire the qualifications to get there, great—as long as you don't feel an underlying sense of I'm not good enough. If you do feel this way, even when you are awarded a doctorate you will be unfulfilled.

A woman with healthy self-worth genuinely celebrates success, and rightly so. She may feel challenged to accomplish something else, but underneath she feels good about her success. She might even say, "That's enough hard work for a while. I think I'll just relax and do something less demanding." She'd still be happy.

Do you appreciate the difference? Women who are always driven to do more are addicted to this behavior. It's like a drug labeled Low Self-Worth. No amount of money and no accomplishment, no matter how big, will wean them from this addiction, because the inner core issue is not being addressed.

About Image

Words favored by the younger set these days are, looking good, cool, far out, awesome and sweet. They often describe how you look, what you've bought, or what you did. Many women base their esteem on how they look. They obsess about their skin, grooming, clothes, body weight and, of course, age. With all the judging and comparing, you would think life was a never-ending beauty pageant.

These women may also have big agendas about looking younger. The packaging has to be perfect. However, low self-worth is built on the cosmetics of fear. Many women think they must be center stage, in full view, clinging to a desperate need to stay visible and desirable. Perhaps they wouldn't worry so much if they knew how little their image mattered to everyone else.

> Daphne walks into the club teetering on strappy stiletto sandals. Her body is sucked into a short skirt and her scooped tee-shirt shows off generous cleavage. Her searching eyes are saying, "Notice me please, otherwise I'm nothing."

Have you ever compared yourself to someone else? If your esteem is low, you will always come up short. Imagine comparing yourself to those beautiful leggy young things on the hottest magazine covers. For most of us it's an exercise in futility.

One of my pet peeves is the television commercial showing twenty-somethings worrying about wrinkles. Give me and every other forty-something a break...please. Or...how about firming and toning from a bottle, usually demonstrated by a youngster with unbelievably tight buttocks and fabulous thighs? I am flummoxed and insulted. Do they think we are that stupid? Does hope come in a bottle containing the elixir for youth and vitality?

Imagine if gray roots became all the rage and crow's feet were esteemed as classic beauty marks. The younger generation would rush to get their roots dyed and the Botox business would go bankrupt. Older women would smile and hold their heads high, thinking, "It's about time—don't I look fabulous?"

Is it any wonder that so many women feel empty inside? We've been seduced by external promises that there is a quick fix for self-esteem.

- If you don't like yourself—get a makeover and buy a new outfit
- If you're not happy with your partner—get a divorce or find a new relationship
- If you're depressed—go to the spa, take a holiday

Maybe you've reached the same conclusion as me. It doesn't work. It doesn't last, and you still feel pretty much the same afterward.

Six Building Blocks For
HEALTHY SELF-ESTEEM

First Building Block – Integrity

Building healthy self-esteem requires integrity. This means honesty—matching who you are on the inside with who you are on the outside. Young children are often more integral than adults. They speak the truth, with no agenda about having to please or displease anyone else. They cry when they're hurt and they get angry when they're upset. There is no holding back or thinking about what others might or might not do.

When you are not being true to yourself, or to others, the fraud is directed right back at you. Your self-esteem takes the hit. Courage and independent thinking are essential ingredients for being authentic. But courage and independent thinking are elusive traits, and this is the reason why so few people are authentic.

Carol says: "I try to impress people when I don't even respect them. I hate myself when I do that, and I often stay silent when I don't agree with what's being said."

Carol needs to speak up and be honest. By silencing her truth, she has become devoid of integrity.

The more integral we are, the more self-respect we earn. Our self-esteem begins to flourish.

Another crucial aspect of integrity is keeping our word. It's not easy. I believe this is one of the prime reasons our world is in such a state. Do you keep your word? All the time?

"Looks aren't everything. It's what's inside you that really matters. A biology teacher told me that."

When you break your word, you break an agreement. There is no such thing as a little agreement. All agreements are important; they are all based on doing what you say you are going to do. The outcome can be war when leaders of countries break agreements. Husbands and wives break agreements, and marriages fall apart. When business partners break agreements the lawyers get rich.

This is a really big point: All broken relationships can be traced back to broken agreements.

Some people give their word without even realizing they have given it, because they treat it so casually. Think about how you feel when a friend breaks her word to you. If she becomes a repeat offender, what does it do to your relationship? How do you feel about trusting and respecting this person? Not very good, I'll bet. You feel let down, angry or upset. Let's turn this the other way. What happens to you when you know you have broken your word? You may beat yourself up, or rationalize why it was acceptable, or apologize to cover it up. But you can only get away with saying sorry for so long. It damages your self-esteem.

Be conscious when you are giving your word. Focus! Treat your word as if it is all you have. Your word is your bond. It is what sets you apart in the integrity stakes. Giving your word means you are being accountable to yourself and to the people with whom you work, play and share your life.

If you want self-respect, if you want to stand out in the business community, if you want great relationships and if you want to be trusted, keep your word.

How often? Every day. Let's take a simple example that challenges many people. Do you show up on time? The answer is yes or no, not "It depends." Being late is another way we sabotage our self-esteem and our relationships. It indicates a lack of respect for someone else's time. If you make a habit of being late, ask yourself why? Is it about control or resistance? What are you making more important than keeping your word?

Hear me, this is huge! Being loose with your word will gradually erode your self-respect and self-trust until it becomes a mere speck on your integrity scale.

I know this because I grew up with little integrity. Back then it was more important to protect myself by telling lies. Always being disappointed taught me not to trust others. Today I strive to walk my talk. I make fewer promises and commitments because I want to keep my word. It's sometimes better to say no, even though doing so can be difficult. But over time, people have learned to trust me, and I have learned to trust myself. I do what I say I'm going to do, with no excuses like, "I don't feel like it."

Second Building Block – Personal Responsibility

When I was a young mother I took little responsibility for anything outside the home. I thought making decisions and paying bills were my husband's responsibility. However, when it came to the other people in my life I would take responsibility for everyone. This included my children and my extended family. That changed when I began to understand the importance of setting boundaries. Over the years I have gradually taken back my power. I am now responsible only to myself. I think for myself and make my own decisions. I even took over paying the bills. How much responsibility do you take in your own life? Are you an active participant, or a bystander? I've discovered that being responsible generates self-esteem. This world needs more participants, not more passengers. Active, responsible people get things done. They are not dependent on society to look after them, nor do they expect handouts. Here's a big question. Consider it carefully and be honest: Are you taking personal responsibility for creating the life you really want, or are you just hoping it will all work out?

Maybe you're waiting for someone else to bring your ship in. Perhaps, if you are like a lot of women, you failed to send your ship out in the first place.

> "When I finally realized how much of a victim I'd become," says Mavis, "I was disgusted with myself. There I was—forty-five years old, divorced and broke. Of course, I blamed him for everything. I would spend more than I made each month, and I was deserted by my friends. I don't blame them. I would whine and complain all the time. Nobody wanted to be with me. I finally woke up and decided to accept responsibility for the situation I was in. It was like flipping a switch from victimhood to being responsible. I couldn't believe the change in me. I felt more powerful, more energetic and more confident. It was like being plugged back into life again. Now I know that I have control of the switch."

Feeling helpless or victimized, blaming others, complaining and remaining passive are great techniques for being stuck with low self-esteem. Letting others think and do for you only makes things worse. If you're like most women, there are probably some areas of your life where you are good at taking responsibility and others that could use improvement. You may be responsible at work, but when it comes to managing your finances or your health—you know what I mean.

We tend to like ourselves more in areas where we take responsibility. The opposite is also true. When we avoid taking responsibility, whether that's with money, health or some other area of our lives, we like ourselves less. If you want to feel better about yourself, start taking responsibility in more areas of your life. Here's an exercise to help you focus on building your self-esteem by becoming more responsible. Below are some stem sentences that will help you discover the benefits of increasing your responsibility. Please take the time to finish these sentences—it may provide a valuable breakthrough for you.

Example:

If I took more responsibility for my body I would exercise three times every week, drink six glasses of water daily and eat more fruits and vegetables.

- If I took more responsibility for my life I would...
- If I took more responsibility for my finances I would...
- If I took more responsibility for my happiness I would...
- If I took more responsibility for my work I would...

Now think of one specific area where you're not taking responsibility. The exercise below will be helpful.

1. Define the situation.
   Example: I do not take responsibility for my health.

2. List the benefits if you don't make any changes.
   Example: I can continue to eat what I want.
   I do not need to take time to exercise.

3. List the costs if you don't make any changes.
   Example: I will continue to put on weight.
   Low energy.

4. What are you pretending not to know?
   Example: I'm very unhealthy; I could be
   at risk for diabetes.

5. What can you do to be more responsible in this situation?
   Example: Take action—start by exercising every day.

6. When will you start?

Here are my own reflections. If I took more responsibility for my life, I'd stop being so busy and relax more. I'd have more fun and enjoy more belly laughs. I'd be kinder and more compassionate to myself. I'd strive for even more integrity and build my self-respect. I'd spend less and save more. I'd live more for today and be happier.

Third Building Block – Boost Your Self-Image

Self-image is the package you have assigned yourself. It is built on your life experiences—how you have interpreted what others said, how they treated you, what you told yourself. Your self-image may or may not be accurate, yet it forms your personal beliefs. A belief is anything we hold to be true. Most of our beliefs are formed in childhood, when our life experience and knowledge is limited. During that time we looked up to significant people—parents, teachers and others in authority—and mostly believed what they told us. Over the years these beliefs formed our attitudes and created our life experience.

Some of our beliefs go deep, to our core, while others lie just below the surface. Some labels—you're a loser!—may be surface-deep in one woman and cut to the core in another. If the second woman has low self-esteem, she could easily interpret this statement as, "I'm not worthy." A self-image of negative core beliefs can become increasingly negative as you grow older, unless you challenge and change them.

As an adult, you have beliefs about everything including your intelligence, competence, image and lovability. Unfortunately, much of what you believe is false. To help you better understand, consider this analogy. Have you ever worn someone else's prescription lenses? When you look through them everything is distorted, badly out of focus. The same is true when you adopt false beliefs. It's like you're wearing someone else's glasses—they distort the true image of you and your life.

Whose perceptions are you wearing? False beliefs limit you. They become the glasses through which you see your world. You don't see things as they are, you see things as you are. The glasses act as a filter, screening out anything that does not match your beliefs.

We don't see people as they are,
we see them as we are.

—Anaïs Nin

Cindy says, "I would like to meet someone nice," but her belief says, "Men can't be trusted." When Cindy goes out into the world she attracts men who can't be trusted. Her glasses let her see only what she believes. One day, if a great trustworthy guy shows up, she won't even notice him. The glasses of her beliefs will filter him out, and Cindy will carry on looking for Mr. Right in all the wrong places. Beliefs create your experiences. They must be constantly examined and challenged.

> At sixteen, Carol Ann was a typical teenager. She occasionally fought with her parents, she liked trendy clothes, her friends were important and boys were starting to be interesting. One day she caught the bus as she usually did, but something happened that day which changed her life. The bus was crowded and there were no seats available. A man standing behind her rubbed himself against her and touched her sexually.
>
> When Carol Ann got off the bus she was no longer a carefree teenager. She was changed. She told herself, "It must have been my fault, the way I was dressed." She also adopted the belief that all men were dirty, and vowed never to be touched like that again.

Painful experiences can change your beliefs. In his popular book, *Self Matters*, Dr. Phil McGraw writes about the ten defining moments that change your life. He is absolutely right. After working with women for many years, there is no doubt in my mind that painful incidents change people, and the consequences can be devastating. The tragedy is that most women do not connect the pain in their life today with events that may have taken place forty or fifty years ago.

Carol Ann is now thirty-five. She busies herself in her work; it is her life. But she is lonely and overweight. She would like to meet someone and have a family.

"After my experience on the bus, I started overeating to ease my pain. I can see that now. I blamed myself for being naive and attractive, so I lost the ability to trust myself. Being fat was my protective shield. It kept men away. I had no idea this had anything to do with the incident on the bus."

The good news is that today Carol Ann has moved on with her life. She has completed therapy to heal her pain and is finally having success with her weight problem.

Eleanor has deep feelings of inadequacy. "My dad was leaving for a tour of duty with the Army, and the day he left he kissed my sister goodbye but not me. As a three-year-old I believed he left because he didn't love me. As an adult, I still struggle with abandonment issues."

Have you created limiting beliefs because of a negative experience? It doesn't need to be something as dramatic as sexual abuse, divorcing parents, a death in the family or bankruptcy. Sometimes a simple childhood experience triggers a false belief. What may be inconsequential to a parent can be traumatic in the eyes of a child.

Do you have a critical or judgmental inner voice? Most of us do. It shows up in two ways—your own self-talk, or what others have said about you. Either way, it has programmed your thinking.

- I'm a hopeless student.
- I'm an awful cook.

- Why can't you be more like your sister?
- Can't you do anything right?

This programming starts early on, from the day you were born. If you were fortunate enough to grow up in a loving, supportive environment, your programming was most likely positive. If you experienced a dysfunctional, critical environment, your self-esteem is more likely to have been eroded by harsh words and putdowns. The excessive criticism my friend Doris received from her mother eventually took hold, and she became her own worst enemy. Just as she could never please her mother as she was growing up, now she can never please herself. Her critical internal voice never stops. "Doris don't be so stupid." "Doris you never do anything right."

Becoming aware of the critical voice gives us a chance to change and stop the old destructive programming that can limit us. When we are aware of this negative voice, we can learn to talk back to it. When you hear the voice, immediately use a strong word or phrase to break the negative train of thought. Cancel! Stop! That's a lie! Garbage! You decide what's best for you. Some people like to wear a rubber band around their wrist and snap it every time they hear the critical voice—it's a great thought-stopper. Practice replacing the critical words with a positive phrase, or use your own affirming statement. I am incredible! I am enough!

Beyond the words you hear and the thoughts you think, the words you speak can significantly affect you. Just as eating junk food all the time can lead to ill health and obesity, the words you use can also have a physical affect. Pay attention to this, otherwise the words you speak to yourself will rob you of power. We have identified some of the most common.

WHATEVER YOU TELL YOURSELF THE MIND ACCEPTS

Phrases	Examples
I have to	I have to pay my taxes.
I should	I should finish writing the paper.
I ought	I ought to start exercising.

These phrases come from feelings of guilt and powerlessness. The truth is that you always have the power to make the choices you want. Replace these disempowering phrases with:

I choose to	I choose to pay my taxes.
I choose not to	I choose not to finish writing the paper tonight.
I will	I will start exercising.

Read these phrases aloud. Notice the difference in how you feel. Have to, should and ought to, create negative energy, whereas choose to, choose not to, and I will, produce positive energy.

I can't	I can't stay up that late.
	Change this to:
	I choose not to stay up late.
I don't know	I don't know how I feel.
I'll try	I'll try to get your message to her.

Often these phrases sound weak and indecisive. Many women say I don't know to avoid or get out of something. To try is a lie. If you ask a friend to meet you for lunch tomorrow at noon and she says, "I'll try," how confident are you that she will show up? Exactly! Be decisive. Either you will or you won't.

| To be honest with you | To be honest with you, I'm really forty-four, not thirty-four. |
| To tell you the truth | To tell you the truth, I've only worked here two months, not two years. |

Using these phrases implies that most of the time you don't tell the truth. It sounds like everything you said up to this point was a lie. For example, how would you feel if the office equipment salesperson explains why his product is one of the best and then says, "To be honest with you, last year's model is a better buy." The word "but" is another negative energy producer. If your boss says, "You really did a great job on those sales calls, but...," the original compliment loses all of its impact. In some cases removing the word "but" is difficult. You can substitute "and" in most situations.

Whether you have developed a mild or severe case of using powerless language, you can change it. Be vigilant. This is a bad habit that can be changed. Start becoming more conscious of the language you use. Fine yourself one

"Can't we just talk without you dissecting every word I say?"

dollar every time you use powerless language. Have your kids help you, they'll love collecting the money; or include them in the game and you can cut your losses. Here are some other suggestions:

- Take a recipe card and draw a line down the center. On one side make a list of the powerless words you find yourself using. Write the more powerful words in the other column. Post it as a reminder.

- Enroll the help of friends; a women's group, or colleagues at the office, and keep each other accountable.

When you use more powerful language, your sense of self will change. How you are perceived by others will also change. You will be treated with more respect, and looked upon as someone who is responsible and decisive.

Don't be fooled by the simplicity of this concept. I couldn't believe how quickly I noticed a shift in myself just by saying I choose to, instead of I have to. Immediately I started feeling more responsible and more in control. Now that I am aware of the power of language I can quickly recognize women who feel powerless in their lives, just by listening to the words they use.

Fourth Building Block – The Competence Factor

Do you have the ability to think, reason and judge for yourself? Do you have a mind you trust? Do you defer to others most of the time? These are important questions to ponder as you continue to build a foundation for healthy self-esteem. Competence is like having internal security. You are self-reliant, you trust yourself to make good decisions, and you allow yourself to make mistakes. Competence builds confidence. You know you are capable, well-grounded and savvy enough to overcome the obstacles that life presents.

We all feel overwhelmed and helpless from time to time. The competent woman knows these situations are not permanent. She is proactive and uses her knowledge and ability to initiate solutions. Unlike Joan.

> "I usually rely on others to make choices for me and I accept their opinions. I was never taught to think for myself. My father made all the decisions for our family, and we were expected to do what he said without question."

No wonder Joan has difficulty building competence. She needs to start thinking for herself. Are you an independent thinker? Do your opinions matter? Are you in the habit of openly expressing yourself?

If you are struggling with feelings of insecurity and uncertainty, this can be frightening. The way to conquer the fear is to push through the anxiety and speak up anyway, believing that your opinions have value. If you keep practicing this, it will become easier. Eventually it will be a habit that feels natural.

To keep this in perspective, it's impossible to be competent in all areas of your life, and you don't need to be. I believe some motivational speakers and self-help gurus are doing women a disservice by telling them to always be confident and upbeat. That's not the real world.

A woman who has been out of the job market for eight years may not feel competent re-entering the workforce. However, she really shines at managing the home. So do yourself a favor—lighten up, you can't be great at everything. In a nutshell, here's what will build the competence factor for you:

- Experience life fully—actively participate.
- Understand that unexpected challenges teach you resilience.
- Take responsibility; think for yourself.

- Make your own choices and decisions.
- Improve your skills, keep learning.
- Trust yourself.

If you have children at home, take heed. Allow them to become decision makers; let them take some risks and make mistakes. By doing so, you are letting them know that you believe in their abilities. Children who learn to be responsible for themselves build their own level of competence.

Fifth Building Block – Self-Worth

Worthiness can be a difficult concept to grasp. It is closely aligned with these other self-esteem principles, but how do you prove it even exists? Worthiness does exist, and you have it. It doesn't matter what you've done, what has been done to you, whether you feel shame or guilt—your worth is fundamental, and it cannot be diminished. If I held up a $5 bill and asked, "How much is this worth?" You would answer $5. Then if I took that $5 bill and crumpled it up in my fist and asked, "How much is it worth now?" You'd answer $5. If I took the $5 bill and crumpled it up, stomped on it, threw it in a mud puddle and then asked you, "Now, how much is it worth?" you'd still answer $5.

I believe unworthiness is a spiritual sickness because our worth comes from God. We are all born with a physical body, a mind, emotions and a spirit. Unworthiness at its core is evidence of a damaged spirit. It's difficult to express love in this condition. If parents have a low self-worth, they may not know how to love. In those unfortunate situations the child shoulders the blame. "I must not be worthy of love, I'm defective, I'm not good enough." This lack of worthiness can be passed on from one generation to the next.

Children in this environment learn that to feel worthy of love they need to act a certain way, to be a "nice little girl." Or love is tied to accomplishments such as getting excellent grades at school. Little wonder we are confused when we are programmed to believe our worth is based on how we act or what we do.

Self-worth comes from who you are, not what you do. You can look for your worth through achievements, by wearing masks and building pseudo self-esteem from external sources, and announce, "Look, I'm worthy." But inside you still feel hollow and unworthy. Your internal critic says, "You are not good enough." As a result, you feel lost and unloved.

As I said before, your worth comes from God. This is a divine gift and does not require validation or proof. It will always be a part of you. It's where your creativity, enthusiasm, peace, love, trust, happiness, joy and wisdom reside. It's your spiritual core and it is invincible. Just know that you are worthy, you are enough—right now.

Can you say that with conviction, really believing it? I am enough! This is a cry from your spirit. Women who know they are enough value the way they are treated and how they treat others. What about your values? Do you allow people to take you for granted or to demean you? Do you treat others with little or no respect? Only when you feel worthy and have love for yourself can you love others unconditionally. Then your love will be unlimited and will flow freely.

Spiritual matters are personal. Individually, we must discover our own definition and meaning. If you feel unworthy, you can always seek God. A spiritual void is an empty feeling. It's like being unplugged from the source. However, the source is always there. It's up to you to re-connect.

Sixth Building Block – Self-Acceptance

It is crucial to have a loving relationship with yourself. It isn't just a good thing, it is absolutely indispensable for a healthy, meaningful life. Of all the relationships you will have in this lifetime, you are the only one who will never leave you. Some of us have bought into the belief that it is selfish, conceited and morally suspect to love and accept ourselves. We are taught to satisfy others and live for everyone else. This is not the moral high ground. Yes, I know we've all had enough of the "me, myself and I" generation. It's not about that.

This is about building self-esteem, by honoring and accepting yourself with all of your faults and attributes. That means loving yourself with compassion and forgiveness. You cannot expect to contribute to the world, to show compassion and love others, when you reject yourself. To fully accept yourself is to embrace all the parts of who you are. It's easy to love the side of you that's generous, compassionate, happy and helpful. But what about the greedy, angry, jealous or envious side of your character? You need to accept these attributes too. If you only accept the good parts you are rejecting yourself, and you will never feel whole. By doing so, you automatically reject others as well.

Humans play a sad game called Projection. We don't accept our hidden traits. We project them onto others. Debbie Ford, in her book *The Dark Side of the Light Chasers*, uses a good analogy: Imagine having a hundred different electrical outlets on your chest. Each outlet represents a different quality. The qualities we acknowledge and embrace have cover plates on them. They are safe: no electricity runs through them. But the qualities that are not okay with us, which we have not yet owned, do have a charge. So when others come along who act out one of these qualities, they plug right into us.

For example, if we deny or are uncomfortable with our anger, we will attract angry people into our lives. We will suppress our own angry feelings and judge people whom we see as angry. Since we lie to ourselves about our own internal feelings, the only way we can find them is to see them in others. Other people mirror back our hidden emotions and feelings, which allows us to recognize and reclaim them. Next time you judge someone else for having a negative quality, take a look at yourself first. See if this same quality is part of your own character, but you haven't accepted it yet.

After working with many women over the years, I realize just how hard we can be on ourselves. I have a request—be kinder and gentler with yourself, become your own best friend. Acknowledge the fact you are human and you make mistakes. Learn to be compassionate and forgiving of yourself, as you would be to a dear friend. Value and love the unique person you are, as you strive to love and accept others.

THE PHOTO

I found an old photo
I was five
With rosy apple cheeks
And shining curly locks
Smiling my widest smile
Showing gums where my two front teeth
Used to be.
I looked into my five-year-old eyes
And I was moved to tears
Because I could see the love and hope in them.
I sobbed like my heart would break.
How could I have abandoned her?
How could I have forgotten to love her all these years?
I rocked her picture in my arms and held her
Close to my aching heart.
I promise never to leave you again
I will love you till the day I die.
This was the start of my healing.

—Fran Hewitt

We'll conclude this chapter with a unique story. It's about my friend Jana, whose changing life circumstances caused her self-esteem to plummet. Knowing the dream she had, I wondered if she would ever turn things around.

The atmosphere was electric!
Her unmistakable voice had everyone on the edge of their seats. Superstar Diana Ross was delivering another stunning performance in the jam-packed Las Vegas auditorium, belting out hit after hit. It was the early '70s and the audience was mesmerized, none more so than twenty-four-year-old Jana Stanfield, sitting near the front, reduced to tears by the diva's performance. These were not tears of joy or adulation. These were heartfelt tears, painful to express: "I was wishing so much that I was the one up there on stage. I knew I had the capacity and talent to perform and it hurt me physically, in my heart, not to be pursuing my passion." This was a defining moment for Jana, one that would send her reeling into deep depression, agonizing over the fact that she had not made better choices. She felt hopelessly sad.

Jana Stanfield's story embraces all of the issues that we have discussed in this chapter: Upon leaving school, Jana chose a large college in Texas to major in broadcast journalism. She thought it would be cool to experience an out-of-state environment. The student population was almost as big as her hometown. She felt like an outsider who didn't fit in. This feeling of not being accepted was something new, and hard to understand. Her parents' marriage was also in trouble. She loved them both, and it was confusing and heart wrenching to see the family break up. They soon divorced and Jana felt her self-esteem plummet. On a scale of one to ten she was in the negative numbers, off the chart. She felt like a failure and was grieving over the split in her family. This was her first real experience of low self-esteem and the impact was devastating. Her kind uncle, a minister, took the time to have lunch with her every week, and provided much-needed counsel.

Jana used a unique strategy called *Three Steps, No Failure* to create a full-time opportunity for herself in the music industry. (You'll learn more about this in Chapter Eight). The transition was slow and challenging. Jana worked as a TV news journalist for four years and became competent at writing stories for her broadcasts. Little did she know this would be an important stepping stone to her future career. Deciding to go out on her own and move to Nashville, the hub of the music industry, was a defining moment. She had no place to stay, no phone and no job. A room in a $14-per-night dormitory was her first home. Gradually she met people and found work as an administrative assistant in a record promotions company.

While waiting for her breakthrough she educated herself; songwriting classes, voice lessons, stand up comedy and dance. She sang for free in the evenings. Open-Mic nights gave her exposure. Before her first performance Jana was shaking so badly she could hardly sing. This was Nashville after all, intimidating, and very competitive. She auditioned for TV shows, talent contests, and Opryland.

Rejection was commonplace. Eventually she made a few recordings with the help of an undiscovered producer and did a series of shows for record companies. Her dream was to secure a recording contract. All of the record companies expressed disinterest. What would you do at this point? Eking out a living from month to month, along with the constant rejection, was eroding Jana's belief in herself. She had suffered a big drop in income compared to her days as a broadcast journalist, and was really doubting her decision to switch careers. Jana took a year off to re-examine her motives. She calls it her, "Lying on the bed, crying phase." To improve herself in every way she attended twelve-step programs and various counseling groups. This helped her to grow emotionally. She started writing and recording again with renewed determination.

The release of her first record, consisting of what she fondly calls her "ten most-rejected songs," was another milestone. Jana's refusal to quit and her step-by-step approach paved the way eventually for a major breakthrough. She wrote a beautiful song called *If I Had Only Known*. Reba McIntyre asked to record it, and sold five million copies! Jana was now performing in front of small audiences and making enough money from the sale of her tapes that she no longer needed freelance work to sustain her.

In the last twelve years she has become a star in her own right with a dedicated fan base, and has sold almost 100,000 CDs on her own without the help of a recording contract. She has performed in Australia, Canada, Thailand and New Zealand, and opened for the Dixie Chicks and Kenny Loggins. Recently she won a major talent contest and sang on the main stage at the Grand Ole Opry, receiving a standing ovation.

Reflecting on her success she says: "I believe in the power of small steps to create great changes. Your ability to focus evolves as you get older. My first focus was to change careers, secondly to become a star. Now I'm focused on being helpful. I've discovered that the more I help people with my music, the more they want to take it home with them." She calls her music, "heavy mental" because it causes you to think, and as thousands have discovered, it's inspired them to pursue their own dreams too.

A Man's Perspective Les Hewitt

Compared to women, men are generally not good at expressing emotion. Most of the time we don't even use words that describe how we feel. Many of my male friends and clients come across as confident and competent. On the surface everything appears under control. Internally, it's often a different story. We do have concerns about money, our families, and our careers. There's also a lot of energy around how successful we are. How are we measuring up compared to everyone else?

Many of us are very competitive and driven to sell more, have more and earn more. Those who work in large companies are often under intense pressure to produce bigger and better results, in order to move up the corporate ladder. Sometimes our backs are against the wall financially, when the economy goes into a tailspin, or we get downsized.

Then our self-esteem is really tested. In these situations, the last thing we want to hear at home is, "Where's the money coming from? Are we going to be able to pay the bills next month?" Despite all of the outward bravado, our confidence can be so fragile that lack of emotional support from the family is devastating. Sometimes we feel scared, anxious and uncertain. We worry about making bad decisions, especially ones that may affect the future of our family. The stress can be so bad that we won't share our true feelings. We just stuff them and play the strong silent type, which does nothing to ease our fear. Be sensitive to our pressures. Like yours, they are real. Avoid blaming. Focus on working together as a team. Everyone needs encouragement, especially when times are tough. Men are no different.

CONCLUSION

Life experiences and circumstances can affect the level of your self-esteem. In Jana's case one traumatic incident (her parents' divorce), combined with the feeling of being rejected at college, was enough to cause a freefall in confidence that led to acute depression. Jana had a good education and a promising career, yet she still felt empty inside. Her real passion was music, but until she rebuilt her self-esteem she was unable to explore and express this unique talent.

You can turn any situation around by working on the six building blocks and enlisting the support of people you trust, respect and like. The lesson is clear. Building a healthy self-esteem is vital for your future well-being and success. One of the biggest payoffs, as we saw with Jana, is that it gives you the confidence to pursue and live your lifelong dreams.

ACTION STEPS

Changing Beliefs

Then, Now and Moving On

Self-Acceptance

My Negative Beliefs and Behavior.

Relax and take a few deep cleansing breaths. Ask yourself the following:

What core beliefs are running my life?
Take a look at all the major areas.

Things I have told myself or believed about myself from others:

my intelligence	my anger
my self-image	education
my worthiness	the opposite sex
my sexuality	labels I have adopted
my success	my beliefs on religion
money	others

Use the two columns on the following page to list these beliefs and the behavior you associate with each one.

My Negative Beliefs	How This Belief Shows Up In My Behavior
_____	_____
_____	_____

Look at your list and ask yourself the following questions:

a. Why do I have this belief?

b. Is this my belief or did I adopt it from someone else?

c. What would happen if I gave this belief up?

To know the cost of holding onto the belief, ask yourself:

a. How long have I believed this?

b. How is this belief showing up in my life?

c. If I still have this belief five, ten, fifteen years from now, what are the consequences?

Beliefs can be changed once you become aware of them. To remove limiting beliefs it's important to challenge your thinking and create a new reality. I believed for years I was incompetent at math, until I met an excellent teacher who tutored me. With patience and lots of encouragement, I discovered not only could I do math, I excelled at it. That was my new reality.

Sometimes beliefs are developed due to traumatic and painful experiences. Uncovering a belief can often bring up emotions. Let go of any painful emotions and feelings involved. Once the energy of the feeling has been released the belief can be changed.

Take the analogy of a brick wall. Bricks are your beliefs and the mortar is your feelings holding them in place. Release the feelings, release the bricks.

Then, Now and Moving On
Traumatic incidents and painful experiences unfortunately are a part of life. Even though it can be painful to revisit these events, it is very worthwhile. What you discover can help you eliminate old thinking patterns, uncover limiting beliefs, and help you become aware how these events can still be affecting your life today. Take time to do this exercise thoroughly. First make a list of the specific experiences you wish to evaluate. Then use the set of questions below to help you review each incident. This may trigger your emotions. If tears come, let them flow. If your stomach hurts, experience it. This is all part of your healing. Give yourself time to remember and reflect. Use a journal to record your answers and any other thoughts.

THEN

What was the incident?

How old were you?

How many years have you carried this?

Describe what happened?

What did you tell yourself?
(About you, the people involved, life.)

What feelings did you have?

What did you need at the time and not get?

NOW

How does this incident show up in your life today?
(Self-sabotage, relationships, overweight, rejection.)

How has it changed you?

How much longer do you want to carry it?

See and feel the price you have paid.

What is your payoff for keeping it alive? Be honest
(Stay a victim, be able to blame and not take responsibility,
don't want to forgive, can continue to judge/hurt yourself.)

If you continue to hold onto this incident for the next five
or ten years, what will your future look like?

Is this what you want?

MOVING ON

a) With conviction, say these statements aloud,
    or to yourself:

    I have paid enough.
    I will not allow him (her, them) to run my life anymore.

    Do this three times. This is the start of a new
    commitment with yourself to move on.

b) Let go of any emotions that come up.

    If you are angry, release it.
    If you are still hurt, cry.

If you still feel stuck after doing this exercise a few times, consider getting professional counseling to help you move on. You
are worth it! To move on—only spend 10 percent of your time
thinking about these incidents (how unfair it was, what you
learned, etc.). Focus 90 percent of your time on getting on
with your life.

Self-Acceptance
Read this exercise twice before creating the experience.

Step One
Imagine someone you love and admire is sitting in a chair facing you. He or she is smiling at you. How do you feel about this person? If this person was to make a mistake, could you, and would you, forgive him or her?

Step Two
Using your imagination, put *yourself* in the chair opposite you. Imagine that you are sitting there smiling back at yourself. How do you feel about her? Do you feel the same way about her as you did towards the first person, the one you love and admire, or is the feeling different? If this woman (you) made a mistake, could you, or would you, forgive her? Are you more forgiving of the other person?

   This exercise often highlights a discrepancy between how we love and accept others, compared to ourselves.

Step Three
Find a photograph of yourself as a child, any age is fine, and place it where you can see it everyday. Let this remind you to be loving and accepting of yourself.

Balance: Challenge of the Century

Women want men, careers, children, friends,
luxury, comfort, independence, freedom, respect,
love, and $3 pantyhose that won't run.

—Phyllis Diller

My sister Anna accepts the reality of being a single mom, raising two sons, three-year-old Ben and one-year-old Henry. As you can imagine, her hands are full. Between the kids' needs and the never-ending running around, she does an incredible job and seems to be coping well. When asked how she created balance, and kept herself sane, she said:

"For me it was all about making mental adjustments. I gave up my high standards around the home. If half of the house is clean at any one time that's good enough. I also decided to accept the fact that I would have less income and less personal time during this stage of my life. I deliberately took the focus off any lack, and concentrated on what I do have. My two boys are healthy and I'm grateful for that and the time we spend together. Friends and neighbors provide invaluable support. Just being able to have a chat on the phone or enroll another pair of hands to help is very satisfying."

Many women think it is impossible to live a balanced lifestyle without being wealthy or enjoying a leisurely retirement. I quite agree—acquiring a satisfactory balance between work and family, with time for personal and spiritual growth, fun, friends, relaxation, household chores, community activities and vacation, is unrealistic and virtually unattainable for most women today.

Managing a busy life is a daunting proposition, despite the latest technologies at our fingertips. The two most common statements I hear are, "I always seem to be rushing because there's never enough time," and "I just wish my life was simpler and more meaningful."

The philosophy of balance still being touted by some self-help experts doesn't fit anymore. "We can have it all, and do it all," they say. But that's not even close to being within the grasp of most women. The word balance implies equality. It suggests spending equal amounts of time and energy in all areas of our lives. But for most of us, that's impossible. For working mothers in particular, family life collides with job requirements. Hassled, hustled and hurried, too many women are experiencing too much stress and feeling out of control. We have become prisoners of time, desperately seeking the illusion of a wonderful, balanced way of life.

There is no one-size-fits-all when it comes to defining balance. In this chapter we will examine many aspects of this, and offer proven, practical solutions. Balance depends on our personalities, and our particular set of circumstances. As women, we go through many stages, including being single, getting married and raising a family. Some of us experience divorce or become widowed, and eventually we all must deal with retirement. Balance differs with each stage.

Right now, balance for you is probably quite different than it is for me. You may be a single parent raising two young children and working a full-time job. Prioritizing your time, having a strong support network, outsourcing and delegating effectively would all be high on your checklist. Spending special time with your children and paying attention to personal care would also be important in order for you to enjoy a good balance in your life.

I'm at the empty nest stage now. Balance for me is having time for my primary relationship with Les, working part time and feeling fulfilled by it. Self-care, spiritual development and staying healthy also get significant attention.

Finding balance involves two main issues—time and stress. Time and stress are inter-related. With more time, you feel less stress. The big question is: how do you find more time and reduce your stress? The bad news is that there isn't any more time. You only get 1,440 minutes every day. What makes the difference is how you use that time. Use it skillfully, and you can enjoy better balance. Waste it and you will feel like you're always on a treadmill, racing to catch up.

Strategies that are successful in the business world need to be adopted on the home front with the same tenacity, discipline and focus. Prioritizing and scheduling are paramount. So, too, is making sure that what you do is in harmony with your values. Delegating effectively and outsourcing will free up more time. Downsizing and simplifying your life will free up more energy.

Making these adjustments requires a different way of thinking. It takes innovative planning and focus. Creating the type of balance that's best for you may require considerable effort. The first step is to clearly define what balance means to you. Then make a list of the rewards you will enjoy for attaining it.

BALANCE IS SOMETHING YOU DESIGN

Blending Work and
FAMILY

Our uncertain economy and high cost of living are causing more women to trade in the playground for a paycheck. Some do not have much of a choice. More single moms than ever before are working to support the family. Family economics often dictate the situation. A divorce may mean a woman is thrust back into the marketplace after not working in a job for years. Or a husband is laid off and his wife ends up being the primary breadwinner, while he becomes a house dad.

Becky, thirty-six, works as a computer programmer and is under a lot of stress. "I know I'm not happy, but I just put the blinders on. I prefer not to look too closely at my circumstances in case I lose hope. But the reality is that my husband's unemployment is threatening our marriage."

Becky's husband, Steve, was laid off from a large IT company two years ago. Up until that point the couple had lived comfortably on their two salaries while raising their son, Jason, who's now three. Steve is still being Mr. Mom. He says he prefers to wait for another position in his field rather than accept any old job just to pay the bills. But Steve feels his manhood is threatened if he does too many "feminine" chores. That means most of the household tasks still fall on Becky's shoulders. Becky is unhappy and resentful. She wishes Steve would make more of an effort to find a job. The intense pressure of being the only wage earner is wearing her out. She is watching their savings dwindle, and money issues have become a constant battle. "The tension between Steve and I is exhausting. When it comes to intimacy, my resentment and anger always get in the way." Becky knows it's time to confront the issue or the marriage will collapse.

Becky's story is not uncommon. When a situation suddenly changes, stress and resentment often occur. Becky's feelings need to be addressed quickly. Steve must agree to take more responsibility by increasing his efforts at finding a job and helping out more at home. Although life may not be ideal, there will be better balance, and their relationship will be healthier.

There is no doubt that the biggest challenge facing many women is the struggle to balance the demands of work with the needs of family. Single mothers have it extra hard, being the sole caretakers and having to meet their financial needs as well. I feel badly for mothers who prefer to stay home but find it necessary to work. Recently I watched a television program on this subject. My heart ached watching one young mother rising at dawn, sadly kissing her kids goodbye as she reluctantly left the house, quietly crying on her way to the office.

On the other hand, many mothers choose to work. They love the job, or the challenge of building a business. It's not so much about making the mortgage payment, they enjoy the creative rush, the thrill of competition. Work is an important part of who they are, and a constant source of nourishment.

Melanie has figured it out. An energetic mother of two, she is president of her own executive search firm. "I have always worked. The fact that I have a family now certainly adds a new dimension. And it's sometimes stressful. But I love my business, I have great clients and I'm motivated. I'm also a good mother and work hard at it. It's tiring, but I do take care of myself. There are days when family comes before work and vice versa, so I've learned to prioritize. There are trade-offs of course. My home is not as tidy as it could be and I don't always cook dinner. We have take-out a few times a week. I know it's not the most nutritious way to eat and I feel a bit guilty at times. However, that's just one of the trade-offs. My business is important to me."

Many working mothers are demanding more creative schedules and flexible hours in an effort to find something that works. This concept is gaining acceptance with progressive employers. They understand that a happy workplace improves productivity and reduces stress. Unfortunately, a lot of organizations still have the outdated attitude that motherhood is a distraction that hurts the bottom line.

An interesting development these days is that more women than men are starting their own businesses, many of which are operated from home base. And one of the fastest-growing employment trends is women working out of their homes. This is a great win-win situation that can provide flexibility and save time.

Gina loves being home with her kids, Tyler, three, and Duncan, four. "I used to work downtown in the main office," she says. "I hated the morning daily commute, leaving home at seven a.m. to be at work by eight. That meant my kids were up really early so I could get them ready for daycare. I was never home before six at night. It was too much for me. I was feeling burnt out, so I approached my boss about working from home. He agreed to a trial period. I haven't looked back since. Working from homeis the best of both worlds. I do have challenges with interruptions and distractions, but it's kept me sane. And my kids are happier.

I'm grateful to be at home, especially if one of the kids is sick. I do feel guilty when I have a report due and both of the kids are demanding my attention. Most days I can focus, but there are times when I can't help noticing the growing mountain of laundry or the trail of muddy feet down the hallway. Mostly it works out well though. My boss is happy that my work gets done, and I'm not feeling so burnt out. The kids are happy to be at home, and we save a lot of money that used to go to daycare, transportation and expensive clothes for work."

Gina has figured out how to make the most of her opportunity, but a word of caution—this situation doesn't work for everyone. Some women find it difficult to switch off their work role and enjoy family time. Even though they are physically present with the kids, their minds are at work. Unless they schedule and prioritize effectively, they feel out of control and inadequate on both fronts. It takes discipline and focus to be totally present in both roles.

The family dynamic has dramatically changed. Compared to the pace experienced by our grandmothers and even our mothers, life today is faster and more demanding. More than 68 percent of women now have jobs. Employers require higher levels of commitment and performance, and kids are involved in more extracurricular activities—women routinely add the job of chauffeur to their growing list of responsibilities. However, working women who hold on to the ideal picture of motherhood are setting themselves up for an exhausting, resentful existence.

When it comes to motherhood, many of us cling to old thinking. We still believe that the gold standard goes to stay-at-home moms. These women can spend more time with their young children because they don't have the pressure of a job outside of the home. Stay-at-home moms volunteer in the classroom, bake cookies and have time to play with their children during the day along with running the household.

The gold standard doesn't work anymore. It needs re-defining. The first shift you need to make is a mental one. Let go of the old paradigm that worked for your mother. In this new world, the old stereotype doesn't fit anymore. You need to abandon traditional definitions. Creating excellent balance today has a lot to do with letting go.

When you work full time, go home to nightly chores and end up with weekends filled with to-do lists, you can't possibly live up to this ideal mom role. When you are not happy, the family is not happy. No wonder balance is elusive.

I hate housework! You make the beds,
you do the dishes, and six months later
you have to start all over again.

—Joan Rivers

Being consumed with your mother role robs you of balance. This can easily happen, especially when you are raising young children. Your kids become the focus—all your attention and energy is poured into this. But it's important to separate yourself from your sleep-deprived, snack-making, diaper-changing role. Wear something other than sweats with that permanent drool stain on the shoulder. If you don't take regular time-outs for you, balance will quickly be lost. Please understand that I am not suggesting you abdicate your role as a mother. Far from it. But can you really have it all? Probably not, especially if you are still hanging on to the June Cleaver standard of motherhood.

Let go. Change your mind about the "perfect mom" model, and tune in to the reality of the world today. There are many ways to be a great mom. Let go of any guilt you may be feeling, and let yourself off the hook.

Running On
EMPTY

Do you still own the outdated belief that household tasks are all yours? If so, you aren't alone—many women who work full time still do most of the work at home. Of course single women do not have an option.

Admittedly, some women seem to enjoy this. It gives them a chance to nurture and build their female identity. But to achieve better balance, working women need to loosen the reins on their traditional time-honored chores. Is it really the fault of the man in your life—the one who controls the remote and clings to his male privileges, instead of offering to help around the house? Or have you set it up this way? Are you contributing to the imbalance?

I'm guilty as charged. I know a lot about this topic from personal experience. When it came to household chores, I built my own prison. My husband Les is an Irishman and an only child—need I say more? His mother waited on him hand and foot, so of course he grew up believing the world revolved around him and his needs. He never learned to cook because there was always a hot dinner before him.

Along came little old me to take over where Mummy left off. Already forging my trail to martyrdom, I insisted on doing it my way, which meant the laundry was ironed and neatly folded, kids fed, bathed and changed, meals were hot and the standard was gourmet. Looking back, I think I was cracked!

Today, I am a recovering house-a-holic. I've promoted myself to Household Director. I delegate and now have time to take a painting class. I love my new position. Les is learning how to broaden his skills, including how to iron a shirt and do a load of laundry. Life is good!

Most men will not volunteer to do half the housework. If both of you are working full time, you must demand that your spouse shoulders an equal portion of the burden at home, unless you enjoy the thought of a second shift after the office. Learn to speak up. Just because women are nurturing by nature shouldn't lead to an assumption by other family members that house work is women's work.

Single parent families carry the bigger load caused by not having a partner. When it comes to the household, everything falls on their shoulders. My friend Marie became the sole breadwinner for her family overnight when her husband passed away. Her two children were still very young and she was incredibly busy building her home-based interior design business. There wasn't much time for doing household tasks.

Marie started delegating any task that her children could reasonably accomplish. Today they are both responsible, competent young adults. Marie took a potentially overwhelming situation and turned it into something more manageable.

Today, creating a happy family life is all about sharing responsibilities and having fun together. Not asking for help with the chores implies that you are accepting responsibility for them, and you end up pleading for assistance rather than having a well-defined agreement in place. Sharing is a much healthier concept, and it will help you maintain lower stress levels.

In olden times sacrifices were made at the altar
—a custom which is still continued!

—Helen Rowland

Here's another important point. If you have a possessive nature for all things household, you are robbing your loved ones of the opportunity to develop valuable life skills. Are you teaching your teenage son to be a couch potato? If so, think of your future daughter-in-law. Are you, by your example, setting your daughter up to be a do-it-all type of wife who will have no time for herself?

Delegating effectively requires that you be a patient teacher until the student has learned, after which you must have the foresight to let go. A mother eagle spends time nurturing her young, but instinctively knows that her most important role is to push her offspring out of the nest, trusting that they will be able to fly. Amazingly, they do!

Avoid the temptation to take over. Lynn says, "I don't have the time to teach my kids how to cook. If they do it, I know it will be a mess. I'll get mad and have to clean up after them."

Okay, so your white socks end up blue and your best wool sweater now fits the cat. Be patient, it will get better. Start by giving up control of the easy tasks, and learn to bite your tongue. Delegating frees up your time. The bonus is that the kids (or people in your office) will feel valued, knowing that you trust them to get the job done.

Delegating Tips (For Home or Office)

1. Be specific and clear in communicating your expectations.
2. Have the other person verify what you said.
3. Demonstrate how to do the task—if necessary, more than once.
4. Be patient—encourage instead of criticizing.
5. Resist redoing the job or over-correcting.
6. Set high standards, but beware of perfectionism.
7. Kids are not adults—give them time to learn.

Family Council

Family Council meetings are great forums for communication and delegation, as well as for handling any prickly issues that come along. For years we had Family Council once a week at suppertime, usually on the weekend. It's an opportunity for everyone to take note of their responsibilities for the upcoming week, and to be accountable for completing assigned tasks. Here are a few guidelines:

1. Set the same time aside each week so a routine is established. This could be right after church on Sunday, or following cartoons on Saturday morning.

2. The length of the meeting is dictated by the ages of the children. Meetings should last twenty to thirty minutes, but younger kids have short attention spans, so set your watch accordingly. Children need to be old enough to communicate, and to do easy chores.

3. Select a chairperson and someone to take notes, especially about who's doing what and when. Using a weekly calendar is helpful for scheduling. You may want to rotate the roles each week.

4. Start on a positive note by asking each person to describe the best thing that happened during the past week. This creates good energy—the rule is that everyone must participate. Kids love to take center stage, so you may want to limit this to a couple of things each, otherwise you might be there all day.

5. Next up is sharing the chores: tidying, cutting the grass, taking the garbage out, walking the dog, vacuuming, watering plants, etc. Be sensitive to what your kids can realistically accomplish. A rule of thumb is to assign two tasks each. Teenagers can handle more.

6. Discuss items not completed from the previous week, and the appropriate consequences.

7. If there is disagreement or issues arise, listen to both sides. When making decisions, be firm but fair. You may want to take a vote on some situations.

8. Avoid dragging out negative topics for too long. Move on to other relevant events such as upcoming holidays, school trips or special needs. To create positive energy, always end Family Council with some good news or recognition.

Another way we created balance was to have a Family Day each week where we all did something together. One person in the family was allowed to choose where we went and what we did. Everyone took turns at this.

Start To Outsource

If you want more time to do the things you really enjoy, outsourcing is the way to go. Yes, it takes money, but for many working mothers outsourcing is not only a potential marriage saver, it's a lifesaver, too. Do you remember the story about Becky and Steve? Becky was resentful because Steve wasn't making much of an effort to find work, nor was he helping out around the house. Steve eventually found a good job, and they decided to use some of his income to outsource. Becky now has a babysitter coming in two evenings a week so that she and Steve can have a date night, plus another evening where they can be free to do what they want. They also hired a house-keeper twice a month. Becky says:

> "I am so much more relaxed about the house being totally cleaned every two weeks. It's taken some of the pressure off. Steve and I really look forward to our date nights. Even though we've had to stretch a little financially, it's been money well spent. Our relationship has never been better."

To free up time while minimizing costs, be creative. Hire the teenager next door to cut your lawn or weed the garden. Ask family and friends for help with babysitting. For years my sister looked after our kids once a week. Is there a retired handyman in your neighborhood who would love to do odd jobs—painting, electrical, fence repair—around the house? It was great when our kids learned to drive. They were happy to do errands just for the opportunity to borrow the car. One of my friends hates going to the mall to shop for clothes, so she avoids the hassle by ordering from online catalogs. She does this on her own time and saves hours in the process.

Break the busy routine, and lower your stress. Outsourcing can also free you from cooking. Have family members share the load, hire someone, or use take-out (there are some healthy ones). It doesn't need to be expensive. The key is to find as many ways as you can to save thirty minutes here and there. This adds up to several hours per week that can be put to better use. It's all about finding balance, conserving energy and creating time to rejuvenate, whether that means listening to your favorite music, having a massage or gardening.

Standards and
EXPECTATIONS

Rethink them. This is a touchy subject for some people, especially perfectionists. I'm not suggesting you lower your standards, just re-frame them in the context of living as a woman in today's real world. Let go of the attitude that, "I'm the only one who can do it right." What drives some women crazy is not the messy house, dirty car, job or even a hectic schedule—often it is their own impossible expectations. People create so many rules about the way things must be done at work and at home that not only are they unhappy, but everyone else around them is, too. Be aware that Ms. Perfect is a pain to live with when she's resentful, irritable, difficult to please and exhausted. Not a pretty picture, and certainly not one that portrays a happy balance. I mean, is it okay that the cookies for the meeting are store-bought instead of homemade? Is it okay that your house isn't spotless seven days a week?

In my opinion, today's society places far too much emphasis on having the perfect house (I don't call it a home) with nearly impossible standards of cleanliness. Unless you have the time to totally focus on cleaning, lighten up! This is another super-high standard that will only add more unnecessary pressure, especially if you are a mother with young children.

Have you seen those television commercials that demonstrate how easy it is to have everything in the kitchen spotless and gleaming? Even when the kids drag mud all over the pristine floor, Mom is right behind with a mop applying the new magic formula, looking perfectly relaxed and smiling! Don't you just hate her? In the real world Mom is busy wiping greasy fingerprints from the front of the stove for the fourth time that day; the baby's high chair is dripping chocolate pudding, and when the kids traipse over the not-so-clean floor wearing muddy boots Mom chases them with the mop, screaming like a banshee.

No, your floors do not need the super-gloss shine every day, nor do your towels require folding just so. Get real—give yourself, and everyone around you a break. Maybe your reality right now is a life of kids, dogs and messy people. Some day that will change. My own kids used to remind me, "Mom, it doesn't need to be perfect!" They were right. Whether you

"Cinderella lived happily ever after until she had kids. After that she was too tired to know if she was happy or not."

have a young family or not, ask yourself, "How much fun am I to live with?" Are you compromising your balance, your relationships and your own happiness by insisting on impossible-to-meet standards? When all is said and done, you'll discover it's your relationships that matter most. Make sure you nourish those more than anything else. When kids look back on their lives they rarely say they're glad the floors sparkled. Instead, they're happy because Mom let go, and allowed them to use the couch pillows to build forts on the floor.

From Chaos To Calm
High stress levels are a serious problem. Managing stress is essential for maintaining balance and having a healthy body. To conserve emotional energy, we need to become clear about which situations we can, and cannot, change. Most working women struggle with something called spillover. This occurs when one area of our life affects another, and it creates stress. If our job involves inflexible hours, a high-pressure environment or a lot of travel, the negative spillover can affect our family life.

On the other hand, having a sick child, finding convenient daycare, dealing with an unsupportive partner or looking after elderly parents can have a spillover effect at work. It's difficult to focus on doing a good job when other urgent matters are demanding our energy and attention.

For most women, spillover is a fact of life. No magic wand will erase it. The best we can do is to learn how to manage each situation, and put a lid on the stress. It helps to keep everything in perspective, and to trust intuition. Later I'll provide some practical tips that will neutralize future stress attacks.

The Juggling Act
Do you ever feel like a juggler, trying to keep all the balls up in the air? Most women do an amazing job of juggling work, kids, home, health, fitness, extended family, bill paying and so on. The list seems like it's a mile long for some women, and still they manage everything. But sometimes life adds an

unexpected ball to the mix. The car breaks down on the way to pick up the kids from swimming, you have parent teacher interviews in an hour and you still need to prepare and pack for tomorrow's business trip. Your supervisor at the office asks you to work Saturday on yet another project that has an impossible deadline. Yes, the unexpected can cause your stress to surge out of control.

The bad thing about negative stress is that the buck stops with your body. Your healthy habits, such as exercise programs and nutritious meals, are usually the first to suffer when you are struggling to cope with a heavy workload. When you are always over-committing, juggling more and more balls, your body finally says, "Enough, I can't handle this anymore."

Brian Dyson says, "Imagine life as a game in which you are juggling five balls...work, family, health, friends and spirit. Work is a rubber ball. If you drop it, it will bounce back. But the other four balls are made of glass. If you drop one of these, they will never be the same." When that happens, the balls all come crashing down and you end up with disease (stress), which is only one step away from disease.

Living a Quality
LIFE

Let's talk about solutions. As always, awareness is the first step. Thinking on paper will give you clarity, so you can make better decisions. One of the most valuable skills you can develop is the ability to ask yourself really good questions. Often simple questions provide the greatest insight. Ask yourself:

1. What specifically am I stressed about?
2. What is the root cause of this stress?
3. What can I do right away to alleviate the situation?

4. Who or what can help me?
5. How can I prevent this from happening again?
6. What resources can I use to learn more?

Another great way to de-stress and improve balance is to adopt the traditional day of rest. Whatever happened to the one-day-off-a-week habit? Remember when stores were closed on Sunday and families had fun together? Now the pressure is constant. We even have a name for it. 24/7. Instead of having a day to breathe and recoup, the weekend pace has women running on empty before the new week even begins. Although it is a different type of busyness, the weekend often leaves us feeling depleted and resentful about going back to work on Monday.

> Gina, the Mom who works from home, makes her day off a priority. "I make sure all of my household responsibilities are taken care of during the week. Often I spend a couple of evenings catching up on the laundry and paying bills because Sunday is a day off for everyone in our family. I protect it. I don't let anything or anyone interfere. This is our day to rejuvenate spiritually and physically, to recuperate, relax and enjoy each other."

It's easy to get caught up in the hectic activity of daily living and lose sight of what you truly value. Unless you schedule this day off, it won't happen. I suggest getting out of the house—it's too easy to get distracted by your to-do list, by feeling guilty about not working on it. Get away if you can. Don't let your mind burden you with worry, guilt or thoughts of work. Learn how to slow down and have fun. Give yourself permission to take this day. It's a gift. You deserve it. All the other stuff can wait. Perhaps it's not really that important anyway.

Once you start doing this, you will be amazed at how well you can manage. This day off will go a long way toward restoring relationships, bringing family members together, encouraging recreation and regaining your balance. It is one of the most important things you can do to help you de-stress and regain balance.

Another time-out strategy that I really enjoy is called Girls Day Out. These are unique memorable experiences meant simply for fun and relaxation. They are special occasions that you can plan well in advance. There's nothing like a group of women heading off for the day and enjoying a few good belly laughs. It's great to be a little silly, to see the little child in us come out to play. Go on, have fun. Meet together for lunch, have a glorious picnic in beautiful surroundings, or go on a hike. No guilt allowed!

Single working Moms often feel guilty taking any time off for themselves. "When I'm not at work I feel I owe it to my kids to be there." The truth is that they will be happier when you are happier. Taking a day off will not only rejuvenate you and preserve your balance; it will replenish your nurturing reserves because you have taken the time to nurture yourself.

It's easy to neglect yourself when you have important deadlines at work, or four kids needing rides to various venues. Making time for self-care is a new way of thinking for some women. Your time is not a luxury, it's a necessity. When you nurture yourself, it does wonders for your psyche. You will feel happier and more generous. Everyone benefits, especially your family.

> *Beware of the barrenness of*
> *an overcrowded life.*
>
> —Anonymous

The same principle applies on the work front. Women think that taking time for themselves will affect their performance. That's right, it will—for the better. Some companies even insist their employees do this because they know the benefits that rejuvenation can have on the bottom line. Creative ideas most often originate during down time.

Many women drive themselves beyond reason, all the while insisting that everyone else, even the dog, gets exercise, eats well and has lots of rest. Keeping yourself healthy, nourished and rested is a huge benefit, even if you are neglecting other areas of self-care. Know your physical limits. The beyond-exhaustion point is too late. Avoid the lame excuses: "But I don't know how to relax," or "I can't relax with so much to do."

Taking enough time is a learned behavior. It involves discipline and practice. The busy stuff of life will always be there. You must learn to hit the stop button each and every week.

The 15-Minute Crossover

Some days when you walk through the front door at home, your husband, the kids and the dog are all eagerly waiting to launch themselves at you with news and requests, even before you've taken off your coat. But if you've worked a full day and your head is still buzzing with meetings and deadlines, you need a mechanism to switch off the office. Here's a good strategy to help you ease out of one role and into another.

The 15-Minute Crossover is an agreement with everyone that allows you fifteen minutes to unwind, change your clothes, take a few deep breaths and have something refreshing to drink, or whatever works for you. Then you are better prepared to step into the role of wife and mother again. If you are able, push the time to thirty minutes and slip in a mini-nap. It makes a world of difference. Even if you don't have a full house when you come home, you should still take fifteen minutes to unwind from the pressures of the day. Don't allow busyness to determine the quality of your life. Take care of you first, and everything else will fall into place.

If you have younger children who are eager to see you, the 15-Minute Crossover may not be desirable or practical. Here's another option. Before you pick them up from school, or daycare, or before you walk through the door at home, close your eyes and take a few deep breaths. Allow yourself to become grounded. Actually feel your feet on the ground. Now, mentally flick an imaginary switch and shut off all thoughts of work, then smile.

Focus on your children. They are one of the most important reasons for living, and they are eagerly awaiting your arrival. Now you are ready!

Do this anytime you are feeling overwhelmed. With practice it will become easier. Remember to smile. This changes your physiology and releases those "good feeling" hormones.

The soft Scottish brogue was still clear in Sharon's voice.
However, she had lived most of her life in North America. "I was superwoman, I wanted it all," she recalls, reflecting on what might have been. "It almost cost me everything I value most in life. I was a career woman, ambitious and good at my job looking after fifty-one retail clothing stores and more than 500 employees. I had no friends outside work and no social life. The hours were insane, averaging seventy a week, and I was on the road one week a month." Needless to say, Sharon didn't have much time to spend with her family, particularly her two girls who were six and eight at the time. Initially her husband was content to cook the meals and take care of the kids, but the marriage was unraveling.

The guilt that Sharon felt was an additional burden. "I'd wake up in the middle of the night and my youngest girl would be lying beside me. She'd always ask, 'Mommy, are you going to work tomorrow?' Then she'd refuse to go to school hoping I would stay home. I redecorated her bedroom wanting to entice her back to her own bed, making it special, but the novelty didn't last long. It was me she wanted. So I made an adjustment. Every morning the girls and I got up early and we'd all go for a walk and say 'hello' to everyone we met. Then we'd have a special breakfast together. At least I was focusing some attention on them. We did this for months."

But Sharon's ambition was relentless. Moving up the corporate ladder was still important. She did this by setting and achieving higher sales targets. Where did this drive originate? Partly from her father, who always told her she could do anything she wanted. The other factor was tragic. Sharon lost her sister in a car accident when she was eighteen. This had a huge impact. The message was clear. "Life can be over very fast. I'd better push hard to make sure I accomplish everything I want."

Two specific events caused Sharon to re-evaluate her hectic lifestyle. One night, returning late from another long day at the office, she sat in her car outside her home, exhausted. As she looked around the street, nothing seemed familiar. She had no feeling for anything. It was almost surreal. She was scared by how detached she had become from everything around her.

The second incident touched her heart. Looking through the family album, she came across a photograph of her first grandchild, only four months old. He was sitting on the floor. Behind him sat Sharon on the couch, surrounded by paperwork, totally focused on her work. "It brought me to tears. There was my pride and joy two feet away, and I was buried in my work."

At that time Sharon was working for one of the largest retail and office leasing corporations in the country, and still breaking sales records. She decided to get control of her life and informed her boss she would no longer be hostage to the company—no more late nights or taking work home. Not surprisingly, he listened. She was creating more business than anyone else. Sharon has learned to set new boundaries. She also knows the expertise she brings to the marketplace. With each new opportunity, she clearly defines her terms—what she will and won't do. Her values are clear. She's learned to take time off regularly and enjoys vacations with her family. As a grandmother of four at age forty-five, she still has a lot of living to do. Today she says, "I live a full life, and it's wonderful."

Prioritize Your
VALUES

As Sharon discovered, another key to creating excellent balance lies in knowing what we value most and making this a priority. We are more likely to stay true to our values when we know what they are, but people are often vague when it comes to defining values. We know some of our surface values, like maintaining good health, but deeper values that are connected to our core remain elusive. Making our values a foundation for everything we do gives us a great feeling of congruency. When our goals, work and relationships are in alignment with our values, life flows more easily. This is the catalyst for creating joy and peace of mind.

The opposite is also true. If we do not integrate our most important values into everyday life, we experience stress, tension and conflict. It's like having a jigsaw puzzle with pieces that don't fit. No matter how much we force them to mesh, they never do. Instead of creating joy and harmony, life feels disjointed, frustrating and meaningless.

To avoid all of this potential angst, let's look at a comprehensive list of values. Not all of these will apply to you, and there may be other values not on this list for which you have a high regard. That's fine—just make a note of them.

I cherish many of the values on this list, especially health, quiet time, family and work. How do I integrate these values into my life? I exercise every day by going to the gym, doing aerobics or walking the dog, or a combination of all three. Exercise not only keeps me fit, it's the best way for me to handle stress and stay healthy. Giving back to the community in some capacity is also important to me.

Values Worth Considering

These are in no particular order of importance. That's up to you to decide.

Family	Quiet time	Opportunity
Work	Creativity	Spirituality
Honesty	Intuition	Independence
Faith	Knowledge	Beauty
Courage	Compassion	Adventure
Fun	Solitude	Tithing
Health	Friendship	Music
Flexibility	Self-discipline	Financial security
Learning	Intelligence	Balance
Playfulness	Generosity	Cleanliness
Culture	Achievement	Enthusiasm
Win-win	Passion	

I also schedule quiet time every day. That's the time I can reflect without interruption. It helps me solve problems and nurtures my creativity. It's also time to connect with God. That relationship is significant to me. He is my compass and provides direction and purpose for my life.

My family and my relationship with Les are important, so family time is a high priority. In our house, meal time has become a focal point for communication. My work provides meaning and helps me to expand my competence and confidence. It also balances my week. Not every day is perfect —the unexpected can knock my best-laid schedule off course. But most of the time I feel balanced and satisfied that I am in harmony with myself.

Integration of your values into your life is the key to balance. When you do this, you may not get your busy stuff completed all the time. You may not be perceived as

Ms. Super-Efficient anymore, but by putting your most important values first, you will feel happier. What would your day look like and feel like if you lived more from your values?

The good news is that you don't need to integrate everything all at once. Pick one or two values to start with, then focus on these for the next few weeks. Make decisions that are centered on these values, and be more conscious of how this affects you each day. You'll likely feel more in charge, more confident and more congruent. That's a lot better than filling your days with too much stuff, feeling bombarded and out of control.

Beat The
TIME TRAP

The focus in this section is on practical tools to help you become more efficient with your time. We all know that time marches on. It cannot be put in a Tupperware container and stored for later use. Once spent, it is gone forever.

Let's start by reinforcing some basics that are essential for good organization. These tips to beat the time trap can be applied equally well at home or in the office.

Set Up A Schedule For Your Day
The secret to keeping your day under control and preserving your sanity is to know what your priorities are before you start. I find the best time to write a schedule is the night before, or early in the morning. Keep it simple. Rank what needs to be done in order of importance, keeping in mind your most important values. Learn to focus on these. Women are natural multi-taskers. That's good in the sense that you can handle several tasks at the same time. However, if you have an important goal to complete, your habit of multi-tasking may end up being a source of distraction.

Patsy the Procrastinator has put off paying her bills to the last day, so getting to the bank before it closes at 4 pm is important. She starts to focus on the task at hand, getting her documents together, but suddenly realizes it's soccer night and Brendan will need his jersey washed. That also means an early supper. Patsy quickly throws in a load of laundry and starts preparing a meal. Her neighbor phones for some advice, so tucking the phone beneath her chin, she stirs the pots on the stove, feeds the dog, loads the dryer, and hangs up as soon as she can. Soon the clock strikes four. Patsy's multi-tasking ability certainly helped in getting lots done, but her lack of preparation and focus is going to cost her in late-payment penalties.

Our daily tasks do not have equal importance. We need to keep asking, "Am I focused on my top priorities?" Too often we surrender to the tyranny of the urgent. Every time the phone rings we answer it, even when we're in the middle of an important project that requires total focus. Avoid interruptions. At the end of the day you don't want a guilty hangover, mentally beating yourself up because you allowed other people to ruin your focus.

Using lists helps to free your mind and your energy. I like simplicity, so I use two lists to keep me on track, my Daily list and my Main list. My Daily list details my priorities and schedule for the day. The Main list includes other tasks that require attention through the week, though perhaps not today.

Depending on my schedule, I usually include a few items from the Main list on my Daily list if I have time to do them. If not, that's okay. I just put them back on the Main list at the end of the day. By focusing on these two lists I can usually get everything done each week.

At first it will take practice to gauge your capacity. Be careful you don't make your list so long, or the tasks so big, that you set yourself up for failure.

You can record your to-do lists on a simple notepad or on any basic organizer. If you like technology, you can choose from numerous types of Personal Digital Assistants (PDAs) that have multiple functions. Knowing what's available and what suits you best is part of your ongoing education. Harness the expertise of someone who is really up to speed with technology and can help you make wise choices.

"You could call me a workaholic if I brought my work home with me...but I don't go home."

Learn to say no more often. Have as much respect for your own time as you have for others. Also, be aware of the time you spend socializing on the phone. It's perfectly fine to socialize, just don't do it when you are in the middle of an important project. Focus!

Avoid Clutter
Effective scheduling will significantly free up more time, but we also have to deal with clutter. Have you noticed how much paper still flows into your life, despite all this

instant-response technology? And if it isn't paper, it's all the other stuff that just seems to grow in the closet, office and basement. Where does it all come from?

One of my breakthroughs was discovering a professional organizer. I didn't know there was such a person; someone who makes a career out of cleaning up messes. What a great idea! Georgina showed up at my home one day ready to do battle with a room that my newly married daughter had vacated. It had been her study/project room and I wanted to turn it into my home office. The clutter was embarrassing, but six hours later it was transformed into an efficient work space, with files and drawers neatly labeled and everything in its place. I was amazed. Below are some practical tips from Georgina's hot list. These tips will help you eliminate clutter and save time.

Tips For The Home

1. Create a place for everything	If you don't know where something belongs, how do you know where to put it?
	If you need that item later, how do you know where to find it?
2. Store similiar items together	Categorization is vitally important when you're getting organized. Keep all bill-paying supplies in one place. Gather craft supplies in one basket. When you need to work on something, everything will be easily accessible.
3. Decide now	Most household clutter results from deferred decisions. "I don't have time to decide where this belongs, so I'll just put it here for now." Decide where it belongs, and put it there immediately. It will only take a few seconds, and it will eliminate large piles of deferred decisions down the road.

4. Dump junk mail immediately

You know what it looks like, so don't even open it. Use the FAT system for all mail:

File it—Action now—Trash it.

5. Be ruthless

If you haven't used an item in the last two years, you are not likely to need it again.

Do you really want a clutter-free, streamlined home?

6. Don't keep buying things

Before you buy something, stop and ask:

Do I really need this?

Have I got somewhere to keep it?

Will I use it?

Do I want to be responsible for storing, cleaning and maintaining yet another item?

Don't shop unconsciously anymore. Some people work on a one-in, one-out system—good idea!

7. Post your grocery list

Post it where other family members can add items when they run out of something. This will save unnecessary trips to the store, and reduce those "How was I supposed to know?" discussions.

Tips For The Bed and Bath

1. Tidy up your closet

Dressing each morning from a chaotic closet affirms that your life is chaotic. Organizers for shoes, hats, sweaters, gloves, belts, scarves, pants, handbags and ties can generate an incredible return on investment by blessing you with more time and less stress in the "search and hunt" process.

2. Be realistic

Don't keep clothes in the hope that you'll lose weight. If you do, chances are they will either be out of style, or you'll want to reward yourself with new items. Get rid of them, and take better care of the clothes you do have.

3. Create a sense of serenity

Your bedroom is where you retreat at the end your day. Shouldn't this space be clutter-free?

If your intimate space is visually disorganized, you have a constant reminder to do something. It requires a lot of energy to suppress these nagging reminders. Clean out under your bed, behind the dressers and even in the drawers.

Are there items in your bedroom that needn't be there?

Assign them new homes in other areas of your home. When you awaken refreshed from a good night's sleep, you don't want to be surrounded by clutter. Any amount of disorganization detracts from your room's serenity.

4. Streamline your morning

Your morning routine should energize you for the day, not wear you out before the day begins. Toss those old tubes of lipstick you no longer use. Experts tell us our makeup needs to be replaced about every six months because bacteria grows on it.

How long have some of those compacts been around?

Clear out your drawers and only put in what is essential to your daily routine. Half-used shampoo that you no longer use—donate it to a homeless shelter, and while you're at it, the shelter could also use all those sample packs of cleansers and shampoos you've been hoarding. You don't need them.

5. Clean as you go

Wipe down the tile after you shower, or better yet, there are excellent products on the market that allow you to spray the tile after showering. Voila! You've just cut your bathroom cleaning in half. Keep a container of disinfectant wipes under the sink for a quick sparkle and shine. Use old dryer sheets to wipe up hair off the floor. This takes about a minute, and your bathroom will look like it's been freshly cleaned every day.

Tips For Handling Paper and Files

1. Set up an action file for sorting mail

This file should be kept on top of your desk (a stepped sorter is best for visual clarity).

Make a file for each of the following categories: DO, READ, FILE, TODAY.

Here are a few other categories you can use as well: PAY, ANSWER, ATTEND (for tickets to an event, or information about a course). These are active files, so paper should always be attended to and moved out of these file folders.

2. Don't overstuff filing cabinets

There's nothing worse than having to file papers in an overloaded file cabinet. Leave enough room in the drawers so that you're not using all of your energy to get a piece of paper in or out. Leave at least three inches of space in the file drawer. More than 80 percent of what we file is never looked at again. Maybe it's time to purge old files.

Time Management Tips

1. Leave some breathing room

When organizing your schedule, don't jam-pack it full of tasks, activities and appointments. If you do, you're going to be running around like a chicken without a head, and you're bound to fall behind every single day. Always leave time for things that take longer to complete than expected, special circumstances, emergencies, traffic delays, phone hold and thinking moments. You should also schedule a few minutes to relax/re-energize.

2. Determine your best time for tasks

Use your most productive time to do your most productive work. Tackle your most difficult or important work during the time of day when you're at your best, and when you're more likely to complete it.

3. Do-it-now

Develop the do-it-now habit. Don't procrastinate.

4. Delegate

Whenever possible.

5. End each day on a good note

Save easier tasks for day's end. You'll be able to complete them, and each day will end on a positive, rewarding note.

6. Get organized and get going

Stop wasting time hoping things will change.

At The Office

1. Word processing programs

Use a word processing program to type long e-mails. That way you can edit and send by a simple cut/paste method or by attachment.

2. E-mail addresses /Reply

Update your e-mail address book regularly. Put "no reply needed" on the end of e-mail. Don't waste time opening thank-you e-mails.

3. E-Mail Handling	Handle your e-mails once or twice a day—no more. Be rigid about the time you spend dealing with e-mails. Often they are time -wasters.
4. Leadership meetings	If you have a leadership role at work, consider stand-up meetings that are no longer than fifteen minutes. Use a small boardroom table to stand around for quick, efficient meetings.
5. Business Meetings	Keep meetings to a minimum each week. Set a specific start/end time, and stick to it. Circulate an agenda in advance. Make sure Action Steps are clarified in the meeting and followed through.
6. Important Phone Calls	When making important phone calls, write out a short agenda and your expectations before you call. Take notes during the conversation about anything that requires specific action.
7. Driving	If you drive a lot in your business, always have plenty of spare change for parking along with extra business cards, stationery, thank-you cards and brochures in the car.
8. Technology	Use technology to help you. For more ideas check out the CD album by Les Hewitt and Mike Foster called e-Savvy: Using Technology To Free Up Your Time, Boost Profits And Reduce Stress! (www.achievers.com Toll Free 1-877-678-0234)

Source: smartWORKS! Professional Organizing Solutions
smartworks@shaw.ca

Review all of these ideas and pick out the ones that appeal to you, then start organizing and simplifying your life. This will free up your time. Letting go of the clutter will create room for new experiences and will release your energy. More time and more energy is exactly what we're looking for.

A Man's Perspective   Les Hewitt

Some men don't get it! What women value highly often doesn't even show up on our radar screen; like a clean home, keeping things in their proper place and having meaningful discussions, (even if it is about work). From this viewpoint, these values are of minor importance compared to a golf game, watching the World Series, or a night out with the boys. I know not all men think like this, but a lot of them do.

The sad truth is that we need to be told about what makes you happy, and told often. This creates a bit of a dilemma. Fran tells me that many women don't like asking because it comes across as nagging. You would prefer us to take some initiative. That seems reasonable. Let me make a couple of suggestions.

Fran would assume that I knew the chores she wanted me to look after at home. Meanwhile, I'm off in my own little world, totally oblivious to her mounting stress. After a couple of weeks of no action on my part, the volcano would blow! Now we have a simple way of handling this. Fran makes a list of the maintenance items she wants me to take care of, plus any other items that require my attention, and gives me a reasonable timeframe to complete everything. She feels good because it's now out of her mind. This works for me, because I know what her needs are and I can fit them around my own schedule. I give her back the list with everything checked off, or an explanation for any item that will take more time.

Family Council is also a great way to communicate—and for men to know what's going on. Do this once a week. Sharing responsibility is a much better concept than pleading for help. I suggest you have a heart-to-heart talk with your husband or partner. Together, set up an equitable agreement that will serve as a framework for a healthy, balanced lifestyle.

CONCLUSION

Are you familiar with the phrase, "her life hung in the balance?" This describes a woman teetering on the edge, hovering between life and death. One wrong move, one bad decision, and game over. Obviously, I hope that doesn't describe your situation. The point I want to make is that creating balance is critical to living the life you really want. If you are always on the edge, taking everything to extremes, it puts incredible pres-sure on you and the people close to you. In the long run, that's not healthy.

Your life is a bit like a balance sheet. It's a statement of accounts, a running tally of how you're really doing. In business, when expenses consistently exceed revenues, a financial crisis is not far away. It's the same with life balance. If your life load does not allow time for rejuvenation, a health crisis may be close at hand. If this describes you, it's time to make changes...now! If you are at a turning point, a critical juncture where the expense column is significantly outweighing your income, then it's time to make corrections. Look at the payoff. A healthy balance sheet inspires confidence and self-assurance. It shows you are in control.

It proves you are using good judgment and common sense. The overall effect will have you constantly smiling because you are in harmony with the world, and with yourself.

*Sometimes the best thing you
can do for others is to care
for yourself.*

—Anonymous

ACTION STEPS

Relieving Stress

Outsourcing

Prioritizing Your Values

These action steps are designed to help you implement the key strategies from this chapter. Pick the best time for this, then focus and follow through.

1. Name three practical ways you can lower your stress, ways that will work best for you. There are many listed in this chapter.

a) _____

_____

b) _____

_____

c) _____

_____

2. Name one time-consuming task you are going to eliminate from your weekly schedule immediately.

_____

_____

3. Name three chores you can outsource, or effectively delegate in the next few weeks.

a) _____

_____

b) _____

_____

c) _____

_____

4. Using the list in this chapter as a guide, write down your most important values. This will require some soul searching, so take your time.

_____   _____

_____   _____

_____   _____

_____   _____

_____   _____

_____   _____

_____   _____

_____   _____

_____   _____

_____   _____

_____   _____

Prioritize this list by drawing a circle around your top five values. Take time to think this through. Now you have a strong foundation on which you can build a purposeful life.

5. Using your daily planner, review your activities for the last week. Did your actions reflect your most important values? What, if anything, is incongruent about your behavior compared to your values?

_____

_____

_____

6. What adjustments are you prepared to make to achieve more harmony?

_____

_____

_____

As always, focus on identifying the necessary changes you need to make, then follow through with appropriate action.

The Benefits of Boundaries

We torture ourselves mentally, physically, and spiritually because of our inability to set boundaries.

—Fran Hewitt

The single best way to improve your life is to learn how to set boundaries. Boundaries create healthy relationships. Not only will your relationship with yourself be more authentic, your relationship with others will be more honest. You will improve your communication skills and feel less resentful. Setting boundaries is a loving thing to do. Boundaries are about self-respect. By respecting how you feel and acting with integrity from those feelings, others will be more likely to respect you. Remember, you are always teaching others how to treat you.

One of the biggest benefits of setting boundaries is learning how to say no, particularly to other people who use up your time. Boundaries stop you from overcommitting, which keeps you free to focus on what you value most. As you become more assertive, you will feel stronger. The result will be win/win, without compromising or alienating your relationships. The benefits of boundaries are clear, yet few women are competent at this. Setting boundaries is especially difficult for us because we are natural caregivers and nurturers. When others ask for help, we seldom refuse. Even when we do set boundaries, they are inconsistent.

Boundary situations show up at home, in the office, with friends and extended family, and within each of us. Let's tackle this challenging subject head on. By the end of this chapter you'll understand how boundaries work and don't work. You'll also have some helpful strategies to simplify your life and make it easier to say no.

Personal
BOUNDARIES

Boundaries can be physical, mental, emotional or spiritual. They define limits. The purpose of personal boundaries is to separate us from others. People who don't have healthy boundaries are often vulnerable, frightened and bombarded by life.

In the external, physical world boundaries such as fences, walls and property lines are easy to identify. Personal physical boundaries include our personal space, our bodies and our sexuality. Physical boundaries may also include things like shelter, money, clothing and time. Mental and emotional boundaries involve our feelings, thoughts, relationships, choices and responsibilities. Spiritual boundaries relate to religion, spiritual beliefs, relationship to God and our sense of purpose.

You need good boundaries for balance, for self-protection and especially to establish inner harmony. You also need them for building and maintaining healthy relationships, and for raising responsible kids. They are an indispensable tool in today's invasive world. If you do nothing else with this book, make sure you absorb and implement the ideas in this chapter. They will have a dramatic impact on reclaiming your life, your time and your primary relationships.

Boundary Checklist

These are warning signs that you need to set boundaries.

❑ You say yes when you mean no.

You say yes to helping with the fundraiser when you want to say no.

❑ You have a hard time being assertive.

Someone jumps the line in front of you at the store. Instead of speaking up, you rationalize that she only has a few items and won't take long—yet inside you are seething.

❑ You give in because you prefer to avoid conflict.

The manager at work is yelling about some project she is waiting for. You are already feeling overwhelmed and know she is being unrealistic, but you stay late rather than confront her.

❑ You find yourself bombarded by life.

Exhausted after working all day, you come home to your other job; kids, rides, meals, phones, e-mail, pets and other chores.

❑ You give past the point of love.

Your elderly mother wants some attention. You take her to lunch, buy her some groceries, and are ready to go home when she mentions how messy her apartment is. You spend the afternoon resentfully cleaning.

❑ You suffer from the disease to please.

"Don't worry. I can do without lunch and get those calls made," you say, just to please your boss.

❑ You feel emotionally, physically and spiritually exhausted.

At the end of the week when you are tired, empty and still not caught up, you ask yourself, "What's the point? Why am I living like this?"

Don't worry if you answered yes to one or more of these questions. You are not alone. Having poor boundaries is the number one reason many women have no energy or feel frazzled, joyless, overburdened, resentful and unhappy. It's insanity to live in today's world without the protection of boundaries. Life and other people will simply push you around. It took me many years to gain this understanding. My own need to please others and to feel loved kept me trapped in an emotional prison. There was no limit to my giving, and I felt guilty when I took care of my own needs. I felt torn on both fronts.

When establishing new boundaries, do not expect your life to change overnight. That would be unrealistic. You would be setting yourself up for disappointment and discouragement. Boundaries take time and setting them with those you love is uncomfortable at first. Be sensitive about this. Slow, steady progress is more likely to succeed—and in turn you will feel encouraged to keep going. Unfortunately, boundaries—like many major life skills—are not taught at school. If you are like most women, you can probably do with some improvement here.

Setting
BOUNDARIES

If you find setting boundaries is difficult, you may be stuck in old programming. Maybe you've heard phrases like these:

- Be polite to others
- Be nice
- Don't hurt her feelings
- Put on a happy face

In other words deny your feelings, always put other people's feelings first and ignore your own instincts—all for the sake of looking good, being liked, or keeping the peace. We are systematically taught to look outside ourselves for validation, always caring what others think or worrying how they might react to us. This robs us of inner harmony, integrity and self esteem. I want to show you my old programming and why it was so difficult for me to set boundaries. The first statement is my misguided belief. Beside it is the truth, what I needed to know.

Do you see any of your own misguided beliefs in this list?

My Old Belief	The Truth
As the woman of the household, I am responsible for everyone's happiness.	Setting healthy boundaries helps define what is and is not my responsibility. Being overly responsible for others is actually selfish, manipulative and disabling.
I can't just think about me all the time.	Thinking about me isn't selfish or self-centered. Setting healthy boundaries is a way to protect and take care of myself.
What everyone else wants comes first; I'll take what's left. I'm not important. It's not okay to reveal my feelings if they rock the other person's boat.	Setting healthy boundaries gives me the right to state my feelings, stand up for myself and ask for what I want and need. My needs are often just as important as the needs of others.
I'm only worthy when I'm doing things for others.	Setting boundaries shows respect for me and increases my feeling of self-worth.
I come gift-wrapped and available for whatever you want and need. I am always nice and ready to please.	By setting boundaries I teach others how to treat me. People know what I will or will not tolerate. I am taking responsibility for the integrity and health of my relationships.
Keep my head down and my nose clean. Get along with everyone. It's important what people think of me. Bow down to those in authority.	By setting healthy boundaries at work, others learn to trust me. I feel more powerful, and my integrity is noticed. I know that being liked is not as important as being respected.

The good news is that you can change these misguided beliefs. I'm happy to report that I've largely been able to shift my old beliefs to accepting the truth and living it. It's taken a few years, but setting boundaries has made an incredible difference to my quality of life today.

Another reason many women find it difficult to set boundaries is that they get stuck in the rut of wanting approval. "But I need you to like me...."

Did you get that? It's so important! The need for constant approval will rob you of your self-respect and self-esteem. Being afraid to do or say something that might disappoint or hurt someone is no way to live.

If you keep collapsing your boundary so that your child, your husband or your boyfriend will love you more, they will eventually stop trusting you, and you will end up resenting them. This is a big lose-lose scenario. Keep reminding yourself that you are of more value to them when you love yourself. You cannot give away what you don't have.

One morning I phoned my neighbor in a panic. "Tara, the clinic just called. They have an opening for me at noon if I can make it. Would it be possible for you to look after my kids? It's okay to say no, I can always call Cathy."

"Yes, of course I'll help, send them over."

"Are you sure? I know I'll be at least two hours."

"No problem. It's a nice day, they can play outside."

"Thanks Tara, I owe you one."

A week later I heard through a mutual friend that Tara resented being burdened with my kids that day. She had made other plans and had to cancel them.

Initially you might think that Tara had put herself out, that she was being a good neighbor. True—except that she didn't really want to help. Underneath, she resented the intrusion and even complained about it to others in her circle.

What could Tara have done to respect her boundaries and our friendship? How do you think I felt about our relationship after that incident? Do you think it affected my level of trust for Tara?

Unhealed Wounds

You may have past issues that are still unhealed, like an open wound. When you decide to set a new boundary this may feel like putting salt on the abrasion. It's painful.

> Gail's father left when she was four. Because of this painful event, she developed a fear of abandonment. Now it was affecting her relationship with Tom, her husband, who she felt was too flirtatious with other women. "I'm frightened if I say anything to Tom he's going to leave me," she says.

Gail needs to set a boundary. Her fear of being abandoned is preventing her from telling Tom how she feels. She stays stuck in her resentment. This is obviously unhealthy for their relationship.

Inner wounds are deepest with your closest relationships. That's why it's more difficult to set boundaries with family and the people you care about. You may not be able to fully heal these wounds—that could take a lifetime. However, having some awareness of them will help you understand why you act the way you do.

Avoid the
EXTREMES

Here are two extreme boundary situations, using the analogy of a brick wall. Both of these situations are unhealthy. See if you can find yourself in either of them.

The first wall is tall and thick. It has no windows, doors or openings. Behind this impenetrable wall lives a woman. She doesn't like to feel vulnerable. The wall insulates her and provides protection. To her, feeling safe behind the wall is vitally important. But the wall isolates her, too. It keeps others away who may hurt her, who may try to get too close, even those who may want to love her. The wall separates her from good people and the joyful elements of life.

You will never have a close relationship with this woman. She is in pain, and she is paying a huge price for keeping herself safe. It takes great courage to step out from behind this wall, to learn to trust again.

Donna was married for ten years when her husband Harvey asked for a divorce. He had fallen in love with someone at work. Donna was devastated. Her neighbor, Connie, stood by her as she went through the painful process. Donna was grateful to Connie and the two developed a close friendship. Then a bomb dropped— Harvey told Donna about an affair he had with Connie during their marriage. Donna's life fell apart again. This second betrayal was too much. Despite Connie's tearful remorse and apologies, Donna never again let anyone get close enough to hurt her. Now she is alone.

The second wall is low and brittle in its construction. It has doors, windows and lots of openings. Anyone can trespass and penetrate this wall. The woman who lives on the other side, Ms. Nice, is a people-pleaser. She melts into the demands of other people. She can be a chameleon too. If you say jump, she will jump, skip, hop and even fall over backward just to please you. What happens when Ms. Nice meets Mr. Dependent or Mr. Controller? Often they get married. Mr. Dependent just loves her. This woman takes responsibility for his life. He never has to grow up. Mr. Controller loves her too. She lets him have his way and he can manipulate her to get all his needs met.

But Ms. Nice is often resentful. She takes on too many responsibilities and feels used. She has difficulty saying no, and is easily persuaded into giving more than she wants. Ms. Nice thinks she is loving, but when she gives, it is out of a sense of compulsion or reluctance. She doesn't understand why others abuse her. She often slips into victim mode, feeling as if she has no choice. She blames her unhappiness on the lack of love and respect in her relationships. In her view, "I do everything for them."

> *Get over the disease to please. Understand you cannot*
> *please everyone. Being able to disappoint others*
> *is crucial to reclaiming your life.*
>
> —Oprah Winfrey

The Lesson

My kids knew they could always come to me for help with their homework. Naturally I wanted them to do well in school and if I could help, great. Their homework became my homework. I was totally immersed in it, staying up late in the evenings long after they had gone to bed. Ten-year-old Jennifer came home from school one afternoon and tossed her English essay on the kitchen counter. I could see the large A in red ink in the top right-hand corner. "You got an A," I exclaimed, "Well done, sweetheart!"

"No Mom, that's your A," Jennifer said quietly. She walked away leaving the evidence burning a hole in the countertop.

I was dumbfounded. She was absolutely right. Constant rescuing and over-zealous caretaking were certainly not the building blocks for healthy self-esteem. My selfish need to be needed was hurting our kids. My own lack of boundaries was unintentionally sending the wrong messages:

- You are inadequate
- You can't do really well on your own
- You don't need to study hard because Mom will bail you out

My beautiful wise daughter taught me an invaluable lesson that day, one I will never forget.

Flexible
BOUNDARIES

As we've seen, unhealthy boundaries can take the form of emotional walls. Healthy boundaries, on the other hand, are more like willow trees. They have a certain amount of flexibility, like the willow bending in the wind. The deep roots, however, provide strength and rigidity so the tree won't fall.

Some of your boundaries need to be rigid, too. These are unshakable—no exceptions:

- It's never okay to hit me even when you are angry.
- It's never okay to cheat on me.
- It's never okay to lie to me.

The woman who sets healthy boundaries speaks openly and honestly about her feelings. She stays true to herself. She is trusted and respected because of her integrity. This woman knows who and what is important in her life, and she is clearly grounded by these values. She has the strength to easily say no to anyone or anything that conflicts with them. She takes full responsibility for her own choices and actions. She never takes responsibility for those who can take responsibility for themselves. This woman loves and respects herself. She knows her worth is not what she does—it's who she is. She fully understands that loving others beyond the point of love leads to resentment. She also knows she is happier and healthier in her relationships when she takes time to care for herself.

Is this woman too good to be true? Not at all. Setting boundaries is a learning process. It takes time, but it can be achieved by anyone who is willing to do the work. Are you ready to create the boundaries that will give you more confidence and control over your life?

"I'll be home late. I've joined a support group for women who need a reason to stay at work until the house is picked up and dinner is on the table."

The Three Freedom FIGHTERS

1. Exercise Your No Muscle

No. It's a small word, but some women have terrible difficulty saying it. Are you one of these women?

We learn to say no at about two years of age. In fact, as a Terrible Two that's our job. As we grow older, it gradually disappears from our everyday vocabulary. We learn that pleasing others and looking good is more important.

Let me share a well-kept secret: learning to say the n-word is your job again if you want to preserve healthy boundaries.

I've been flexing my no muscle now for several years and have almost mastered it, although my need to feel useful sometimes gets in the way and a yes slips out. However, most of the time I'm dynamite at saying no. This is from someone who always caved in to telemarketers, always gave at the front door, always volunteered when asked, and generally felt the need to be involved in just about everything, usually to the point of exhaustion. It's important to understand the reasons for your resistance to saying no. This is part of the cure. Here's something that will really help if you still have nagging doubts about saying no when it's in your best interest to do so. Before you say yes, check your intentions. Simply ask yourself: what is my intention if I agree to this request? Is it to genuinely help out, to look good, or to automatically repeat old patterns that always cause me stress?

> Checking our intentions is a great way to observe the self-sabotaging games we all play.

Why Don't I Say No?

Check if you have any of the following symptoms:

❏ When you say no you automatically feel guilty.

❏ You are seeking approval, because it matters to you what people think.

❏ You have a high need to feel useful.

❏ You believe that it's selfish to say no to anyone, or at the very least, not good manners.

Here are some tips to help you say no. These tips have all been thoroughly field-tested, and I'm happy to report that they work. To improve your skill level, I suggest writing the following responses out on a 3 x 5 card. Keep it beside your phone at home—that's where most of us get bombarded with requests. You can also design a cue card for work. Refer to the list often and keep practicing until your answers become automatic. One day you will hear yourself saying no in a strong confident voice—and it will be music to your ears.

Tips To Help You Say No

Tip #1 – Buy Yourself Time To Think

If you're a knee-jerk yes person, this is especially important. Be assertive. Learn to use phrases like, "Let me check my calendar first," or "I'll get back to you in a couple of days," or "Let me think about that, I'm not ready to make a decision right now." Each of these answers gives you more time to think through the request so you can make the decision that's best for you.

Tip #2 – Create Policy Statements

Corporations have policies that sound like they are cast in stone. You and your family can too. A banker will say, "Our policy is not to divulge client information over the phone." End of story. The phrase "We have a policy" sounds official—you've obviously given this serious thought. Callers usually won't argue and if they do, simply repeat the phrase more firmly, or hang up.

We have a policy not to support telephone solicitation.
We have a policy to only support children's charities.
We have a policy not to volunteer in the evenings.

Here's another good response:

Our portfolio for charitable donations is over-subscribed at the moment. Thank you, and good luck in your fund raising.

Tip #3 – Shift The Focus Back To You

This is not about you; I need to say no for me. This is my personal favorite. When you say this sincerely, with empathy for the other person's situation, and use great eye contact, it is magic. Just about everyone will understand and support someone who says no for their own personal reasons.

Tip #4 –Know Your Priorities and Stick To Them

Once again, check your most important values. If having supper together as a family is a high priority, say no to all interruptions. That includes cell phones, TV, reading materials, salespeople or urgent e-mails. It's difficult enough to find time for meaningful conversation, so put your foot down.

Tip #5 –Keep It Simple

You don't need to give long-winded explanations or make excuses about your decision to say no. That can make you vulnerable. Keep it short and simple. If you are feeling weak or unassertive, don't attempt to convince the other person by rationalizing, or even worse, telling half-truths. This usually comes back to haunt you. Buy some time instead.

Tip #6 –Tackle Easy Situations First

Avoid confronting Aunt Betty if she's your toughest case. Instead, say no to the saleslady demonstrating the latest perfume, to the survey marketer on the phone, or to the clerk who wants all of your contact information. Build up gradually from there. Develop the habit of saying no at least once every day. Before you know it you'll be ready to take on the world.

When I was still in the learning phase of how to say no, one of my tests was when a young paperboy came to our door selling new subscriptions. We rarely read newspapers, but his bright eyes, freckled face and hopeful smile got to me as he enthusiastically described how he wanted to win a bicycle for selling the most subscriptions in the neighborhood. How could I say no to that? I folded.

Avoid difficult situations as much as possible until you're ready. The first few times may not be perfect. That's simply because your no muscle hasn't been flexed enough yet. Keep practicing. Also watch out for the guilt demons—those little voices that chatter in your head after you've said no.

- How could I not give to that worthy cause?
- How could I not help out on the local community council this year?

Tell those guilt demons to shut up! Stay focused on your new habit and eventually they will leave you alone. Soon you'll notice your confidence level increasing, and you will feel stronger and more assertive. That will add valuable bonus points to your self-esteem while staying true to yourself. As you can see, there's a lot to this saying no business. It's vitally important that you master it. Review this section as often as you need to, until you feel fully prepared. Then go have fun with it.

Judy just couldn't say no to salespeople. A knock at the front door would send her into near panic. One of her biggest challenges was saying no to Mr. Zippy.

Mr. Zippy was a jovial round-faced entrepreneur who sold door-to-door from the back of his truck. His forte was delicious meats and fish, conveniently fast frozen so you could make supper in a zip.

Judy would initially choose two boxed items, but she always ended up buying the super special of the day. She would find herself standing behind a small tower of boxes, handing over a $300 check. "In the end I had no more room in the freezer. I had enough zippy meals to feed the entire neighborhood for a year!"

Needless to say, Mr. Zippy loved knocking on Judy's door every month.

"One day I was out digging in the garden when I spied Mr. Zippy's truck driving up the lane. I leaped into the lilac bushes hoping he wouldn't notice the cloud of blossoms I'd created. I peeped out a couple of times to see if he had gone. I felt so stupid. Here I was, a grown woman hiding in the lilac bushes because I couldn't say no."

The good news is that Judy finally learned to say no. Mr. Zippy was shocked when she said it the first time, even before he'd stepped inside the door. In fact, she said it to him every time he called after that. And now Mr. Zippy no longer calls. Judy loves her new-found power, and it's saving her money.

2. Choose Your Timing

When I was at home raising the kids and volunteering or working part-time, most of the household chores fell on my shoulders. I accepted this and felt it was a fair division of work. Then I went back to work full-time.

The transition was exhausting and it took me a while to wake up to the fact that I was still doing most of the household chores. No wonder I was feeling resentful and burnt out. I sat the family down and told them how I felt, and how I wanted everyone to share in the necessary tasks. They initially responded favorably, then there was resistance, then finally after a couple of months I noticed how they had adjusted to doing their part. I love boundaries!

First, choose the best time to sit down, face to face, with the individual or people you want to talk to. It could be your husband, boss, co-worker, elderly parents, family or friends. Prepare for this meeting. Think about what you want, and why. What is the specific outcome you desire?

The quality of strength, lined with tenderness,
is an unbeatable combination.

—Maya Angelou

Make a list of benefits that the other person will receive as a result of your new boundary, but focus on your own need, and be strong. This is an important discussion so make sure you are not interrupted. Find a quiet location.

These types of conversations are sometimes uncomfortable because you are concerned about a negative reaction or heated argument developing. Be totally sincere with your words and use good eye contact. Express your feelings at the start. To prepare the other person and minimize any immediate defensive reaction, here are a few suggestions on how to start the dialogue:

- I want you to know how I'm feeling right now
  so you will know how to handle me. I'm upset
  (worried, anxious, angry) because...
- I want to talk about me and my relationship to you...
- I realize I haven't been honest with myself lately,
  or with you...
- I'm concerned because you haven't been getting
  the best from me recently...
- I want to feel happy and have some balance
  in my life again...
- What I'm going to say is difficult for me,
  and you may feel some resistance at first...

What you don't want to say is anything that lays blame on the other person. That's a sure-fire way to have a short conversation.

- It's your fault that I'm so upset...
- You never listen to a word I say...

Get in Touch With Your Feelings

Can you be emotionally honest with yourself when you have no idea how you feel? I don't think so. Many of us are so busy just living, or so focused on others, that when it comes to feelings we are totally disconnected. Making this situation worse, we are taught that expressing emotions is bad.

- Don't be angry.
- Stop crying.
- Stop being so emotional!

Feelings are just feelings. They are automatic responses—we need to express them. Because we don't like certain feelings, such as anger, hate, jealousy or bitterness, we condition ourselves to avoid expressing them. Not realizing the potential damage to our health and relationships, we hope they will disappear.

But low self-esteem and a lack of self-respect are too high a price to pay. When we set boundaries, it's important to be emotionally honest and take responsibility for our feelings.

Start by becoming more aware of your body. Tune into it. Do you feel a knot in your stomach or a restriction in your throat? Do your shoulders feel burdened, weighed down? Is your chest tight? Body awareness can help you understand what you are feeling and where you need to set boundaries. By accurately tuning in, you can discover where you are giving your power away. That knot in your stomach could be fear. The restriction in your throat alerts you to words that need to be spoken. Sometimes the need for more space may cause a tightness in your chest. Your body is always talking to you—listen to it.

I like to play a little game. Throughout my day I ask myself, "How are you feeling?" This keeps me tuned in, mentally and physically. I've also noticed that I'm getting much better at expressing my feelings to others. Familiarize yourself with words that describe feelings; happy, sad, frustrated, excited, peaceful, worried, distracted etc. Practice this.

Vent Your Feelings, Then Talk

If you feel like a volcano ready to erupt with anger, it's not a good time to set a boundary. Anger, or any other intense emotion, polarizes communication. We use attacking language, or we start whining like a victim. Often that triggers a similar reaction in the other person and a fight ensues. It's impossible to think clearly when you're in the heat of a battle.

I strongly advise you to first go off somewhere to vent. Let it out. This is healthy. Repressing your anger is not. You're just stoking the volcano when you stuff your emotions. When I'm home, if something or someone is really pushing my buttons, I march upstairs to the bedroom, grab my pillow and punch it for all I'm worth, or... I go for a long walk. Physical activity helps me let off steam. Some progressive companies have a stress-release room equipped with a good old-fashioned punching bag for their irate employees.

Here's another tip if you happen to be in a supervisory position at work. When a staff member corners you and uncorks her volcano, force yourself to listen quietly. Don't say a word, just listen and care. She (or he) will give you a verbal laundry list of complaints and eventually run out of steam and be quiet. Then, and only then, do you say: "Are you just here to vent your feelings, or do you want me to take action on this?"

More often than not you will receive a sheepish look and the response will be, "No, I just needed to get that off my chest. Thanks for being a good listener."

I'll never forget the time I sat in front of a group of hostile women, outnumbered twenty to one. It looked like a lynch mob. The atmosphere was extremely tense. They had been mandated by the government to attend my workshop as part of a training program for people re-entering the workplace. I didn't know it, but my program was one of many that this group had been required to attend. These women were upset that this was yet another personal development program, when what they really wanted was to learn practical office skills. It was obvious they were not willing to participate or cooperate in any way. They'd had enough personal work and I became the scapegoat for all their pent-up anger and frustration. So I let them rant and rave and let off steam. It was one thing to criticize my program, I drew the line when they started attacking my character.

I felt this was completely uncalled for. Trembling with suppressed anger, I first set a boundary with my emotions. I deliberately chose not to play their game—no attacking or shouting. Using the more honorable discipline of quiet humility, I decided to leave them with a few memorable words. When I opened my mouth, however, all that came out was a high-pitched squeak. Sometimes being emotional sucks!

Somehow I left the meeting with my dignity intact, but inside my anger was boiling over. Back at my hotel room I erupted. Dignity and decorum thrown asunder, I pummeled an overstuffed chair. It was the best tantrum I've ever had, and it felt sooo good!

3. The When-Feel-Want Technique
Whether at work or at home, good communication is important when you are setting boundaries with others. This technique will assist you in being clear when expressing what you want.

When... (describe the behavior)

I **feel**... (describe your feelings)

I **want**... (state what you want)

For example:

- **When** you come home from work you disappear into your office downstairs.
- I **feel** ignored and unloved.
- I **want** you to ask me about my day.

- **When** I have an urgent deadline...
- I **feel** pressured.
- I **want** you to become more sensitive about this by not adding more to my already full workload.

A word of caution: if you're expecting total cooperation when you first set up a new boundary, think again. You may be setting yourself up for a major disappointment. Let's face it, we know it takes time for people to adjust to a new situation. Some women are really ticked off when their brand-new boundary is ignored, but unless the situation is absolutely intolerable, consider giving the other person a little wriggle room. Old habits die hard when it comes to adults. And teenagers? Some have selective hearing. Often they don't even remember what you said yesterday.

Obtaining agreement for a new boundary is a form of negotiation. To maintain healthy integral relationships, adults need to regularly negotiate boundaries between themselves. Focus on making it a win-win. One thing you don't want to do is isolate your family and friends by being too rigid. Like the willow tree, you need to be flexible. Getting everything you want some of the time may be sufficient. Check your position by asking these two questions:

- How important is this?
- How far do I want to take it?

Curfew Consequences

Consequences are often the only way we can get cooperation and have our needs met. My son was late again. In fact, it was well past his curfew. Being a typical mother, I was sleeping with one ear open, listening for his safe return. By the time he noisily entered the house in the wee hours, I was tired and angry. "You are grounded for a month!" I yelled.

Be careful what you set up. That consequence didn't affect him nearly as much as it affected me. Having a cranky, moody teenager in my space for thirty-one long days was nearly unbearable. When you set consequences, make sure that you are willing to enforce them. Be certain the impact on the other person is greater than on you. Don't threaten to leave a relationship if you're not ready to do so. Don't say you'll quit your job if that isn't your intention. Making hollow threats can backfire on you later. Think through your consequences first, don't make them in the heat of the moment. Consequences often take creativity—remember, your goal is to change the behavior. If you aren't prepared to follow through, the other person will not be motivated to change. The secret is in the follow through.

> *Be committed. Do what it takes, and you*
> *will have what you want.*

—Dr. Phil McGraw

A Man's Perspective   Les Hewitt

I think men have an easier time setting boundaries than women do. One of the main reasons is that women are natural caregivers. This instinct is not automatic for all men.

However, where we have more difficulty is being on the receiving end of a new boundary. I remember Fran telling me years ago that she would no longer accept last-minute projects from me. This included everything from typing, banking and creating Power Point slides to ironing a shirt. At first I was in denial. However, when she firmly said no the next time I dumped one of my urgent requests on her plate, I realized she was serious. It was humbling having to make phone calls apologizing for the fact that I would not be able to make my deadline. This led to a good discussion—fortunately I listened.

She explained the pressure she felt when I surprised her with last-minute work. This disrupted her schedule and made her feel resentful. Fran was right. I realized that the longer I maintained this bad habit, the more damage it would do to our relationship. Since that time, Fran has created other boundaries and even though I have had to make adjustments, the benefits far outweigh any discomfort. She is more assertive and happier overall. To me that is good for our marriage.

From a man's perspective, I think women need to set more boundaries. The men in their lives would really prefer them to be happier and less burdened. Because men tend to be solution oriented, I would suggest you sell the boundary as a benefit to a problem.

CONCLUSION

As a woman I know how difficult it is to set boundaries. Today I can say with pride that I am adept at setting boundaries, but it wasn't always that way. Understanding what boundaries are, and implementing them in my life, has helped tremendously. It starts with self-knowledge. Knowing myself better has uncovered why I do what I do, and revealed the intentions and motivations behind my action or inaction. I now understand why I was unable or unwilling to set boundaries in the past. Focusing on how I feel supports this new skill. If I feel resentful or used, it usually means I have given more than I want to give, and I need to set a boundary. If I feel guilty, it probably means I have set a boundary that is making me uncomfortable, at least initially. When that boundary is necessary, however, I've learned to breathe through the guilt, and eventually it passes.

Learning to respect myself as an equal to everyone else is a factor. Understanding that other people are not more powerful nor more worthy than me (and vice versa) has also contributed to my success.

So has learning the difference between martyrdom and selflessness. I can now give with generosity, and care for others without feeling deprived, used or resentful. I maintain my self-respect and self-love in the process. Although my nature is to love and to give, I adopted a tough-love approach in my closest relationships. I learned to set boundaries, and was determined to follow through.

You can do this too. The benefits to your life, and to those you love, are worth the effort. There is no race to do it all today. Make a commitment to get started, and follow through.

ACTION STEPS

Relationships

Boundaries

Saying No

Use these steps to implement the key chapter strategies.

1. Who in your life intrudes into your boundary? Candidates include children, in-laws, spouse, boss or strangers. You may feel resentful around them, or perhaps you feel like a doormat.

_____

_____

Why do you sacrifice yourself for these people? Knowing the answer to this will help you understand your motivation.

❑ I don't want conflict.
❑ I want to feel needed.
❑ I like to please.
❑ I cannot say no to them.
❑ Other reason.

READER/CUSTOMER CARE SURVEY

We care about your opinions. Please take a moment to fill out this Reader Survey card and mail it back to us.
As a special **"thank you"** we'll send you exciting news about interesting books and a valuable **Gift Certificate.**

Please PRINT using ALL CAPS

First Name _____ MI. ___ Last Name _____

Address _____

City _____ ST ___ Zip _____

Phone # (___) ___ — ___ Fax # (___) ___ — ___

Email _____

(1) Gender:
___ Female ___ Male

(2) Age:
___ 12 or under ___ 40-59
___ 13-19 ___ 60+
___ 20-39

(3) Marital Status
___ Married
___ Single
___ Divorced/Widowed

(4) Did you receive this book as a gift?
___ Yes ___ No

(5) How many Health Communications books have you bought or read?
___ 1 ___ 2-4 ___ 5+

(6) How did you find out about this book?
Please fill in ONE.
1) ___ Recommendation
2) ___ Store Display
3) ___ Bestseller List
4) ___ Online
5) ___ Advertisement
6) ___ Catalog/Mailing
7) ___ Interview/Review (TV, Radio, Print)

(7) Where do you usually buy books?
Please fill in your top TWO choices.
1) ___ Bookstore
2) ___ Religious Bookstore
3) ___ Online
4) ___ Book Club/Mail Order
5) ___ Price Club (Costco, Sam's Club, etc.)
6) ___ Retail Store (Target, Wal-Mart, etc.)

(9) What subjects do you enjoy reading about most? Rank only **FIVE.** *Use 1 for your favorite, 2 for second favorite, etc.*

	1	2	3	4	5
1) Parenting/Family	O	O	O	O	O
2) Relationships	O	O	O	O	O
3) Recovery/Addictions	O	O	O	O	O
4) Health/Nutrition	O	O	O	O	O
5) Christianity	O	O	O	O	O
6) Spirituality/Inspiration	O	O	O	O	O
7) Business Self-Help	O	O	O	O	O
8) Teen Issues	O	O	O	O	O
9) Sports	O	O	O	O	O

(14) What attracts you most to a book?
(Please rank 1-4 in order of preference.)

	1	2	3	4
1) Title	O	O	O	O
2) Cover Design	O	O	O	O
3) Author	O	O	O	O
4) Content	O	O	O	O

TAPE IN MIDDLE; DO NOT STAPLE

BUSINESS REPLY MAIL

FIRST-CLASS MAIL PERMIT NO 45 DEERFIELD BEACH, FL

POSTAGE WILL BE PAID BY ADDRESSEE

HEALTH COMMUNICATIONS, INC.
3201 SW 15TH STREET
DEERFIELD BEACH FL 33442-9875

FOLD HERE

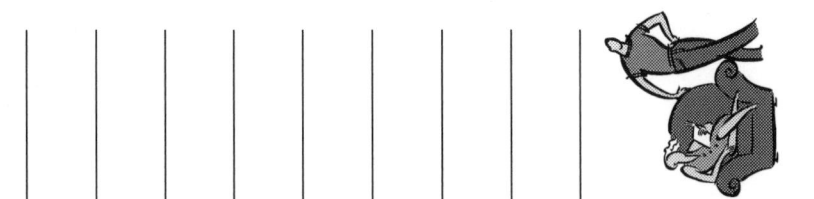

Comments:

_____

_____

2. Whose boundary do you not respect? Perhaps you intrude on their privacy, you don't respect their no's, you manipulate them to get what you want, or you shout them down.

_____

_____

_____

_____

3. Who is good at setting boundaries?

_____

_____

_____

How do you feel about this person?

_____

_____

_____

What positive qualities do you see in him or her?

_____

_____

_____

4. Write down the names of the people with whom you will choose to negotiate new boundaries. Concentrate on one of these relationships starting this week. Take your time. Easy manageable steps are more likely to succeed.

_____   _____

_____   _____

_____   _____

_____   _____

5. What other boundary issues besides relationships came to mind as you read this chapter? These issues can include protecting your values, or your time.

_____

_____

_____

6. List some of the benefits you will enjoy by implementing successful new boundaries.

_____

_____

_____

_____

_____

Do everything you can to maintain these new disciplines.

Eliminate the Four Burdens:

Perfectionism, Guilt, Worry and Resentment

*Travel lightly my friends. Give up
your unconscious pain and habits; they weigh
you down. Accept your birthright
to be joyous and free.*

—Anonymous

Of all the personality traits I struggle with, perfectionism has been the most difficult to overcome. I call myself a recovering perfectionist. My husband and kids are recovering too—from me.

The crowning moment occurred when my best friend caught me ironing my six-year-old son's boxer shorts. She screamed! That got my attention. I always thought I was just fussy—but then I questioned what else was over the top? As I look back on my life as a perfectionist my biggest regret is not for the lost opportunities, nor for the unnecessary, insane pressure I put on myself. My main regret is for not being silly enough with my kids, for not allowing them to wear what they wanted, for scolding them sometimes when they made a mess on the floor. I'm also chagrined for allowing my standards and rules to take precedence over my husband's happiness. My controlling nature and need for order could have permanently damaged the relationship closest to my heart.

Besides perfectionism, there are three other burdens that rob us of joy—guilt, worry and resentment. Combine these burdens with perfectionism, and we have a deadly mixture that is poison to health and happiness. Life is a constant battle between the negative forces that hold us back and the positive energy that provides us with fulfillment and peace of mind. Let's start by clearly defining the characteristics of each of the four burdens. Then I'll provide some powerful antidotes to help keep you burden-free. The most important of these antidotes is forgiveness.

Perfectionism:
A DOUBLE-EDGED SWORD

Perfectionism
Perfectionism can be both constructive and destructive. It's a double-edged sword. Constructive perfectionism is practiced by the woman who sets healthy goals and focuses her efforts on achieving them. She has a high work ethic and strong reasons for meeting her objectives. She wants to do well in her field and is prepared to give her best effort. In the process she learns about her strengths and weaknesses, and where she needs to make adjustments. Self-discipline is her friend. If everything goes according to plan she may even create a perfect result. When she eventually succeeds, she takes time to celebrate and includes the people who helped her on the road to victory.

If you want to be a top achiever, going the extra mile is both necessary and smart. In today's competitive world, you cannot drift to the top. Many benefits come from creating habits that improve your focus, concentration and self-awareness. You will experience a surge in confidence, be able to easily sidestep distractions and often achieve a substantial financial reward. All of this is good.

The other side of the sword is destructive perfectionism—a compulsive striving toward unreasonable standards and an inability to feel satisfied. The result never feels good enough. You feel like you're always falling short. Even when the destructive perfectionist is certain to hit her target, instead of celebrating she makes the target bigger and extends the timeline. She never feels satisfied.

> Tanya spent three hours every day for a whole week preparing for a fifteen-minute presentation. She had rehearsed numerous times and covered every eventuality, but she still felt unprepared.

Are you excessive in your preparation? Do you feel that your accomplishments are never good enough? Do you find that with your high standards you are hard to live with?

The perfectionist measures her worth in terms of productivity and accomplishment. Despite exerting tremendous effort, in her mind she never measures up. The emotional cost is high. It comes in the form of self-doubt, stress from the self-imposed pressure to outperform, disappointment, frustration, fear of making mistakes and a fear of being humiliated. Eating disorders such as bulimia and anorexia are linked to perfectionism. So are depression and suicide. Perfectionism is a very painful burden.

Little Miss Perfect

How do people become perfectionists? Some children are born with a predisposition to perfection. It's an inherited genetic trait. More common, however, is parental influence. Children quickly learn, directly or indirectly, that they aren't good enough.

- Your B grade on the exam was good, but an A would have been better.

- You did a pretty good job cleaning up your room, but next time put things away properly.

Children interpret these messages to mean that their value is based on their achievements, and the approval of others. Children of hypercritical parents feel that only when they are perfect, are they valued and loved.

Over time, these children may create the belief that being perfect is the only way to live. As adults they no longer need to please Mom or Dad in a direct way, but they still demand perfection in themselves. And indirectly, of course, they may still want to prove something to their parents.

Another factor is a chaotic upbringing. Alcoholism, divorce, abuse, constant relocation or chronic illness often cause children to seek order and control. They do this by being good, by being neat and tidy, or by becoming high achievers, all in an effort to cope with the chaos. Again, this often carries into adulthood even though they no longer live in a state of flux.

Two Perfect Traps

Perfectionism is either directed at yourself, directed at others, or both. The former—inwardly focused perfectionism—occurs when women are too hard on themselves, pushing relentlessly to achieve unrealistic goals. They don't dare make mistakes. Failure is a reflection of their worth. They see failure as proof of incompetence. Letting go and being easier on themselves is difficult because they internalize failure. Self-oriented perfectionism is a form of self-rejection.

Perfectionists can also impose ultra-high standards on others. When this happens, relationships often suffer because it seems like other people are always letting them down. They become frustrated because other people fail to meet their demands. Wanting others to do their best is one thing, but expecting perfection is setting them up to fail.

Binocular Vision

When you look through binoculars everything is magnified. Perfectionists magnify their imperfections and perceived flaws. They focus on one negative piece of feedback, ignoring thirty that are positive. When you minimize the positives it's like looking through binoculars the wrong way. The positives are so far away they appear insignificant.

> Debbie did an incredible job for her company bringing in the biggest sale of the year. Everyone congratulated her, but all Debbie could think about was one error— forgetting to mention the new, improved warranty. Her persistence, the magnitude of her accomplishment, and her well-deserved recognition were ignored, even though her error didn't affect the outcome. In her mind, it just wasn't good enough.

Perfect Illusions

Perfectionism is rampant today. No wonder so many career-driven women are unhappy. On the outside they appear to have it all—success, great lifestyle, fabulous looks. However, on the inside it's a different story. In many cases they feel desperate, frustrated and unhappy. Peace of mind and a sense of satisfaction elude them. Striving to be perfect all the time is exhausting. Barbra Streisand, a well-known perfectionist, says, "Demanding perfection is a cold way to live. Imperfection has humanity in it."

If you have fallen prey to this trap, cut yourself—and those you love—some slack. Being perfect is an illusion.

> Melissa was always impeccably dressed and groomed. Every morning she walked into the office looking like a fashion model. Her workmates bristled with envy. How did she do it? She had three little ones at home all under the age of eight, and still managed to look great.

One Friday at an important management meeting, Melissa was presenting at the front of the boardroom. When she turned around to demonstrate her Power Point slides, everyone focused on the red Velcro roller embedded in her hair. We all loved Melissa a little more that day!

Perfectionism dishonors us. The sad fact is that as a perfectionist, we may be controlling our feelings of inadequacy, but we're no joy to be with. Think about someone you know like Melissa, who never has a hair out of place, does everything well and thinks she is always right. How do you feel being around this person? Exactly! It's not a lot of fun.

A good question to ask a perfectionist is, "How is it working for you?" If perfectionism was classified as an emotional disorder, I believe more women would seek the help they need to free themselves from its destructive grasp.

Rigid Thinking

Perfectionists frequently have difficulty making decisions. This is due to their tendency to evaluate using extremes. Everything is black or white. Shades of grey do not exist.

For me, black-and-white thinking almost ruined a uniquely memorable experience. For almost a year I had been planning a special vacation. I wanted to fly to Ireland and go on holiday with my two sisters. No husband, no kids—just me. I could hardly wait. But wait I did. Something was holding me back from booking a ticket. Why was I stuck in indecision and inaction? I wanted it to be perfect. In my mind I wanted a guarantee before I would go. I wanted sunny weather, affordable shopping, delicious food and my sisters to be in great form, with no mood swings or fighting. I was stuck because I wanted the perfect holiday, yet most of what I wanted was out of my control.

Then a friend asked me, "What would a less-than-perfect holiday look like?" What about a grey picture instead of the ideal blue-sky picture?

Hmm, I thought. The sky could be grey, it might even rain some of the time. I might not shop as much as I'd like to and the food could be mediocre. To my surprise, when I thought about the grey picture I realized that I still wanted to go. It would be a great holiday no matter what. That day I booked my flight. There was a happy ending, too. I had a brilliant holiday. It turned out blue-sky perfect after all.

Start accepting shades of grey and give up rigid thinking. It can keep you trapped in indecision. Perfectionists miss out on good opportunities or choose to ignore them. Their indecisiveness is an avoidance tactic. They also penalize themselves by analyzing everything to death instead of taking calculated risks.

175

The Nag

Learn to separate yourself from your perfection by giving it a name and identity. I call mine The Nag. She is the critical voice in my head driving me to distraction. The Nag is perfect, always well put together, intelligent, witty and never, ever wrong. She is also a bitch, and nobody likes her. Every day in some capacity she shows up in my life. When I'm aware she wants center stage, I challenge her. It drives her crazy when I ignore a crooked picture on the wall, or leave a damp towel on the bathroom floor, or deliberately do something that is less than perfect. I have also started saying yes to assignments for which I am unprepared. This really gets her goat! Every time I challenge her she loses power over me. She is miserable—but I have never been happier. I've decided I'd rather be happy than perfect.

Monitor Your Expectations

Having expectations is healthy. Just don't expect to control every outcome and have everything your own way. Unmet expectations keep perfectionists frustrated and miserable. One way to check your expectations is by uncovering your *shoulds*. Here are a few examples of *shoulding* on yourself:

- I should always be prepared.
- I should never look untidy or unkempt.
- I should always be calm.

On others, *shoulding* sounds like this:

- You should do as I say.
- You should do it properly or not at all.
- You should always respect your elders.

Make a list of the expectations you have, for yourself and for others. You'll find it enlightening. Look for similarities between the two. Often what we demand of ourselves we also demand of others, realistic or not.

Perfectionists are into making rules. They have rules for everything. Rules for cleaning the home, driving the car, having things in the right place, when to eat, what to wear and what to buy. At the office, perfectionist bosses have high expectations and rigid rules. Do you have too many rules in your life? Do most of these rules make you feel bad? Too many rules suffocate relationships. Here's a big question: What's more important, your relationships or your rules?

The longest journey is the journey inward.

—Dag Hammarskjold

I used to think that I couldn't be happy unless my dinner party was perfect—superb atmosphere, great food served piping hot, artistically set table, fresh flowers, the best wine, lovely background music, everyone getting along and enjoying each other's company. At the end of the meal I'd suddenly realize: "I forgot to serve the gravy!" When you're upset, chances are it's not your husband, your kids, the boss, the food or the wine. What's upsetting you are your own inflexible rules.

Anthony Robbins, the noted author and business coach, says, "You may be winning but feel like you are losing because of your unrealistic standards. It's not whether your rules are right or wrong, but whether they empower or disempower you. Have you set up the rules so that it's impossible for you to win?"

Challenge Your Expectations

One solution is to challenge your expectations by doing an honest reality check. Ask yourself:

- What is my expectation?
- What is my *should* about it?
- What payoff do I get by having this expectation?
- What is my payoff for not having it?
- What would happen if I let it go?

Brenda's expectation was to be respected by her bosses at work. She always went the extra mile, putting in longer hours than everyone else. She had a management role and demanded a lot from her staff. This resulted in high productivity and upper management respected her performance. However, Brenda's staff found her to be cold, demanding and unapproachable. Behind her back they called her Bitchy Brenda. Although Brenda liked the work, she felt lonely and didn't like the way her staff reacted to her.

Let's analyze this: Brenda had her expectations met because she earned the respect of her bosses. Her *should* was: "I should always work harder than everyone else." Did she get a payoff? Yes, her demanding management style created productivity.

When Brenda eventually decided to let go of her expectations and be less demanding, she discovered that her relationships with staff members significantly improved. She became more relaxed and started taking a genuine interest in the people around her. Productivity actually increased and staff turnover, which had been about average, dropped.

Not surprisingly, Brenda still enjoyed the respect of upper management. By letting go of her expectations about performance and focusing on her relationships, Brenda ended up with a much better payoff. What expectation could you let go of to improve a relationship?

Bedtime story ending for realists:

So the prince and the princess lowered their expectations and lived reasonably happily ever after.

—Anonymous

Find Your Freedom

If you want more peace and harmony in your life I strongly suggest you fire The Nag. To help you find your freedom, here's a practical checklist:

1. Being a perfectionist is nothing to be ashamed of. Acknowledge your frustration and pain.

2. Accept the fact that you have a choice in every situation. You can choose what you want to strive for and you can choose when you want to settle for less.

3. Set realistic standards and goals. Talk this over with someone you trust.

4. Be alert every day for The Nag and vigorously challenge her. Gradually she will lose power.

5. Determine the underlying beliefs driving your compulsion. Ask yourself, "What will happen if it's not done right?" What will happen if you go shopping without wearing any makeup—will you survive?

6. Experiment with your standards. Choose an activity and instead of insisting on 100 percent, see what it's like doing it to an 80 percent standard or even 60 percent.

7. Check to see if you have a major need for acceptance. "When I'm perfect, I'll be accepted." If your belief centers on this, you need to work on self-acceptance. What will make you feel better about who you are?

8. Keep asking yourself, "What's more important, my relationship or my rules?"

9. Change your thinking. Here are some examples:

From: When I achieve perfection, I will find inner peace.

To: When I let go of perfection, I will find inner peace.

From: I must be perfect or I'll be rejected.

To: I'm perfect when I make mistakes
     because this shows others that I'm human.

From: If I make a mistake I'll be humiliated.

To: If I make a mistake I will learn from it.

From: There is a right way and a wrong way to do things.

To: There are many ways to do things.

From: If I demand that others do things my way,
     I'll be happy.

To: If I help another person do their best,
     we will both be happier.

> Perfectionism is like walking toward
> the horizon—you'll never get there!

The Three Energy Vampires:
GUILT, WORRY AND
RESENTMENT

Stacey is excited because Friday has finally arrived. Only one more day at work. Tonight she's leaving on a ski trip to the mountains with her friends. The forecast is for mild temperatures, sunny skies and a fresh snowfall—ideal conditions. She leaves her apartment feeling energized and happy at the thought of a fun-filled weekend.

Her car is slow to start, requiring several attempts before the engine eventually comes to life. This problem has been getting worse but Stacey hasn't had time to have it checked. She's also concerned that fixing the car might result in a big bill and her cash flow isn't healthy at the moment.

By the time she arrives at the office she's running late. The security guard, an older gentleman with a friendly smile, signs her in. Stacey makes a mental note that she hasn't called her father this week. He's a frail eighty-three-year-old who lives alone. She feels a pang of guilt. Lately, she's been worried about his ability to cope. When she sits down at her workstation a memo from her boss is on her desk. It's blunt—"Where is the report that was due yesterday?" Now she feels guilty about having left work early to pick up a few things for the weekend trip. Stacey realizes that she may need to work into the evening to get her work caught up, messing up arrangements for the weekend. She feels resentful at the possibility. Her mood has changed, and her energy is low. She can't wait for this drag of a day to be over.

Mainly through her own choices, Stacey has created a downward spiral. Sucked into this whirlpool, she finds it difficult to pull herself out. Her positive energy has been replaced by the negative burdens of guilt, worry and resentment. If she doesn't make some quick decisions, the spiral will grow deeper. People who are superstitious claim that bad things often happen three at a time. Possibly. But bad things may not stop at three. Negative attracts more negative—it's a chain reaction. Negative thinking fuels the burdens of guilt, worry and resentment. Where the mind goes, energy flows.

To reverse a downward spiral you must act quickly. First, become aware of what's happening. Then take action to correct the situation. Stacey realizes that *she* is causing her dilemma due to her negative thinking. The thought of ruining her carefully planned weekend motivates her to take action. She apologizes to her boss, avoids interruptions for the rest of the morning, and works through lunch. The report is on his desk by two o'clock. Instead of continuing to feel guilty about her father, she calls him and invites him over for supper the following Tuesday. She also books an appointment to have her car checked while she's away.

Stacey took control by focusing on what needed to be done instead of letting the energy vampires suck her spirit dry. As she left the office, her boss congratulated her on an excellent report. Stacey could feel her positive energy building as she looked forward to a great weekend. She had successfully exchanged the downward spiral for an upward one. Let's look more closely at these energy vampires, and see what we can do to keep them out of our lives.

Guilt

This is not always a negative emotion. It can be a healthy reminder to our moral conscience when we are acting unethically. If we value honesty yet knowingly lie to a friend to save her some embarrassment, a guilty voice reminds us that it is better to tell the truth. This type of guilt monitors our misdoings and teaches us to be wiser and more loving.

Unhealthy guilt is a different story. This type of guilt excessively punishes us for mistakes; it would have us doing penance for eternity. At times everyone is selfish, hurtful, fearful and acts without thinking about the consequences. We all make mistakes. Yet some women believe they deserve to suffer permanently. They lock themselves up in an emotional prison and throw away the key. They attach indelible labels to themselves: I am bad. I am guilty. I deserve to be punished. Those labels keep them frozen in their conviction. Instead of feeling a sense of remorse or regret for their behavior, they choose the more damaging sentence of guilt. This inflicts a direct hit on their self-esteem, and creates more labels such as, I am worthless. Some of the manifestations of unhealthy guilt are depression, shame and anxiety.

> Judith was depressed. Even though the affair she had at work was long over, guilt still consumed her. Her best friend, Lana, knew the situation and was concerned about Judith's failing health. It became so bad she threatened to inform Judith's parents. Judith's tearful response revealed the depth of her anxiety. "Please, please don't. I couldn't face them. I'm so ashamed."

Do you believe you deserve to suffer when you make a mistake, do something inappropriate, or hurt someone? If you answered yes, consider these questions: How long must you suffer? What length should your sentence be? When is enough? When your time has been served, are you going to unlock the door to your mental prison and set yourself free, or will you still choose to be miserable? Some people take the view that if they hurt someone else they deserve to be hurt too. The truth is that even long-term suffering cannot reverse the bad deed or cure the guilt. Continuous self-condemnation actually intensifies the guilt.

Sincerely showing remorse and apologizing for your wrong-doing is a better option. This acknowledges that you are aware of the pain you caused. It also shows that you learned a valuable lesson and won't repeat the same mistake. Guilt is a crutch for some people: I'm guilty, I'm hopeless, so don't expect anything else from me.

A few years ago my younger sister reminded me of an incident when we were little. Mom had entrusted me with Trish's bus fare to make sure she got home from school. Instead of giving it to her, I spent the money on a sticky bun! She had to walk home by herself. I'm not sure what was going on in my nine-year-old head at the time. Did I want to punish her? Was I being greedy? Maybe I was just hungry. None of that really mattered. All I remember was my deep feeling of guilt. Many years later I apologized, she forgave me, and we both had a good laugh. Yet inside I still felt uncomfortable. I wanted to do something special for her to resolve the issue in my mind, once and for all. Along with a luxurious terry bathrobe and wonderful aromatherapy bath salts, I sent a written apology and asked for her forgiveness. She was delighted, and at last I felt free.

The Judgment Horse

As adults we are good at pointing fingers at ourselves. We look back at earlier situations, the ones we feel we should have handled better, and sit in judgment. Often this is inappropriate and cruel; especially when the criticism is directed at our own childhood behavior.

- I should have known better.
- I was so naive and stupid.
- Just thinking about what I did makes me sick.

These are strong words. How easily we forget, or don't understand, that children and teenagers are not fully equipped with maturity and wisdom. Often they don't appreciate the consequences of their actions, and they use hurtful behavior out of fear, or their own pain. I believe it's not up to us to judge ourselves or others. Better leave that to a higher power. Feeling guilty is bad enough. You don't need to paralyze yourself by being judgmental.

Empathy and forgiveness, for yourself and others, can help free you from this unhealthy energy-drainer. Empathy is feeling the impact of what the other person has experienced, and feeling how that is affecting you as well. It's feeling an appropriate level of sorrow and regret, without being overwhelmed with guilt and judgment.

Pervasive Guilt

Another type of guilt subtly eats away at us, weaving its way into the fabric of our everyday lives. Triggered automatically in many situations, it especially likes to infiltrate the lives of working mothers. I call it Pervasive Guilt. Think about it. We feel guilty about going to work and guilty for enjoying that work. We feel guilty for not staying home and when we do, we feel guilty because we'd rather be somewhere else. We're guilty again when we spend money on ourselves instead of Johnny, who insists he must have those new Nike runners.

Okay, so you blew the diet this afternoon demolishing that double chocolate cheesecake, and now you're suffering a major guilt attack. Delicious at the time, it now feels like a lead weight congealing alongside the guilt in your gut. Then there's your guilt for not spending more time with Mom and Dad, even though they drive you crazy.

> *Guilt is the price we pay willingly for doing what we are going to do anyway.*

—Isabelle Holland

Guilt—it's all around us. We live and breathe guilt and just can't seem to shake it. Every day we need to guard against the pervasive guilt permeating our existence. But how? One strategy is to watch out for those negative *shoulds*. Remember them? They keep popping up in all sorts of situations.

- I should always be available for my kids.
- Good mothers shouldn't work.
- I should be more loving to my parents.

Every one of those statements is dripping with guilt. Tune in to your guilt by being acutely sensitive to the words you use. Monitor yourself for one whole day by writing down every *should* you utter. With practice you'll get so good at this

185

preventative maintenance that every time you or anyone else uses the 's' word you'll hear an alarm bell ringing in your ears. Be on the alert. This pervasive form of guilt becomes an automatic and symptomatic emotion, yet most women are not aware of it. Pervasive guilt is energy-draining and mood-changing, so stamp it out.

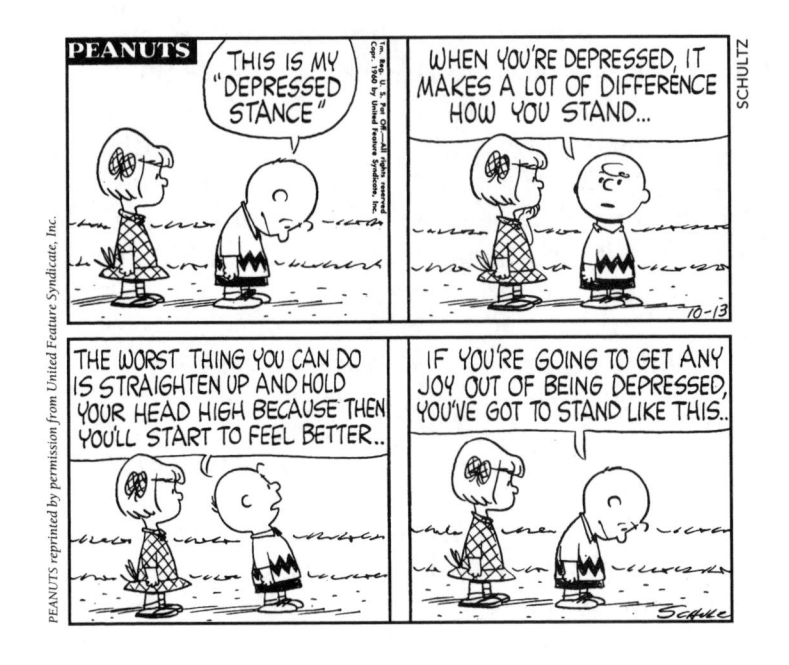

Worry

Worry is another energy vampire. Like guilt, worry is so much a part of our thinking process that we don't even notice we are doing it. Worry promotes doom-and-gloom thinking. By worrying, we torment ourselves with disturbing thoughts and images of what we don't want to happen. Fretting this way contaminates our thoughts and feelings of well-being. It can immobilize us so badly that we are unable to take action.

Worry is the misuse of our imagination; it is projecting something negative into the future that hasn't happened yet, and 95 percent of the time it never happens anyway. Do you lie awake at night worrying about your bills?

> *If you can solve your problem, then what's*
> *the need of worrying? If you cannot solve it,*
> *then what is the use of worrying?*

—Shantideva

So why do we do it, if it's such a waste of time and energy? It's simply a bad habit. Taking on the energy vampires is like going into battle. To be successful, you need to be fore-warned and fore-armed. As my mentor Jim Rohn says: Learn to be a warrior instead of a worrier. Here are some suggestions to beat the worry habit:

1. Be conscious of when you are worrying. Have others act as spotters to help you. Kids enjoy this: "Mom, you're doing your worry thing again!"

2. Pause. Focus on your breathing. Take a deep breath and allow your body to relax. Slowly count to ten. Let the tension go. Repeat this process two or three times if necessary.

3. Take action. Reframe your thinking. Ask yourself: "What can I do?" If I'm lying awake worrying because my teenage son isn't home yet, I can call his cell phone.

4. Stay focused on the present. Stop your mind from catastrophizing or futurizing. If you find yourself fretting, get busy. It will distract you. Find something else to occupy your mind.

5. If you've had a major crisis, naturally you have concerns. Get support. Talk to a good friend, a pastor, or a professional counselor. Sharing your burden helps to release it.

6. Just let go. There are certain things we cannot control so it's pointless worrying about them. Many people find comfort in their faith. If you are one of them, turn your worries over to God, and let Him handle them. Prayer is powerful.

7. Use a journal to capture your feelings. Probe to find the source of your worry.

I have an imaginary pair of scissors. When I find myself obsessing over something, I mentally cut it off with my scissors. Use your own imagination. Be creative. Learn to trust in yourself—life will go the way it's supposed to go. Remind yourself that you are competent and can handle most situations, but you can't do anything about situations outside your control. Joy is the absence of worry, so focus on joy; it's more beneficial to your health.

Jane has a worry box. It's a cardboard shoe box labeled Worries. She writes all her worries down at the end of the day and places them in the box. Once a week she schedules a specific time to do her worrying. She pulls out each piece of paper and reads it. Worries that are no longer of concern she throws away.

When the time is up, she places the remainder back in the box. Sounds silly, but it puts her worries into perspective. After a while she started scheduling her worry time for 5 a.m. Sunday. Usually she sleeps through it, missing her allotted time, and postpones her worrying for another week. Eventually she plans to kick the habit.

Resentment

Resentment, the third energy vampire, is insidious and directly affects relationships. You know you are feeling resentment when you harbor animosity against someone. Perhaps you are holding a grudge, are really angry or feeling upset about a particular event. There is either a deliberate unwillingness to forgive the other person, or an inability to let go

Resentment comes from the Latin *resentive*—to feel over again. Resenters rehash and relive the anger. This does more harm to the resenter than to the other person, because it's like a self-fed poison eating away at the resenter's soul. There are a multitude of reasons why we become resentful. Check to see if any of these situations apply to you:

- ❏ You agree to do something and end up feeling used or taken for granted.

- ❏ You have unmet needs and feel ignored or rejected.

- ❏ Others have let you down in some capacity.

- ❏ You see others getting ahead who haven't worked as hard as you.

- ❏ You feel that you are the one who always makes sacrifices in a relationship.

- ❏ You've experienced divorce, infidelity, being mistreated or abused.

One of the biggest challenges in relationships is infidelity. When this occurs, it is extremely difficult for most people to overcome their resentment.

"My first reaction after discovering Bill's affair was to divorce him," admits Allison. "Then I tried to come to terms with it; we had three children and too much to lose. I know my attitude toward him prior to his affair may have contributed to his temptation. I've accepted my part in that; now it's time to rebuild. Bill is working hard on our marriage and says he loves me and doesn't want a divorce. He has begged for my forgiveness and I believe he is remorseful. I want to have a great relationship, but my resentment keeps getting in the way.

It's been three years since his affair, and our relationship is much stronger. Bill is so attentive now. He has become the husband I always wanted. I still get angry when I remember, though, and sometimes I push him away. Will I ever forget?"

Resentment is an understatement of the pain and anger experienced whenever memories of the infidelity come to mind. Even after a reasonable time has passed for reconciliation, resentment often lingers. All might be forgiven, but forgetting may never happen.

The resentment associated with the painful memory can be overcome with time and the rebuilding of trust. Many marriages do outlast the scars of infidelity.

Games People Play

Resentment comes in many forms. Everyday situations can cause us to withdraw, and everyone has patterns or games they play in relationships. When resentment occurs, these games become evident. Can you spot yours?

❑ I will refuse to play with you. I will withdraw and fume in silence, but watch out for my revenge.

❑ I will get back at you by keeping score. I will keep track so I can gain leverage.

❑ If I can't win, then nobody will win. I will become a problem and you will know all about it.

- ❏ I will never forgive or forget. I have a long memory and I will remind you of all your past mistakes. You will never be sorry enough to please me.

- ❏ I will attack and react. I will be in your face and on your back; nobody messes with me.

- ❏ I am right, period. I will get you to see my way, no matter how it affects you.

It's healthy to become angry and voice our feelings when we feel we have been wronged. It becomes a problem when we connect it to self-righteousness, adopting a superior position of I'm right, you're wrong. Instead of confronting the other person and being assertive, sometimes we prefer revenge. We feel that by getting back at him or her, it will cancel our pain.

> "Frank should be helping out more around the house," complains Doris. "He knows how I feel about this. It shouldn't be any surprise to him when I refuse to be intimate."

Notice the *shoulds?* Doris may have a legitimate complaint. However, using her resentment to punish her husband will not create a win-win. It will probably make him resentful too. Instead of resolving the issue with honest communication and perhaps some compromise, the relationship will become even more strained.

Take The High Road
How to let go of resentment:

- For a specific issue, first put it in perspective by asking, "Is this worth getting steamed up about? Am I over-reacting? Is something else the root cause of my resentment?"

- Look for a rational solution to the issue. "Who do I need to talk to? What action must I take to have my needs met?"

- For significant issues, especially situations where you have harbored your resentment for a long time, write a letter. Release your anger and express your feelings clearly. You can always choose not to mail the letter.

- To release your anger, use the Total Truth Process at the end of this chapter. Note: it is often advisable to have professional help from an experienced counselor when doing this.

- Be more aware of when you first start feeling resentful. Normally there is a buildup over time. The sooner you can identify this, the better. When you do, take action. Deal with the situation by speaking up, or doing what you need to do.

- Work on your self-esteem, so you can be more accepting and loving of yourself and others.

- Develop a good support network of friends who can give you honest feedback when you are holding on too long to negative feelings.

- Believe in yourself. Develop your strengths and be assertive. Do not allow others to belittle you.

- Maybe this is the most important: learn to let go and forgive. This is the higher road.

Life is an adventure in forgiveness.

—Norman Cousins

Learn to
FORGIVE

Those energy vampires—guilt, worry and resentment— can suck the energy from your day. Forgiveness is a powerful antidote that will totally re-energize you. Forgiving is an exercise in compassion; it requires you to make a decision. It's also a process. The conscious decision to forgive is followed by an act of will. In the process you will be able to convert your suffering into psychological and spiritual growth.

Forgiveness is an honorable process because it replaces wrongdoing with goodness. It creates benevolence through goodwill and generosity. In some situations—a brutal rape, for example—it's hard to imagine putting aside thoughts of anger or revenge and replacing them with the gifts of love and mercy. Yet some people do.

I used to think forgiveness meant erasing past wrongs and superimposing happier memories. It was difficult for me to forgive because I felt I was losing face and being diminished —that my wrongdoers still had the upper hand. By withholding forgiveness I believed they would suffer more. Then I realized that I was the one who was suffering.

When I finally understood the power of forgiveness, it was truly enlightening. I discovered that I'd have a lot more freedom and feel happier if I released my past burdens, including my own mistakes. Over the years, I have witnessed many incredible stories of forgiveness. I'm sure you have too. It's often beyond comprehension how some people embrace this higher road when such heinous acts were perpetrated against them or their loved ones. I believe a higher power is at work, demonstrating grace where it is most needed.

It was a typical busy morning.

Quickly downing tea and toast, Annette Stanwick's mind was already racing through projects at the office. Her role of vice-president of medical affairs at the prestigious eye clinic was demanding, yet stimulating. The ringing telephone jarred her train of thought. Picking it up she heard her youngest brother, Rick, his voice trembling: "Annette, Soren has been murdered!"

In that moment her life changed forever.

Her brother Soren, a long-distance trucker from Idaho, had been hauling a load of potatoes and reached the delivery terminal early. He decided to rest in the sleeper of his truck until the plant opened and was found dead that morning, two bullets buried in the side of his face and head.

"My heart felt like it was being ripped out of my body," recalled Annette, remembering the guttural sounds of her anguish echoing throughout the house. "Murder doesn't happen in my family! How could anyone intentionally take the life of my brother? I wanted the world to stop. Anger consumed me. Thoughts of the murderer bombarded my brain. The hours passed. I methodically packed a suitcase, getting ready for the long drive to Idaho for Soren's funeral. My husband and I spoke little; the miles passed slowly. When the words from the song, *God Is Watching Us from a Distance*, played on the radio I exploded and began screaming at God. "How could you watch from a distance and allow this to happen?"

Annette Stanwick is a woman of strong faith, but her beliefs were being tested to the absolute limits of her endurance. For more than a year there were no clues in the case—no suspects, no arrests. It wasn't easy. Grief counseling walked her through the pain. Sometimes Annette's imagination would play tricks. She would see the word *Murderer* written across the foreheads of men standing in line at the grocery store. Then, during a particularly sleepless night, she had the sensation that God was giving her a strong message, one she didn't want to hear.

"I love your brother's murderer as much as I love you and your brother!"

Annette fought this possibility all night, but finally God won the battle, and she fell asleep with a deep sense of peace.

The soul-searching continued. Annette belongs to a Christian motorcycle association. Out on the open road she found solace riding her powerful motorcycle. Before going on a ride she made a practice of choosing a word that would help heal her pain. One memorable day she chose the word acceptance. Earlier that day she had received more gruesome details about the murder, too sordid to stomach. In full flight she throttled through the pain, yelling at the top of her voice for understanding. After her emotion and anger had subsided, the message was even more challenging:

"Forgive them, for they know not what they do."

The last part of those words provided a breakthrough. She realized that the murderer didn't know her brother, or how much he was loved by his family, or how much he would be missed. He just wanted Soren's truck. Her brother stood in the way and was killed for it. Accepting the rest of those words—forgive them—was another matter. Impossible! Another agonizing wrestling match with God ensued. Finally, exhausted, Annette heard these words:

"Forgive, and you will be forgiven."

A few weeks later she received news that the police had found the murderer. Travis, the man who pulled the trigger, had confessed and would be sentenced to life in prison. Would she like to be at the sentencing and present a victim impact statement? Annette decided that she would.

The courtroom in Virginia was packed that day. Travis sat facing her, dressed in a bright-orange prison jumpsuit, his movement restricted by leg irons and chains. She saw a young man who looked sad, depressed, ashamed, afraid and alone. Slowly and methodically, Annette told him of the torment and suffering she and her family had experienced. She continued:

"In spite of the pain and sorrow of the last nineteen months, I have learned some important things. Travis, it is only by the Lord's unconditional love and forgiveness He has so graciously given to me, that I am now able to look at you through eyes that see beyond the hideous thing you have done. Here, in the quietness of this moment, I am offering you God's love and forgiveness. I am also offering you my love and my forgiveness."

When Annette left the courthouse that day, she felt as though a heavy burden had been lifted from her shoulders. The nineteen months of pain and turmoil had drained her physically and emotionally. Now at last she felt free!

It's said that everything in life happens for a reason, even though sometimes the circumstances are so painful that reasoning seems out of the question. Annette's life took another dramatic turn in the aftermath of her brother's murder. She was given the opportunity to tell her story to the inmates of a prison near her home. The impact was amazing, with many of the men reduced to tears. Annette is an inspirational and motivational speaker who now works with prison lifers, delivering a series of workshops. (e-mail: clay-ann@shaw.ca) God has packaged her abilities and pain, and turned them into a powerful ministry.

> *To forgive the unforgivable is the highest form*
> *of love. In return you will be blessed*
> *with peace and compassion.*
>
> —Fran Hewitt

HAVE YOU NOTICED THAT THE WORD forgiveness is grounded by the word give? By forgiving we give ourselves a gift. We choose to let go of the past, in the hope that by doing so we will make a better life in the future.

What Forgiveness Is Not

Four misconceptions surround forgiveness. These false impressions held me back for many years, and in my experience they stop many women from being able to forgive. These misconceptions are:

Denial/Forgetting

In some situations, time never fully heals bad memories. Forgiveness is not about ignoring pain or the wrong that was done to you. Your reality cannot be denied.

Excusing

Forgiveness isn't letting someone else off the hook. You are still holding him or her responsible for the wrongdoing, and rightly so.

Compensation

Forgiveness does not seek an apology. You are not asking for validation for your pain, or any other form of compensation. It is unconditional and personal. You may wait a lifetime for compensation and never receive it.

Condemnation

Blaming, adopting a one-upmanship position, or feeling morally superior has nothing to do with forgiveness. These attitudes are about you being right. They will keep you stuck.

You will remain a victim unless you avoid these four misconceptions. They keep you powerless. Don't allow the pain of the past to become a permanent crutch in your life. To remind yourself, memorize this statement: I am forgiving you because I've paid enough. Now I am ready to move on.

I was abused by a pedophile when I was eleven years old. Many years ago I chose to forgive him, and I know within me that I have. Today the thought of this man does not bring up anger or resentment, hatred or revenge. His image now makes a harmless transition through my thoughts, and I am at peace with the memory.

I do not deny what he did to me, nor do I make excuses to condone his sick behavior. I haven't condemned him to hell and I don't expect to ever get an apology. Instead, I have let go and chosen to heal. Now I'm realizing that I have been rewarded for this past adversity, because I can share it and empathize with so many others in my seminars. This is invaluable as I reach out to touch others where they hurt.

How To Forgive Yourself

Everyone is human. We all make mistakes that need to be forgiven. By forgiving yourself, you are choosing love over judgment. That's a good choice. You are also sending notice that moving on with your life is more important than remaining in the emotional prison of self-condemnation.

There is nothing you have done that cannot be forgiven, no matter how bad you think it is. Offer yourself the olive branch of compassion and choose to love yourself instead.

As a child in Ireland, I grew up believing I was going to be a saint, or at least a nun. In my mind I pictured myself heading off to the convent to join the Medical Missionaries of Mary. Of course I never came close to being holy enough. I would beat myself up unmercifully for every little infraction that took me further from my goal. It was a great relief when the convent burned down, because it meant I didn't need to be so good anymore.

We are so hard on ourselves, and we sometimes set such high moral standards, that it's no wonder we suffer. Here's a five-step process to avoid this trap.

Steps To Forgiving Yourself

Step 1: Accept What You Did
Take full responsibility for your action or inaction. Confront the situation head on, no excuses or denial. I suggest you journal your thoughts. This will bring clarity, and help purge the memory. Allow yourself to be emotional. Release any pain you have; shed some tears if you need to.

Step 2: Confession
Confession is one of the oldest and best methods for unloading heavy burdens. It works. Confess to God, or someone else, what you did. Nothing you have done, no shame deep enough, can separate you from God. Talk to Him, let Him know your remorse and regret. Reconcile your relationship with God if you need to. Telling someone else is a bonus. We share our humanness by showing each other that we make mistakes. Letting go of the pain with someone you trust will prevent you from making excuses or living in denial.

Step 3: Give Up Self-Flagellation
There is no value in continuing to punish yourself, even though you feel you deserve to be condemned. Remaining a victim will negatively affect the relationship you have with yourself and with others.

Step 4: Make Amends If Appropriate
A sincere apology or a verbal olive branch may be all that is required. Perhaps you need to return something or pay back money that you owe. A word of caution—for every choice there is a consequence. Sometimes you can create more damage by the way you make amends. Be discerning. It's imperative that you proceed with the right intentions, having no expectations about the outcome.

Step 5: What Did You Learn?
Mistakes have a habit of reoccurring unless your eyes are wide open. I believe all of life's experiences are designed to teach you something. If you have blinders on you will miss the lesson and its significance to your life.

I find it easier to forgive others than to forgive myself. Some of this I'm sure stems from my perfectionism, from being too hard on myself. As I get older, I am focusing more on self-acceptance. As a result, I've noticed that having compassion for myself is becoming easier.

Learn to forgive yourself. Travel through life lightly, unburdened by guilt. It's one of the best gifts you can give yourself, and those you love.

How To Forgive Others

Perpetrators have power over you for as long as you are unable, or unwilling, to forgive. They occupy space in your mind, and play with your emotions.

Forgiving wrongs done to you gives you an opportunity to grow and heal. But forgiveness is not simple, it's a complex process. For some people, professional help is required. Others can do it on their own. Below is a series of steps to help you forgive others. Implementing these ideas may be all you need.

Steps To Forgiving Others

Step 1: Make The Decision
It is essential that you first make the decision that you want to forgive the one who injured you. This is a courageous, heroic choice.

Step 2: Take Responsibility
Realize that it is your responsibility to heal yourself. Nobody else can do it for you. Unforgiveness saps your energy and may even make you ill. Studies have shown that heart attacks and cancer can be linked to the retention of anger and resentment.

Step 3: Confront Your Pain
Journal about your pain and who you want to forgive. Confront and recognize your hurt. Allow someone else to validate your pain; a good friend, partner, pastor or therapist. When you receive empathy and compassion, you can heal faster.

Step 4: Take A New Perspective
Be willing to find a new perspective about the person who wronged you. This is not condoning the behavior or making excuses for the person. The fact is that people hurt other people because they have been hurt themselves. They act out of their own pain. Ask yourself:

- What was their life like growing up?
- What was their life like at the time of the offense?

These two questions helped me understand my father's angry behavior, where he was coming from and why he acted as he did. I was able to forgive him by separating him from his behavior.

Step 5: Acknowledge Your Part
Acknowledge the part that you played in the wrongdoing, if any. This will help move you from being a victim to taking some responsibility. Forgive yourself for this part. (In some situations, in a brutal rape for example, you would be completely innocent and in no way responsible.)

Step 6: Learn From The Pain
Seek to learn from your pain in order to stop any reoccurrence in the future. Did you gain anything in your life as a result of this pain?

Step 7: The Total Truth Letter
When you are ready, use the Total Truth template and write a letter to the offender. There's no need to mail it. Express your thoughts clearly and honestly, starting with your anger. Write about how the offender hurt you. Get mad. Allow yourself to fully express your feelings. Anger is the place to start. Then follow the steps through hurt, fear, regret and wants to forgiveness. This is where you will find emotional completion.

Step 8: Closure
You can use the letter symbolically to bring closure to the forgiveness cycle. Some women like to bury it or burn it, others like to tear it into pieces and let the wind take it. Create a ceremony that is meaningful to you. Close your eyes and see the link between you and the offender being severed. You are now freed from this memory. Visualize the person you are forgiving being surrounded by the love of forgiveness.

Step 9: Release Expectations

Let go of any expectations you have for the offender. Forgiveness may not lead to reconciliation. That may be desirable but it is not a requirement. Forgiveness does not depend upon repentance by the offender. In reconciliation, both the victim and the injurer need to be mutually committed, and this may not happen. You may not choose to share the fact that you have forgiven him or her, let alone express this in a face-to-face setting. If you do choose to share your forgiveness, check your intentions, making sure they come from love, not pain.

Step 10: Practice Forgiving

Think of forgiveness not so much as an act, but as a lifestyle. Make a practice of forgiving. As soon as you realize you are injured, forgive. You will feel freer and healthier. Conserve your energy for living rather than wasting it on resentment and pain. When you can see the hurt child in others, it enables you to forgive faster.

Step 11: Give Thanks

Last, but certainly not least, you can ask God to help you forgive. He is the great healer and forgiver, and is deeply concerned about your well being.

Four Reasons To Forgive:

- To heal your body—eliminate your toxic
  thoughts and anger.

- To heal your heart—let go of thoughts of revenge, or
  feelings of ill-will, and begin to love unconditionally.

- To heal your relationships—explore the potential
  for reconciliation or re-connection.

- To heal your life—pain should not define you.

Do what you need to do to make all of this happen for you; this is your opportunity to grow and heal.

The Total Truth Letter

To help you move through anger caused by a childhood event or a more recent one, start by reflecting on the person who is making you angry. Then write a letter to that person.

This letter has specific stages. Each stage will assist you in moving from anger through to forgiveness and love. This is emotional completion. Find a private space in which to do this, and experience all of the feelings. Get emotionally involved. This is an important step, to help you release those negative feelings. When writing this letter follow each step of the Total Truth process at the end of this chapter. Give each portion of the process equal attention. If the person you are angry at is dead or unlikely to cooperate, you may simply choose to throw the letter away. If that person is willing to participate, have him or her write a letter too. You can exchange letters or read each other's letter aloud, with feeling and intensity. This lets each of you know you have been heard and understood. It also facilitates healing the relationship.

A word of caution—if you are writing the letter to get back at the other person, your intentions are not pure. You are acting from revenge. It's about you being right. Remember—there are consequences to every action, so let go of any expectations.

Letter to a Parent

Anger: I am feeling so angry with you! I hate it that you drink so much and tell other people how to run their lives. You don't even try to straighten out your own. I am so pissed off with your pretense of having it all together, when you obviously don't.

Hurt: I hurt that you don't care more about yourself. All you seem to care about is that bottle. I'm hurt that maybe you don't care about me and Robert, now that Ted is gone. I'm hurt that you're so drunk; you don't appreciate the things I do.

Fear:	I'm afraid that you might die if you don't quit drinking. I'm afraid you might lose your job. I'm afraid you'll stop loving me because you're hurting so much. I'm afraid you're not going to be there when I really need you because you're too drunk.
Regret:	I regret that I do not understand. I regret that I don't help you more and try to comfort you when you're depressed. I am sorry I don't see the love in your actions.
Wants:	I want you to be happy. I want you to feel good about yourself. I want you to know I am here if you need me. All I ever wanted was a good family. I want you to get help and stop drinking.
Forgiveness:	I love you very much. I care about what happens to you. I forgive you because you have been through so much and I appreciate when you are there for me. I care what you do with your life. You are appreciated more than you know.

Source: Facilitating Skills Seminar – Jack Canfield

It took me many attempts to write a letter to my sexual offender. I finally accomplished it when I was thirty-four, more than twenty years after the experience. My tears washed away my words and my anger. On paper, I uncovered layers and layers of pain, letting go of my hate. I knew I had forgiven this man when I saw him a few years later and realized that I held no ill will against him.

Forgiveness is different with my father. Over eighty now, he still knows how to inflict pain. I want to forgive him for my own well-being, and also to rebuild our relationship in the little time he has left. Forgiving is sometimes a daily process.

A Man's Perspective
Les Hewitt

When was the last time your husband, boyfriend or a male supervisor asked you to have a serious face-to-face discussion about perfectionism, guilt, worry, or resentment? In my experience, working with many male clients, the answer would most likely be never.

These are subjects men avoid, because we might end up feeling uncomfortable, and we don't like anything that stirs up our emotions. Begging for forgiveness is usually not high on the macho man's agenda—unless it is a last resort as his long-suffering wife marches out of the house with her suitcases and the kids in tow.

In the business world these topics are often referred to as soft subjects, as if they have nothing to do with the bottom line. They are thought to be best reserved for the analyst's couch. But as a woman, how do you get a man's attention if one or more of these issues is affecting you?

First pick the right moment, when he's more likely to be receptive. To start, use an attention-getter. For example, if Alice wanted to talk to her husband John, she could say: "John, if there was something really bothering me that could affect my health, would you give me your undivided attention?"

If all goes well, he will say yes. Assuming he does, follow up with this: "Well, there is something I'm concerned about. I just want you to listen, without interrupting or asking me any questions until I'm finished, okay?" That would certainly get my attention. Then make the most of the opportunity. Setting the stage for good discussion is often what men and women don't do. The next time you feel overburdened and need to unload, test this technique. I think you'll be pleasantly surprised.

CONCLUSION

Life presents enough challenges without us adding more burdens to our load. We can flip the switch on guilt, worry and resentment once we become aware of them. To prevent those downward spirals, make the choice to eliminate the energy vampires. Your life will become lighter and more positive.

If you struggle with perfectionism, challenge it every day by being less than perfect. Uncover any unfulfilled need from childhood that drives it, and fill that need using the awareness you have as an adult today.

The path of forgiveness is the best way to travel unburdened. Often it is the only way to unchain yourself from the past. Give yourself the gift of forgiveness so you can be free to live the life you really want.

ACTION STEPS

Handling Guilt

The Total Truth Process

Pick the best time to implement these strategies, then focus and follow through.

1. Think of some action you have taken, or failed to take, about which you feel guilty.

_____

_____

_____

_____

2. What is your belief, or *should*, about this action?

_____

_____

_____

3. What is unrealistic about that belief or *should?* (if it fits, use "except when...")

_____

_____

_____

4. How can you get rid of the guilt? (usually by changing the belief or taking action)

_____

_____

_____

5. What do you truly feel sorry for?

_____

_____

_____

6. Is there any corrective action you would like to take? If yes, what will you do and by what date?

_____

_____

_____

_____

_____

_____

The Total Truth Process

Use the stem sentences below to help you get in touch with your anger, hurt, fear, remorse and wants. The goal is to end with forgiveness, but do not be alarmed if you are unable to forgive. You may need to go through this process many times. Know that each time you are helping yourself and your relationship.

NOTE: This exercise may trigger painful emotions. The assistance of an experienced professional counselor is advised for people who have deep issues to resolve, or for anyone who is in therapy.

Choose a quiet place where you will not be disturbed. Take your time. Go through each step in sequence as outlined.

1. ANGER

I'm angry that...
I hate it when...
I don't like it when...
I'm fed up with...
I resent...
I can't stand...

2. HURT

It hurt me when...
I feel hurt that...
I feel sad when...
I feel awful about...
I feel disappointed about...

3. FEAR

I am afraid that...
I feel scared when...
I am afraid of you when...

4. REMORSE, REGRET, ACCOUNTABILITY

I'm sorry that...
Please forgive me for...
I'm sorry for...
I didn't mean to...

5. WANTS

All I ever want(ed)...
I want you to...
I want(ed)...
I deserve...

6. LOVE, COMPASSION, FORGIVENESS AND APPRECIATION

I understand that...
I appreciate...
I love you because...

I forgive you for...
I forgive myself for...

Thank you for...
I love you when...

Source: Facilitating Skills Seminar – Jack Canfield

The Deceptive Triangle:

Image, Health and Money

Measure success with a single word—love.

—Sir John Templeton

Have you ever been tricked? Most of us have been oversold, duped and deceived more than once. Maybe you suffered a mild April Fool's prank (my kids loved to rig the hose in our kitchen sink, giving me a cold shower when I turned on the tap) or perhaps you paid too much for something thanks to an overzealous salesperson.

Do you remember the story about Helen of Troy? She was captured by the Greeks and held captive in the city of Aphidna. The Trojans dreamed up the idea of building a huge wooden horse to rescue her. They parked it outside the city gates and than sailed off. The Greeks gleefully brought this curious 'gift' inside the city walls. Of course they didn't realize that some of the Trojans were hiding inside the horse. During the night the soldiers crept out of the horse and opened the gates for the awaiting army, who conquered all and rescued a grateful

Helen. The Trojan Horse was one of the greatest tricks ever played, and it worked brilliantly. There are other situations in life that also involve trickery and if you're not wise to them they may conquer and destroy you too. Image, health and money are three that will require your full attention. You need to educate and arm yourself to avoid being deceived.

At first glance it seems that a good image, vibrant health and financial strength are positive attributes to vigorously pursue. Absolutely! But like most things in life this intriguing triangle has a negative side. The truth is that we are being sold a bill of goods when it comes to image, health and money.

We are becoming paranoid about image. Largely through the media, today's society says we must look a certain way to be deemed successful. Our figures, skin, weight, clothes, hair —even our eyebrows, fingernails and feet—are scrutinized.

As far as health is concerned, the news is equally bad. We are saturated with conflicting information. With so many books on nutrition and health, diets, weight loss programs and supplements, who do we believe? Where do we start? It's totally confusing, like being in the middle of a maze from which we can't escape.

The money game is another big con job. We have been duped into thinking we must have everything now, and as a result we have become a nation of reckless spenders. Buy now, pay later— even years later! Interest rates? Don't worry about 21 percent, we can handle it. Our kids head off to college and are immediately bombarded by credit card companies who offer free gifts and tantalizing incentives. Many of our young people are thousands of dollars in debt within a few months, facing years of worry and guilt. Let's get back to common sense.

That's what this chapter is about. We'll tackle the deceptive triangle from all sides. You'll gain heightened awareness and compelling reasons to make the best possible choices in your life. You'll learn how to enjoy the many benefits of having image, health and money on your side.

We'll also talk about the importance of successful habits, and how to create them. Good habits are like a protective coating that you apply every day, to ensure positive results.

Accept Your Body
IMAGE

Grin and Bare It—Get Naked

You're thinking, "Has Fran lost her mind? Getting naked is the last thing I want to do!" When it comes to body image, millions of women have lost their minds.

The majority of women don't like their bodies, and the problem seems to be getting worse. Feelings of inadequacy are fueling a huge industry that is joyfully reaping the benefits. Looking good and feeling good are definite money-makers.

Many of us blame the mirror for the image we see. Maybe we have a little hail damage on our thighs, our bikini days are over, and perhaps our buttocks are headed south along with our breasts. So what? Don't get stressed out about it. What is this obsession with image? Of course we want to look our best and stay youthful, firm and healthy as long as we can. But why are so many of us so self-critical, seeing only our defects and misplaced curves? One of the main culprits is the media—magazines, movies, television and advertising. We are totally bombarded.

- Look ten years younger in five minutes.
- Have the body you want in two short weeks.
- Finally a diet that works—eat cabbage.
- Remove those wrinkles forever.

Just take a look at the magazine covers on the newstand. Models portraying the definition of beauty are all tall, skinny, gorgeous twenty-somethings with bodies like goddesses and sparkling white teeth. Little wonder women feel down about themselves. The media don't provide many role models to restore our drooping self-image.

Advertising constantly infers that our worth is directly related to how good we look. Many women are driven to close the gap between reality and what the media portrays. This has caused explosive growth in the lucrative cosmetics, botox, plastic surgery, weight loss and pharmaceutical markets, creating multi-billion-dollar profits. It seems that the more insecure women feel about their image, the more they will spend to fix it.

As Loretta La Roche says in her book, *Life Is Not a Stress Rehearsal*, "The tombstone no-one wants is: Here lies Jane Doe. Four days a week she worked out to an exercise routine she hated, and she only ate foods she believed were good for her but didn't really enjoy. Here she is anyway."

Sadly, anxiety and feelings of dissatisfaction about body image cause some women to take drastic measures. Fad diets, diuretics and other quick-fix weight-loss gimmicks are now commonplace. To achieve the right look, some people resort to binging and purging, excessive exercise programs or starvation diets. It's getting to be so bad that we feel guilty when we eat an occasional chocolate bar or have a brownie with our Starbucks.

We are driving ourselves to distraction! This constant need to live up to an unrealistic image is taking a heavy toll on our emotional and physical well-being. And what about our sex lives? "What if he sees my stretch marks, or notices my cellulite?" These hang-ups are extremely distracting—instead of enjoying intimate relationships we are preoccupied with covering up or dimming the lights. It's absurd, yet tragically true. How can we get comfortable with our bodies again, accepting ourselves just the way we are?

The answer has to do with self-acceptance. That means liking ourselves, no matter what shape or size we are. Don't be deceived—turn off the dull roar of the media blitz. See it for what it is. Corporations profit from our low body image, marketing products that may not be helpful or healthy.

Other cultures do not suffer the same pressures we do.

Simone, originally from Florida, moved to the French region of Provence as a woman of twenty-five. She has lived there now for twenty years. "Right away I noticed how different the women were. They have confidence, and they show it in how they present themselves, in how they dress and how they walk. It doesn't matter if they are pretty or even what weight or shape they are, they look comfortable. It's an attitude. They are sexy and attractive based not so much on how they look on the outside, but how they feel on the inside."

When you focus on your own ideal of a healthy body image, you will have a much better chance of reaching your goals. This means understanding what styles look good on you, knowing how to enhance your best features, working to reach a healthy weight for your body, and eating whole healthy foods.

Be an independent thinker, it just might save your life. Going back to basics is what it's all about. Cultivate a healthy appreciation for your looks and the body you have, and take the best care of it. Don't throw out the mirror yet.

Nurture Your Body
HEALTH

I'll make this simple and practical. Assuming you are like most women, you probably want to improve something about your body. The following strategies for improving your lifestyle are used by thousands of supremely healthy women. No matter what physical condition you are in, these ideas will make you feel better and look better. This is a lifestyle plan—not a diet. It will enhance your body image and give you more energy to live the life you really want. Everyone knows that eating nutritiously and exercising regularly is preventative maintenance, so let's start by looking at the obstacles holding us back.

What prevents us from making changes to our diet and fitness plan when we know those changes would help us live better and longer? Three primary reasons for this procrastination are:

1. Busyness—anything that saves time and effort.
   We eat fast food on the run instead of nutritious,
   home-cooked meals that take longer to prepare.
   We don't make exercise a priority, so we can never
   find time for it. We prefer driving to walking and we
   take the elevator rather than using the stairs.

2. Denial—we blindly forge on, avoiding the
   obvious, knowing that we are out of shape
   and headed for health problems. Don't even

mention going for a routine checkup or mammogram—we haven't got time and we don't want to know if anything is wrong, even though statistics show that one out of eight women will be diagnosed with breast cancer.

3. Ruts—we're stuck in old habits. When we haven't exercised in ten years, it takes a much greater effort to start. Complacency is subtle. It gradually sneaks up, and before we know it we have succumbed to its deceptive charms.

Are you stuck in unhealthy routines? Before the end of this chapter you'll learn how to dump those bad habits for good. Making better lifestyle choices is all about motivation. In Chapter One we looked at desperation and inspiration, the two major motivators. You're more likely to be motivated when the doctor says, "Change or die."

At her heaviest, Jackie Winter weighed 240 pounds. The fact that she was five foot three didn't help. A hair-dresser, she was on her feet most of the day. This was putting extra pressure on her knees and was not only painful, it was threatening her livelihood. Being single and the sole provider of income, Jackie had battled her weight problem since puberty and had attended numerous dieting programs, some of them extreme. On several occasions she had lost more than fifty pounds, but she could never sustain the loss for more than a year.

Her new doctor advised her to exercise regularly. Jackie had heard this a thousand times before, but this time the doctor added, "I don't want to be treating you for diabetes the next time I see you." This was a serious, unexpected consequence. The thought of losing control, of being under doctor's orders for the rest of her life, shifted Jackie's thinking. It was a critical moment.

In the next ten months, due to the help of an excellent fitness and nutritional coach, she lost sixty-five pounds and had no trouble keeping it off. Her energy and confidence received a much needed boost. She is looking forward to eventually reaching an ideal weight of 135 pounds. Jackie is in no rush and has developed a realistic plan that suits her pace of life. She says: "My coach Laura, has the perfect blend of enthusiasm and intelligence. I trust her implicitly. This ability to trust is another shift for me. I used to believe if people thought I was unattractive then I wasn't acceptable. Also, when I was a lot younger I attracted the wrong type of sexual attention. I viewed men as predatory and untrustworthy. Now at fifty-eight, men don't regard me as a piece of meat anymore. I'm more like furniture—however, I'd like to be nice furniture!

I now realize that freedom comes from daily discipline. Making better choices has changed my life and allowed me to be comfortable with who I am."

I had the good fortune to meet Jackie's coach, Laura Simonson. Laura had her own challenges. As a top caliber athlete, and an award-winning body builder, health issues were far from her mind. She started a new career in real estate, and for seven years she drove herself hard to succeed in this highly competitive industry. The long hours and stress eventually took their toll. Her health suffered and for almost six years she was ill with chronic fatigue and hypoglycemia. To get out of this downward spiral, Laura learned everything she could about natural health, fitness and self-empowerment. She left her real estate career to pursue a lifelong dream. Years of research and hands-on experience resulted in her own revolutionary lifestyle program called "Live It!" She now coaches people in several countries who are transforming their eating and fitness habits with exceptional results. I asked Laura to share her wisdom with us in this chapter. The nutritional science of Laura's program is in alignment with the 2003 recommended food pyramid issued by the Harvard School of Public Health.[*]

Make The 1 Percent Shift

The diet and fitness industries spew out mass amounts of misinformation about miracle menus and fast fitness programs. These messages cause us to question the simplest topics. What is healthy to eat? What kind of physical activity is best to shed weight? We are being led down a garden path by health and fitness advisors linked to pharmaceutical and equipment corporations. What happened to good old common sense?

We have been taught that we can change our bodies in ten days, but this type of quick fix is a carefully planned marketing myth. Changing your lifestyle is not a race. Can you make a 1 percent change in your diet or fitness—per day, per week, per month? Just a 1 percent shift? I know this is something I can handle, and I'm sure you can, too. Everything vital and permanent in life is worthy of patience.

I feel healthy. I could lose ten pounds to be my ideal weight, but I'm not fretting about it. However, I am in the dangerous waters of complacency. Before I met Laura, I hadn't thought much about my future well-being. I did not have my eye focused on prevention, nor did I think much about aging. I was just going along hoping I would be happy and healthy in my later years. Laura has wakened me up to the fact that the time to start taking action is now. That means taking responsibility and getting serious about how I treat this body of mine. What lifestyle changes can I make today to increase the probability of a healthy future?

Simply put, good health is about the food we eat. Fitness is essentially about breathing. The third factor is water. Food, Fitness and Water—how simple is that? Let's get back to basics.

---

*http://www.hsph.harvard.edu/nutritionsource/pyramids.html

Take Charge of Your
DIET AND FOOD

The Carbohydrate Connection

What comes to mind when you think of a carbohydrate? Do you see white bread, fresh from the oven? A big bowl of Mama's pasta? Mashed potatoes? Or do you see a field of greens and baskets of fresh-picked fruit? Here's an assumption: you saw something white. From kindergarten to high school we are taught to follow our government food guides. For some reason, passed on from food guide to food guide, fruits and vegetables are not referred to as carbohydrates. We have been carbohydrate-conditioned to believe that a carb is white.

Another myth is that all carbohydrates are evil. We may have developed habits using comfort foods to make us feel better, but carbohydrates are not bad. Some, such as white bread, white rice and white sugar, do have some evil tendencies, but only when we include them three times a day. I am getting wiser about avoiding white carbohydrates. I still buy the occasional French loaf, but mostly I stick to whole grains and brown.White bread can be difficult on the old bowel. It puts mine to sleep.

Carbohydrates today are defined as high-glycemic and low-glycemic (glycemic refers to sugar content). Naturally present in abundance around the world, carbohydrates are the main source of fuel for energizing our bodies. Carbohydrates keep our engines running. They also provide us with vitamins, minerals, antioxidants, enzymes, fiber and phyto-nutrients necessary to general health. Natural carbohydrates are the key to health, weight management and disease prevention.

Laura recommends choosing carbohydrates on the low-to-medium glycemic scale. These include natural foods such as apples, berries, slow-cooked oatmeal, legumes (beans, peas,

219

lentils), whole grains, most vegetables, and nuts or seeds (which are also protein sources). These will sustain your energy, whereas high-glycemic carbohydrates will give you a quick boost but leave you crashing later. Low-glycemic carbohydrates will benefit you by balancing your blood sugars and insulin levels. They will also prevent fat storage. This is great news for women wanting to shed weight.

Eat food that remembers where it came from!

—Unknown

My son had a problem with feeling sleepy during the day. A healthy twenty-one-year-old, he would often nap in the afternoons, even after a good night's rest. Laura told him to watch his carbohydrates. She rightly suspected he was hypoglycemic (low blood sugar). He soon discovered that by eating the right carbohydrates and increasing his water intake he felt much better, with lots more energy. I think there are many women with this condition. They brush it off as too much stress or being overburdened. Eat the right carbohydrates and feel the difference. If you feel listless or sleepy shortly after eating a meal, check what you ate.

Ratios and Amounts
My mother equated food with love. She would heap our plates with love, saying, "Children in Africa are starving, so eat up." Therefore I felt guilty having food to eat and guilty if I didn't clean my plate.

Take a look back and see if you have retained any messages around food and eating. Often these beliefs block us from changing our food patterns.

Cut back on the amount of food you eat. When eating out don't finish everything on your plate, no matter what Mom said. Portion sizes in many restaurants today are so huge that even Arnold Schwarzenegger needs a doggy bag. Have you noticed how the term super-sizing has crept into our vocabulary? We're being constantly up-sold—encouraged to buy combos of this, that and the other. We eat too much and it isn't healthy. We have become a society of overeaters.

I have difficulty cutting down on my serving portions. My husband has complained a few times that I give him too much food. He's right. I love food, the flavors and textures. I enjoy cooking. Now I'm usually only cooking for the two of us, but I often forget. Old habits die hard.

Laura teaches that a ratio of 50 percent carbohydrates, 30 percent protein and 20 percent fat is best. A healthy balance includes low-glycemic carbohydrates such as salad greens or vegetables, lean protein such as fish, poultry, eggs or legumes, and essential fats such as sesame, olive or flax oils, perhaps served in a dressing or sauce. Brown rice or whole wheat pasta is better than white rice or white pasta. This is a healthy, balanced meal.

Healthy snacks should also be balanced. When eating an apple, have some almonds too. Have low-fat yogurt and fresh fruit together, or fresh vegetables with low-fat dip, or perhaps a small protein energy bar. I grew up Irish, a meat-and-potato girl. In Ireland the potato is sacred. Without potatoes, it's not a complete meal. But now I realize that potatoes can be high-glycemic, especially if baked. What a choice! Do I neglect my very roots? For me, the answer is moderation.

Another confession: my mother insisted on serving porridge. She knew it was good for us. What she didn't know was that I wouldn't eat it. I'd get up early to prepare the porridge pot, dirty a bowl pretending I had eaten mine, and have toast instead. Porridge is one food I still refuse to eat. Sorry Mom.

The pH Perspective

All foods have alkaline, acid or neutral properties. Vegetables and fruits have an alkaline effect on you. Lemons, oranges and tomatoes are acidic, but they are alkaline-forming in your body. Conversely, steaks are alkaline but acid-forming inside you.

Both alkaline and acid foods are necessary, but making approximately 80 percent of your diet alkaline will help prevent illness. When the amount of acid residue is too great, an imbalance occurs and your immune system becomes compromised. This imbalance causes metabolic acidosis or ketosis, which occurs in high-protein diets. Acidosis increases your risk of cardiovascular damage, weight gain, diabetes, premature aging, certain cancers, osteoporosis, allergies, asthma, arthritis, lactic acid buildup (gout), poor nutrient absorption and more.

When I heard that cancer cells cannot survive in an alkaline environment, I was convinced. During my battle with breast cancer I decided to only eat small amounts of protein, mostly fish. I did this for over a year. After that I added chicken. Today I am back to eating everything, but slowly weaning myself from acid-forming foods like red meat. It's a slow process. You would think that after my health scare I would be more motivated. I guess it shows that for change to be permanent, it has to be done slowly.

Examples of acid-forming foods include beef, pork, chicken, most dairy products (milk), fried foods, coffee, sugar, artificial sweeteners, alcohol, antibiotics, pesticides, preservatives, shellfish and peanuts. In the acid-neutral category we find whole grains, legumes, soy, almonds, seeds, yogurt, fish, turkey, eggs and goat cheese. These are preferable over the acid-forming foods in the previous list.

Examples of alkaline-forming foods include most vegetables, such as broccoli, green leafy vegetables, cabbage, carrrots, sweet potatoes, yams, cucumbers, bell peppers, squash, tomatoes and most fruits such as apples, oranges, lemons, bananas, cantaloupe, strawberries, blueberries and natural organic dried fruits.

Don't panic if many of the items on the first list are in your diet. Remember that you are making a lifestyle change. It's not a race. Start eliminating acid-forming foods, 1 percent at a time. It could save your life. Essential fats necessary for energy, disease prevention and weight management are found in salmon and flax, olive, walnut, sesame, almond, grapeseed and canola oils.

Fiber Fitness—Add Fiber To Your Diet

I know, I know, you've heard this before. However, eating foods that are full of fiber will help you shed weight quicker, reduce food cravings, balance your mood swings and increase your energy while significantly reducing the risk of diabetes. Would you rather fill up on a high-cholesterol breakfast or have a healthy bran muffin? The importance of dietary fiber in the prevention of disease cannot be overstated. As part of the body's waste removal system, fiber helps transport everything from digested foods to unwanted hormones. I used to think bran was one of the only ways to get fiber. This is not true. Eating vegetables and fruit will do the trick.

Some people take oat bran in everything.
They become so stopped up with fiber they don't go
to the toilet for a month. When they finally do,
they pass a wicker chair.

—Loretta LaRoche

Fiber can be divided into two categories—insoluble (bran type) and soluble (broccoli and apples type). Each type functions differently and provides different health benefits. A balance of both is best. A high-fiber diet is not only great for disease prevention, it also helps absorb food and slows the entry of sugar into the blood, thus stabilizing insulin. It enables your body to better use the food for fuel, rather than for storage as body fat. As a bonus, it fills you up.

Fiber is found only in plant foods, including fruits, vegetables, beans, whole grains, nuts and seeds. Unfortunately, many of us find that getting enough fiber in our diet is difficult. In fact, most people consume only half of the recommended twenty-five grams per day. But if you eat mostly natural foods you will probably get the right amount of fiber. Eating right is one of the keys to good health. For more information on nutrition see the Resource Guide at the back of this book.

Understanding Cholesterol

Knowing your total cholesterol is a good thing. But knowing your LDL and HDL levels is even better.

LDL (low-density lipoprotein) is considered the bad cholesterol. I find it easier remembering the L stands for lousy. Bad cholesterol clogs our arteries.

HDL (high-density lipoprotein) is known as good cholesterol. Remember H stands for healthy. This lipoprotein keeps our arteries clear.

| LDL = Lousy | Normal Range | 2.20-3.40 |
| HDL = Healthy | Greater than | 0.090 |

Body Mass Index

This is calculated by dividing your weight in kilograms by your height in meters. Body Mass Index is one of the most accurate ways to determine if those extra pounds mean a potential health risk.

20-25	Healthy Zone
25-30	Increased Risk Zone *(you need to lose some weight)*
30 +	High Risk Zone

Source: Personal Health Planning Institute

Keeping An Eye On Your Health

I met a woman who claimed she hadn't been to the doctor for at least ten years. She said fear kept her away. She didn't want to know if anything was wrong with her and preferred to live in denial. This is a very dangerous game, especially when we can prevent so many progressive diseases if we diagnose them early enough. It is every woman's responsibility to be smart about her own health. A monthly breast self-examination is a must. If I had been more diligent with this perhaps I would have discovered my cancer earlier. Skin cancer is another concern. Do a skin self-examination periodically and have anything suspicious checked.

Surprisingly, not everyone goes for a yearly medical and physical check-up. For prevention this is essential. Make sure you include a yearly mammogram.

The recommended age to start is forty, although I personally think thirty-five is better. A pap smear and pelvic exam, complete blood work, urinalysis and cholesterol screening should all be included. If you are older than fifty, I would suggest having a rectal exam and stool blood test annually, and a home density screen to check for osteoporosis. Good health is all about being proactive and taking responsibility. There are two more major topics we need to talk about—fitness and water.

Enjoy Physical
FITNESS

When you think of exercise do you picture a beautiful, lean blonde doing a workout on the fitness channel? Or do you see yourself on one of those machines at the gym, panting and sweating heavily? Cardiovascular activity is a crucial aspect of getting fit, but many women don't know much about it. Here are some fast facts:

- As a woman, your metabolic rate naturally decreases after the age of thirty. Hormonal and lifestyle changes are the usual culprits. But if you build lean muscle, you will naturally increase your metabolic rate, no matter what your age.

- If cardio is your only activity and you are not eating sufficient calories, you may be cannibalizing your own muscle, which decreases your metabolic rate and sets you up for instant weight gain if the cardio is stopped.

- One half-hour session with weights can easily consume more calories than a moderate period of cycling, brisk walking or jogging. Your body will burn calories faster for up to two hours after a strength-training session.

- At rest, each pound of active muscle tissue burns thirty-five calories a day, while a pound of dead fat burns only two calories per day.

- You won't look like a bodybuilder. Women don't have the testosterone that builds big, bulky muscles. Your chances are about as good as growing a mustache.

- A combination of weight training, cardiovascular activity and stretching is best for proper fitness. Doing only one activity is not as beneficial as a diverse, effective and fun combination.

- Muscle is the engine that burns fat. It increases your metabolic rate and it builds and maintains strong bones. It can also improve your posture. If you want to shed weight or maintain your ideal weight, replace your old beliefs with this fact—muscle is the engine that burns fat.

For many years I went faithfully to aerobics class. If I could just huff and puff enough, I thought, I would keep the weight off. Typically I did thirty-five to forty minutes of cardio followed by five minutes of abdominals and stretching.

If I had known then what I know now, I would have spent more time flexing my triceps and biceps, and stretching for longer periods. My cardiovascular workout is still a major part of my training schedule, but now I include weights. This is a great way to burn unwanted calories, reduce stress and keep my body stronger.

> *Two little girls were standing near a large*
> *weight scale. One says to the other,*
> *"Don't step on that, it will make you cry!"*

—Anonymous

Les has been a jogger most of his life. Even in freezing cold weather he's out there doing his run. Lately he has started lifting weights. He says he's doing it to look good for me. Now we have a competition going to see who is more buff!

There are many ways to get fit. The great thing about building muscle is that it doesn't require a lot of time. You may find that ten minutes in the morning is all you need.

Weight Training

Training with weights will create resistance in the muscles you are working. This resistance builds more muscle. Although there are many ways to cause resistance, I recommend that you keep it simple by doing weights at home or by using dumbbells, barbells, fit balls and weight machines in a fitness facility, where they will be able to set you up with a customized program. Be sure to select the right program to best suit your lifestyle.

Building healthy abdominal muscles will help keep your back strong. There are many great exercises to strengthen your core muscles too. With all of the fun equipment you can purchase for home use, there's no excuse. You do not need to buy expensive equipment—handheld weights, rubber tubing and a fit ball will do the job just as well.

I often use a fit ball instead of a chair while I'm on the computer. I bounce up and down on it on occasion to energize my body. It's fun, and it keeps my muscles active.

Depending on your fitness level, I strongly recommend that during your first week you use light weights to minimize muscle stiffness and unnecessary pain. The last thing you want to do is set yourself up for failure.

There are many great resources for weight training, especially if you can get to a gym where a professional trainer can build a program for you. If you just want to do something simple from home, check out the library or the internet for books on weight training. Most important, make it fun! Remember that you are building lean muscle that will keep you healthy, lean and strong for life.

Sally's new health plan has inspired her to change her lifestyle, but she finds that it is an ongoing job. "I started by doing weight training and walking for forty-five minutes on a rotation for the week. I have worked up to doing weights occasionally and running four miles daily. My morning starts off at 5:30 a.m. with time for myself. This plan also inspired me to do something I didn't think I could do because I was in a bad accident seventeen years ago that had left me with a head injury. I was also paralyzed on my left side. Through hard work and determination I have recovered well from this because of my new healthy eating habits. I felt so energetic that I trained and ran three miles in a sprint triathlon this past weekend."

Cardiovascular Training

Cardiovascular activity is the key to building a strong heart and healthy lungs. Typically this activity is aerobic (aerobic means "with oxygen"). Aerobic activity includes a jog without stopping, a power walk, a high-impact aerobic class and swimming laps without stopping. Cardiovascular activity can also be a mix of aerobic and anaerobic (circuit training with weights and stationary bike, basketball, tennis, volleyball or any stop-and-go activity). To achieve an effective metabolic rate, it is best to do at least twenty-five minutes of cardio before breakfast, or as early in the day as possible.

I know this early-morning routine isn't possible for everyone. Just get your body moving. Find an aerobic activity you can do at least three days a week. Remember the 1 percent rule. If you are not doing any activity now, start by taking a walk twice this week. As a bonus, become aware of any situation that will keep you active. If there are stairs at work, take them. Walk to the store instead of driving. Ride a bicycle. Find as many ways to move your joints as possible. When it comes to recreation, do what you enjoy, whether it's a racket sport, hiking, throwing a frisbee, swimming, playing golf or skiing. It's all good.

I took up rollerblading a few years ago. It's phenomenal exercise. I did it despite the fact that I suffer from motion sickness and any speed makes me dizzy. Flying along on those blades I felt like I was thirteen again, roller skating on the pathways in Ireland, free as a bird. Then one day I hit a tree root and fell flat on my bottom. I thought I was going to pass out. A handsome young man happened by and helped me up. Now the blades are collecting dust in the basement. There are safer ways to exercise!

*The best exercise in the world
is the one that you will do!*

—Covert Bailey

If you want to shed weight, do a cardiovascular activity that provides an adequate amount of aerobic intensity (a powerwalk, jogging, a stationary bike or bike ride along a path, a swim or a step class). Spend at least twenty-five minutes at moderate intensity. Moderate is when you can speak fairly easily without losing your breath. This is best for weight management.

If you are focusing on maintenance, fitness or endurance, do a cardiovascular activity that provides you with a more intense amount of aerobics. You will be breathing heavier. During a twenty-five minute workout you will want to stay in the high-intensity range most of the time.

I highly recommend you find someone to exercise with. A workout buddy makes it fun, and you can keep each other accountable. I have a walking buddy. Her name is Eileen and we walk my dog Rafferty in the evenings. Eileen insists I go walking even when I am dog tired (sorry!). She's good for me. Some women prefer the group setting of a regular class rather than going to the gym alone. Attending a class can be more motivating, and chances are you'll be missed if you don't show up.

Cardiovascular activity is all about breathing. Breathing oxygenates our bodies and gives us life. Most people are shallow breathers. Cardiovascular exercise helps us breathe deeply. Practice taking three deep breaths every day. Breathe from the

"Step 1: Apply Miracle Cellulite Cream to problem areas.
Step 2: Run ten miles."

nose right down to the diaphragm in your navel area. Let the air out slowly through your mouth. Often when I am sitting at a stoplight I practice deep breathing. It's a great habit—might as well do something healthy while waiting for the light, and I usually feel calmer about the wait.

As you get older, stretching your body is always a good thing to do. Stretching is crucial for keeping joints supple, and muscles relaxed and active. Follow a good stretching routine every day to keep your body younger for longer. A good time to stretch is right after you've exercised, while the muscles are warm. Laura suggests stretching for five minutes in the morning and five minutes at night. I have never been flexible. This was obvious when my friend Eileen dragged me to a yoga class. I watched others bend and pose in alarming positions. I did my best. My efforts were often only good for a laugh and I realized I'd never be a pretzel. I believe if God wanted me to touch my toes he would have put them on my knees!

The Magic of
DRINKING WATER

Water Wow!

As outrageous as it seems, drinking water may be the single most important catalyst in shedding weight, increasing energy and preventing certain diseases. If we think of this logically it makes sense, because more than 70 percent of our body is comprised of water.

Depending on the study, it is believed that more than 75 percent of our population is chronically dehydrated. Not just dehydrated, but chronically dehydrated. This is not good. We seem to have replaced Mother Nature's beverage with soda, coffee, milk, juice and beer. Once again, we've become victims of the food industry marketing giants, convincing us to drink anything but water.

Get this—every time you drink a liquid other than water, your body reacts quickly to dilute it with your internal water stores. This causes a shortage, unless you've consumed large amounts of water that day. So each time you drink a beverage other than water, drink another glass or two of water to counteract it. This solution can help the millions of people who are chronically dehydrated. How very natural and simple. Water can play a life-changing role in your quest for great health. Strangely, you will notice as you start drinking more water that you become thirstier than before. Why is this? On the surface, it doesn't make sense. But here are the facts:

- Water suppresses the appetite naturally and helps your body metabolize stored fat.

- A decrease in water will cause fat deposits to increase, while an increase in water can reduce fat deposits. This alone should catch your attention if you want to shed weight.

- Your kidneys can't function properly without enough water. The liver has to help the kidneys, so it works harder. But one of the liver's primary functions is to metabolize stored fat, so it cannot handle this excess work.

- Drinking more water prevents fluid retention.

- Water rids the body of waste and toxins— especially important if you are shedding weight or changing lifestyle.

- Water can help relieve constipation but since we are now eating enough fiber we're okay, right?

- Water is Mother Nature's greatest beauty tonic.

- Drinking more water reduces overnight hunger pangs.

- Drinking more water can prevent fatigue, headaches, sinus problems, allergies, breathing difficulties, joint discomfort, neck and back pain, sleep disorders, impotence, depression and brain dysfunction—wow!

- Water helps maintain proper muscle tone by helping muscles in their natural ability to contract.

- Natural thirst returns. This is why you are thirstier even though you are drinking more water. Your body is loving it and telling you it wants more.

Adding even more impact to these already fabulous water facts, researchers in the Center for Human Nutrition at the University of Sheffield conducted a study showing that women who stayed sufficiently hydrated reduced their risk of breast cancer by 79 percent. This was new information to me.

Water is especially healthy and tasty if it is purified—ask your local water company for advice. I suggest that you drink at least eight glasses of water a day, and enjoy the life-changing benefits. Don't worry if it takes some time to get used to doing this. When I first started this regime I would pour a glass of water and forget it. By the end of the day I would have four or five glasses of water scattered all over the house.

> "Mazie, you are 101 years old. To what do you attribute your longevity?"
>
> "I make sure I get up every morning."
>
> "And how do you do that?"
>
> "I drink six glasses of water before I go to bed!"
>
> —Anonymous

I now have a full water bottle in the car every time I go out, and I have developed the habit of drinking two glasses after I exercise. This is automatic. In the morning (and often in the evening) I drink a large cup of warm lemon water made by squeezing fresh lemon juice into warm water. It does wonders for the complexion and it helps cleanse the liver.

Making A Food Journal

To make your body and health dreams real, you may find it helpful to start a journal. Write down a plan of action, whether you have a weight goal, a goal to change your diet, to build muscle or just to drink more water. During the first week, push yourself to keep a detailed food journal for three days. Write down what you ate, how you felt after you ate it, and where you ate it (at home, at work, in a restaurant or in front of the TV).

Victoria Moran, a New York-based motivational speaker and author of *Fit From Within*, says, "Keeping a food journal forces you to be accountable for what you're putting in your body. It also provides you with a clear picture of the food patterns that keep you from reaching your weight goals." Not surprisingly, the article also stated that many people who journal actually double their weight loss goals.

Laura recommends taking supplements (also known as macro-nutrients and micro-nutrients), even while eating a healthy diet. She believes strongly in their benefits and contributes her continued great health today to their effects. Micro-nutrients particularly are deficient in our food supply today.

So far in this chapter we have based much of the information on Laura's excellent health and fitness program. But it's only the tip of the iceberg. For more on this topic, please check out Laura's information and other resources available in the Resource Guide at the back of this book.

Having lots of money isn't much good if you don't have the health to enjoy it.

—Les Hewitt

Money
AND YOU

Money is the last component of our deceptive triangle, one that is potentially devastating.

Mary, fifty-four, is newly widowed. Her husband Jim died suddenly of a massive heart attack. Her two children, Jack and Marianne, are both married with families and live out of state. It is now a few weeks after the funeral, and Mary is receiving a visit from Jim's lawyer, Ben, who is also executor for the estate.

After being seated, Ben takes a moment to collect his thoughts. His voice is soft and apologetic, "Mary, I've gone over Jim's will and papers. As you probably know, he left all of his material belongings to you except for a few personal items he bequeathed to the children." Ben pauses. "But I'm sorry to say there isn't any money. In fact, there are some debts to be paid plus $100,000 left on the mortgage. As for the life insurance policy, apparently Jim cashed it in three months ago when he needed an urgent injection of capital for his business."

Mary's face pales, her expression one of disbelief. "But what am I going to do? I have very little savings and haven't worked in years. Who will pay the bills?"

Twenty minutes later, as Ben lets himself out, he can hear Mary quietly sobbing as her new reality starts to sink in. Mary had always left everything to do with money in her husband's hands. She was brought up that way. Women raised the family and ran the home; men brought home the paycheck. Recently, Jim had complained that the economy was in a slump and appeared stressed, but he had always pulled through before. Mary prided herself on having tightened her belt before, making do with less. These occasions were always short-lived. Soon she could buy the clothes she wanted and look forward to nice vacations again. Jim had never talked about money and she felt it wasn't her place to ask. He hadn't placed restrictions on her spending, either. The credit cards worked fine, although it came as a shock when she discovered the overdue balances were costing 21 percent interest.

Sadly, Mary is not alone. Thousands of women, perhaps millions, have surrendered money matters to their husbands, partners or advisers. They have no clue where they stand financially. That's why we need to talk about finances and forever dispel some of the myths that exist when it comes to women and money. A comprehensive treatment of investment strategy is beyond the scope of this book. Several excellent information sources are listed in our Resource Guide—they will provide more detail on how to handle the day-to-day details of your money. Here I want to discuss the fundamentals. Follow this simple checklist and you will have a great foundation upon which to build security and ultimately, financial freedom.

The Road To
FINANCIAL SECURITY

Financial freedom is the wonderful ability to make choices about what we want to do in life without the restrictions of money pressures. This doesn't mean we need to be wizards at making money, or that we must own profitable businesses. Women with modest incomes, single parents, and those who don't have a higher education can still create long-term financial security. Here's how:

Take Responsibility For Your Money

If you are single or raising a family on your own, this is straightforward. You are the breadwinner, provider and custodian of your financial affairs. If you are in a long-term relationship or married, with or without children, the situation may be different. Communication is the key. Openly discuss your feelings about who's in charge of the various money roles and how you will share responsibility.

In my case, I'm happy to pay the household bills, utilities and house insurance. I budget for groceries and other maintenance items. Les and I have a joint personal account and he looks after taxes, cars and other insurance policies. I have a separate bank account just for me, as does Les. This gives me a sense of independence. I'm responsible for managing my account and knowing what needs to be paid and when.

You might think, "Doesn't everyone do that?" The answer is an emphatic "No!" Many women, like Mary, avoid taking any responsibility for their money. Make sure you don't make the same mistake.

Confront Your Fears

The number one fear that women have about money is that they will be broke when they are old. Financial expert and bestselling author Dr. Judith Briles says, "Statistics show that for every one hundred women and men who reach sixty-five, only two are financially independent.

The reality is that whether you are rich, poor or in between, the person you need to rely on to keep you from the poorhouse is you—your creativity, your imagination, your intuition and your smarts." Other big fears about money for women include:

- Losing money.
- Looking stupid.
- Talking about money.

- Making mistakes and failing.
- Borrowing money.
- Creating and sticking to a plan.
- Investing.
- Not trusting themselves.
- Sticking with people who give bad financial advice.

Do you show up anywhere on that list? Your upbringing is usually the main factor influencing your money habits. Most women would like to have more knowledge and insight about money, but grew up in homes that avoided any such discussions. There were surface talks, but rarely any meaningful instruction. Take some time to write down your fears and beliefs about money. How are these holding you back? How do you feel about debt? What is your risk tolerance when it comes to investing? Old negative beliefs will keep you stuck. As I mentioned before, you can beat this by stepping into your fear. The best way to do that is by implementing the next step.

Become Financially Intelligent

Learn how money works. It's not that complicated. There are many courses you can take from the most basic, how to balance your checking account, to sophisticated investing. Check with your local community college. If you don't have time to take a course, numerous books will teach you everything you need to know. Some of these books are listed in our Resource Guide.

As well, many of these books are now on CD, so you can save time by learning while you drive. The internet is a vast storehouse of financial information. Invest one hour per week in home study. If you feel lacking in knowledge or understanding about money, set a realistic goal over the next few months to educate yourself. Maybe you read one book or meet with a friend who is really good with money, and pick her brains over coffee. What you don't want is to get caught in the middle of a financial crisis caused by bad choices that could easily have been prevented with a little knowledge.

Do A Reality Check Now

The financial truth is often intimidating, so people tend to avoid it or deny that anything is wrong. Sticking your head in the sand is not the way to get out of your money problems. Some women will blame their husbands, partners or friends who gave them bad advice—anything to avoid reality. If you are struggling financially, a totally honest appraisal is essential. Many people are living in a fantasy, instead of the real world. Schedule a time to do this appraisal thoroughly. If someone else at home is involved, do it together. The most important thing is to accept what is. That's the groundwork you need to lay out before you can design a healthier plan for future prosperity.

Write out in detail where the money goes every month versus what actually comes in after taxes. You'll be amazed at some of the ways your money is slipping away. That double latte every day is costing you a few thousand dollars a year! Maybe that's okay, maybe it isn't. Are there more important priorities? This exercise may be difficult, especially if the debt is substantial. The good news is that you can immediately start working on a new course of action based on the truth. In the long run your honesty will pay much better dividends than before.

Look Ahead, Know What's Coming

The danger with a hectic, multi-tasking lifestyle is that one week just blends into the next, and suddenly, before you know it, half of the year has gone. Many women tell me this is their reality. What's worse, when you're immersed from week to week you can't see the bigger picture. As far as your money is concerned, you need to look down the road to see what's coming in order to avoid surprises. Ask yourself what major purchases or payments will be required in the next two years:

a new car, home renovation, college tuition, family wedding, medical expenses, a unique vacation to celebrate a special anniversary, or maybe a significant contribution you want to make to a church or charity.

Have you put a plan in place for what this will cost? Or is it a fingers-crossed, hope-you-make-it plan that might create another deep financial hole from which it could take years to recover? Consider the type of lifestyle you want to have in the years ahead. Is it realistic, based on your current financial situation? Can it be simplified? As you'll see in the final chapter, money doesn't guarantee happiness. There are many options.

Dump Your Bad Money Habits

We spend money constantly, which means we develop spending patterns. When we continually make bad choices about money we end up with all sorts of negative circumstances. For example, if we are always late filing our income tax and paying our credit cards or anything that creates interest penalties, it's like taking a roll of twenty dollar bills out of your purse and setting them on fire. That's crazy, you say. Why would anyone do that? Exactly!

Write down all your bad habits that revolve around money. You may have been doing some of these for years. You must write them down to see the truth unmistakably laid out in front of your eyes. Then select the one that is hurting you the most. Make a commitment right there and then to stop this behavior. No more late payments, frivolous spending, impulse buying or paying too high a price. From now on it's simply not acceptable.

Create A Better Plan

For some women it's not a matter of having a better plan, it's having any plan at all. Every financial adviser emphasizes that planning is where you must start if you are serious about improving your financial health. A good plan always starts with the end result in mind. What's your top priority?

Getting out of debt, creating enough investment income that you can stop working in the next five or ten years? What type of lifestyle do you want? Maybe you just want to get the credit cards under control. Do you have a grander vision that includes lots of travel and a stimulating social life? Is there a part of you that longs to do something creative or artistic, but lacks the money that would free you up to pursue it?

As far as investing goes, diversification is key. Having all your eggs in one basket like the stock market can be risky, depending on when you need to pull your money out. Cover yourself by spreading the risk. Consider real estate, bonds and money market accounts to balance your portfolio. Get sound advice, which leads us to the next step.

Tap Into The Best Expertise

This is absolutely crucial. You can't be expected to become a financial genius all on your own unless you plan on making a career out of it. Even then you will need help. As far as advice goes, find people you trust implicitly, for whom you have the utmost respect. If you genuinely enjoy that person's company, that's a bonus. Your financial adviser must have credibility. Don't take advice from someone who does not have a successful track record managing money. Take your time. Ask lots of questions. Do your homework. If you are going to entrust someone with making your hard-earned money grow, you must be as sure as you can be that you've picked a winner. There are no written guarantees. Just minimize your risk. Your female intuition goes a long way here. Trust your instincts, they are usually right.

Depending on how complex your financial situation is, consider cultivating excellent relationships with an experienced accountant, tax specialist, broker and banker. Having a personal mentor is also a great idea. This is someone with vast experience who is in a position of financial strength and is willing to coach you. If you are wondering where to find people like this, the answer is simple: ask. Put the word out. Keep asking. You are never more than about six people away from the person you need to meet.

Pay Yourself Every Month

This is one fundamental that will never change. It's a difficult concept to grasp for women who are used to putting everyone else's needs first. Every month after you write the rent check or pay the mortgage, make the next one out to you. If you are married or in a relationship, be assertive about this.

Do not let your husband or partner take total control. Get involved and agree on a unified strategy. Save or invest ten percent of your gross income if possible. If you are not able to do this, pick a smaller number. Remember, it's developing the habit that counts, not the amount. Your needs are important. When it comes to retirement, if you don't plan to take care of you, who will? Remember Mary? She learned the hard way. Be smart, the clock is ticking.

Stick To Your Plan

For most people this is the hard part. It helps to focus on the end result, and the freedom your financial discipline will bring you. Money problems are one of the main causes of divorce. Poverty is certainly no fun. The fear of being a bag lady weighs heavy on many women. These are all good reasons to stick to your plan. Use whatever stimulus it takes to motivate you, whether it is the fear of loss or the joy of financial freedom.

Teach Your Kids The Basics

Educating children about money is a parent's responsibility. Teach your children the value of a dollar. Give them clear examples of bad money habits and have open discussions around the supper table. As they get older, make them save for what they want. They will respect you for this later. Introduce them to the concept of giving and being charitable. A good example, even for a young child, is to explain that a dollar is best split up as follows: 10 percent for the government (taxes), ten per cent for charity (people who are less fortunate), 10 percent for saving or investing (helping your money grow), and you get to keep the remaining 70 percent. Label four glass jars accordingly, and have them deposit the appropriate amounts when they receive or earn any money.

> *Do what you love and the*
> *money will follow.*
>
> —Marsha Sinetar

Passion and financial prosperity are closely linked:

Greta couldn't believe her eyes. The automatic teller machine had just displayed the news that the twenty dollars she had requested was not forthcoming because the amount exceeded her balance of $1.17. As good as broke, she and her sister Janet held a garage sale the next day to raise funds. Among the items sold were Janet's car and wedding dress. The sale brought in $9,000.

If you had a dream, would you be prepared to quit your full-time job, risk everything, and put yourself $80,000 in debt, not to mention saying goodbye to any social life for fourteen months? Many people would say no, that's too big a risk. Not Greta and Janet Podleski. These two enterprising sisters, from Ontario, Canada, dreamed of creating a unique cook-book to help people become healthier by eating nutritious, delicious low-fat meals.

Like every business, it started with an idea. However, it certainly was not a typical start-up. Both sisters had good jobs, Greta in a government office and Janet as a marketer for an international high-tech company. When Janet married, Greta moved in with the newly weds, primarily as a cook because her sister was, by her own admission, "a domestic dummy." Greta, who loves to cook, served up delicious meals and didn't mention the fact that they were all low-fat. When this became known months later, Janet's husband said, "You should write a cookbook." The more they thought about it, the more they liked the idea. They were the perfect team: Greta the master cook and Janet a whiz at marketing and writing.

The day of commitment came when they both made a pact to resign from their full-time jobs on the same day. Each checked with the other every couple of hours to see if they had quit yet. The answer was no, until late afternoon when Janet finally took the leap of faith, followed quickly by Greta. Now there was no turning back.

Their credit cards were maxed out and the debtload climbed rapidly. There would be no income for fourteen months. Working out of a tiny basement office with pages of recipes spread all over the floor, the task ahead seemed daunting. There were many times when they felt like quitting. But deep down they both felt strongly that they were supposed to be writing this book. However, more bad news was to follow when eight publishers turned down their manuscript.

The turning point came when they read an article about author David Chilton, who had self-published *The Wealthy Barber* which went on to sell more than two million copies.

They set up a meeting with him and one of his first comments was, "I know nothing about recipes, I can't even cook tea!" His sense of humor matched theirs, and after David's mother gave a hearty thumbs-up to the tastiness of their meals, the girls brokered a partnership with the successful author. Now they had financing and were able to self-publish their first cookbook, *Looneyspoons*. It landed on the shelves a few months later. The results were beyond their wildest dreams. *Looneyspoons* hit the bestseller list in the first week and stayed there for eighty-five consecutive weeks!

Crazy Plates, their second cookbook, was also received by the public with great enthusiasm. Currently their combined book sales total 1.3 million copies. Their latest venture is a line of frozen meal kits, all low-fat and ready to serve in fifteen minutes. The response has been tremendous, even winning a Best New Product award in the grocery industry. Janet and Greta are big dreamers who simply would not quit. Their passion is to make a significant contribution to people's health and wellness. They encourage women to discover their own passion and to stick with it. In the end, they say, good things will happen. They are certainly living proof that passion combined with courageous action produces big dividends.

Your Habits Will Determine
YOUR FUTURE

Now that you understand how to overcome the negative aspects of image, health and money, let's add an insurance factor that will guarantee you enjoy the best results. It's called successful habits. This is the glue that holds everything together, day by day. Habits are the daily disciplines that determine whether or not you will end up with a positive mental image, vibrant health and financial freedom.

Here's an important fact to remember. Successful people have successful habits, unsuccessful people don't. It's that simple. You can apply this strategy to any area of your life that you wish to improve, and reap wonderful rewards.

First, let's define habits. Simply put, habits are something you do often, until they become easy. The longer you repeat the behavior the easier it becomes, until eventually you do it unconsciously. For example, I wanted to increase my water and fruit intake. I would get off to a good start for a couple of weeks and then I'd forget. The problem was that I was too sporadic—I needed a plan. I decided that every time I went to the gym I would bring a large water bottle and one piece of fruit, with the promise to myself that they would both be gone before I returned home. This worked like a charm. I am now totally unconscious of packing them in my bag and it's automatic that I consume them. That habit is now five years old.

We are all creatures of habit. Most of our normal daily behavior is habitual. The first ninety minutes of my morning, from the time I wake up until I'm in work mode, involves habits that are automatic: bathroom, shower, make-up, dressing, preparing breakfast, reading, washing up, checking the to-do list. None of these habits require major decisions.

What about you? When you wake up do you immediately think, "I wonder what my habits will be today?" Of course not. You simply do what you do, and get on with your day.

Good Habits Produce Better Results

Jim Rohn once gave me an insight that I have never forgotten. He said, "Fran, always remember, the results of your bad habits won't show up until much later in life." He had a word for the results; he called them consequences. I've discovered this is true. If we keep making bad choices about our health or money, the consequences probably won't occur immediately. It takes time for cholesterol to build to the point where it causes a heart attack. Lung cancer doesn't manifest its deadly consequences with a single pack of cigarettes. It takes years. The result is still usually fatal. Some women have bought into a "spend-now, save-later" fallacy. They think that one day they will start putting away money. They intend to do this, but it never happens.

The consequences of your bad habits can be heart-breaking. You may end up in poor health or working during the years that you planned for retirement. For some people it's even worse—destitute and broke, they end up requiring assistance to survive. To avoid these nasty scenarios, here's what you can do:

List Your Bad Habits

- Write them down; you know what they are. Consider every area of your life—fitness, relationships, work, money, eating, driving, sleeping, communication, punctuality, following through on your promises, etc.

- Be specific—clearly define each one.

  For example: I hit the snooze button five times in the morning before I finally get up.

- Select one habit that you really want to change.

Assess The Consequences

- Opposite your bad habit, write the long-term consequences if you continue this behavior.

  For example: Sleeping late on a workday can get you off to a bad start. You are rushing, you miss breakfast, your stress levels increase because traffic is backed up. You arrive at the office tense, out of breath and still fuming at the stupid guy who stalled when the stoplight turned green. Repeated tardiness may get you fired and you are labelled unreliable.

- Think about the long-term consequences of your behavior, not the outcome tomorrow or next week.

Clarify Your New Habit and Take Action

- Defining a better habit is easy. Just write down the opposite of your bad habit.

  For example: Get up on time. Do not hit the snooze alarm once, never mind five times.

- Alongside your new habit, write three action steps that will turn this desired behavior into a reality.

  For example: Immediately swing your legs out of bed when the alarm goes off. (I know this sounds too simple, but it works!) Have a friend phone you at the exact time you want to get up. Buy a new clock with a horrendously loud alarm bell on it, and place it on the opposite side of the room. The point is—do something that will jumpstart your new behavior.

- Finally, list all of the positive benefits you will enjoy once your new habit is well established. In most cases this takes thirty to ninety days. Getting up on time soon becomes automatic, and you won't need an alarm. You will be more relaxed and can ease into the day, instead of being jolted into it. Reducing stress affects your long-term health, and being on time for work shows your integrity. You'll be thankful for making the adjustment.

No Exceptions Policy

One final note about creating successful habits. The longer you have maintained a bad habit, the harder it is to break. Creating new habits, especially exercise programs, are difficult at the start. The first few weeks will really test you. There will be times when you want to quit. Don't! Develop a No Exceptions Policy, and stick to it. If you do, the rewards will far outweigh any initial discomfort.

My husband Les always had a weak spot for cookies. He'd have a few cookies at lunch, a few more at supper and a cookie snack before bed. One of his goals was to lose eight pounds and reduce his waist size by two inches. At a routine check-up he mentioned this to his doctor, whose response was, "That's easy. Stop eating cookies and lift a few weights." The timing must have been right—Les stopped eating cookies that very day, and he hasn't had one since! He also does fifteen minutes with hand weights every other day. He made it a No Exceptions Policy, despite aching muscles at the start. In six weeks he dropped nine pounds without any other changes in diet, and now comfortably fits into a thirty-two-inch waist size.

Daily discipline combined with desire and a No Exceptions Policy pays off, no matter what habit you want to change.

The secret to getting ahead is getting started.

—Mark Twain

A Man's Perspective
Les Hewitt

In my coaching business I meet a lot of men who talk openly about their money concerns. This is unusual, because in the real world men generally do not discuss their personal finances. Money is often a reflection of their success and most would prefer to keep that private, especially if they are struggling.

Men, like women, are worried about cash flow. They feel anxious about the future and express concern that they aren't spending enough time with their loved ones. The image of success is important for many men.

We feel we have a reputation to maintain, and even if there is a financial crisis going on, we'd rather pretend to the world and our families that everything is fine. Many of my male clients say they won't talk about money at home because they know their wives get concerned about finances, and they don't want to alarm them.

My feeling is that it's much healthier for the relationship when husbands and wives share their concerns openly. When I first started my business money was tight, and we were living on a hope and a prayer rather than following a well-designed plan. Fran was incredibly supportive and that did a lot for my confidence. We worked together as a team and talked about our needs. If we needed to cut back on spending, it was a joint decision.

Women are good at building support networks and maintaining family ties, whereas men tend to be loners. Our egos prevent us from being vulnerable and we can put on a pretty good act to mask the pain. However, under that façade there is a human being, often fragile and too worried to discuss reality with friends and family. When anxiety is high at work, the office doesn't usually provide many hugs or pats on the back. Be sensitive at these times. Men appreciate encouragement and support when they are highly stressed.

A final word about money. Make sure you educate yourself. The more financial intelligence you acquire through education and asking questions, the less likely you will be to end up in dire straights like Mary did. Set some money goals for yourself. If you are married, create some exciting objectives that will involve both of you financially. Women on average live seven years longer than their male counterparts, so it's wise to be financially savvy.

CONCLUSION

Be kind to yourself. Life is not about perfection. Love, appreciate and accept yourself just the way you are. Sift through all the misinformation and high-pressure trickery and become an independent thinker.

Be responsible for your health and keep your eye on future wellness. The body you have is the only one you'll get, so treat it with the care and respect it deserves.

When it comes to image, health and money it can be difficult to change old habits, and new habits take time to cultivate. However, anything worth achieving is worth working for. Wishing for change is not the same as making it happen. Do what you need to do. If not now, when?

ACTION STEPS

Image, Health
and Money

Successful Habits

These Action Steps are designed to encourage you to make one adjustment in each of the four key areas.

1. Image
Go out with a friend for lunch. Dress like you normally would. However, do not wear any makeup. Do not tell your friend about this exercise. Afterwards, record your feelings and observations. Ask yourself how comfortable you were without makeup. Generally, do you wear makeup for yourself or for others?

If you would not take the challenge, ask yourself why not?

_____

How much emphasis do you place on what others think of you, in this and other areas of your life?

_____

2. Health
What one decision have you made that will improve your health?

_____

_____

Specifically, how will you implement it?

_____

_____

3. Money
What one decision have you made that will move you closer to financial freedom?

_____

_____

Specifically, how will you implement it?

_____

_____

4. Successful Habits
Name one new habit you are going to create in the next few weeks:

_____

_____

What will be the greatest benefit of doing this?

_____

Be Happy
On Purpose

Success is liking yourself,
liking what you do, and liking
how you do it.

—Maya Angelou

In this chapter we will investigate why some women achieve great success, how they are able to focus on what they want, and the techniques they use to get there. I'll introduce you to four unique, dynamic women, all at different stages of their lives, each of them happy with their choices. We'll take a close look at happiness, and how to bring more joy into your life. To conclude, we'll examine another important aspect of creating a meaningful life, the power of purpose.

To live the life you really want you must first figure out what that means. Many young women drift into the workplace without much planning or forethought. Sometimes a friend or parent will influence the decision. Years later they are stuck in a job that they don't enjoy, or one that has limited opportunity for advancement. Many, as Thoreau said, are living lives of quiet desperation.

Are you crystal clear about what you want from life? Have you identified your top priorities? Who do you want to spend more time with? What places do you want to visit? What goals do you want to accomplish? Or have you settled into a routine where one week seems to blur into the next and there's never any time to think or plan? When you are stuck in routine maybe life is okay at one level, but at another level you still have dreams, even if they are somewhat faded. These dreams can include things you'd like to do and experience, or feelings you'd like to have.

We've already discussed how much the busy pace of life affects balance. It also affects our focus and our future. The shocking reality is that only 3 percent of men and women have actually taken the time to consider their future. That means 97 percent of us are just going through the motions from week to week, with no plan for living the life we really want. No wonder so many people end up in their senior years regretting all the things they could have done, never took the time to do, or were simply not aware of as time slipped by.

- If only I had traveled more. There are so many wonderful places I wanted to see, but never did.

- If only I had spent more time enjoying my family. Now the kids are gone and have their own busy lives. I don't see much of them anymore.

- If only I had put away a little money over the years, maybe I wouldn't need to work so hard now.

Where do you stand on this? Is life just passing you by or are you ready to create a new picture? Wouldn't it be better to establish some new disciplines now, instead of ending up with regrets later? Years ago my friend Jim Rohn jolted my thinking on this when he told me, "The pain of discipline weighs ounces, whereas the pain of regret weighs tons."

Schedule Time
TO THINK

This is an important first step. No matter how busy you are, to create a better future you must have a picture of what you want, and that requires real time to think. You can't plan a better life by thinking on the run. I know you're probably a great multi-tasker, but this is serious business and requires uninterrupted time, a notepad and 100 percent concentration.

Two methods can be used to create your Big Picture. The first method is simply to make a list of everything you would like to accomplish within a certain timeframe. A one-year plan usually works well. Most of us can think about the next twelve months fairly easily. Some people create three-year, five-year and ten-year plans. Personally I find these difficult. Choose the timeframe that works best for you. To stimulate your thinking ask yourself some direct questions:

- What's my reality?
- What do I want to do in the next year?
- What do I want to have?
- Where do I want to go?
- What contribution do I want to make?
- Who do I want to spend my time with?
- What do I want to learn?
- What do I want to become?
- How much do I want to earn, save and invest?
- How much time off do I want for fun?

- What will I do to create optimum health?

- What do I want more of that I'm not getting now?

- What do I value most at this stage of my life?

- What will I say no to (something that is no longer acceptable)?

- What do I want to do this year, just for me?

- How do I want to feel at the end of this year, compared to now?

Add more questions to this list if you wish. Creating an exciting picture for the year ahead, and beyond, requires reflection, analysis and insight. There is no quick-fix way to do this. Schedule at least one whole day to clarify what is important to you and what is not. If you have a family, it's a good idea to include them in this exercise because they will be affected by the outcome. Kids enjoy this, especially anything to do with fun and vacations.

Put your thoughts and decisions on paper. Then prioritize what is most important. For specific objectives like buying a new car or renovating your home, set realistic timeframes. If you have never done this type of planning before, you will find it both enlightening and stimulating. At this stage don't worry about how you are going to accomplish everything on your list. Unusual clarity is simply creating a very clear picture of what you want and why you want it. When this is complete you can start creating a plan of action.

By the way, give serious thought to why you want to accomplish these goals. Powerful reasons drive us to succeed. They give us the energy to push forward, especially when obstacles get in the way. For example, you might want to send your aging parents on a special trip, somewhere they longed to visit but couldn't afford. Picturing the joy this would bring them, especially if it is going to be a surprise, could be all the motivation you need. Even if it stretched you financially, you'd probably figure out a way to make it work. It's amazing how creative we become when there's a strong reason.

Create Your Own
PICTURE

Setting goals in this manner may be too linear. For some women it's too structured, too black and white. For the second method of creating your Big Picture, instead of making lists create an actual picture. You still need to make decisions about what you want. However, you can make your plan more like a road map, a visual image of where you are going. Use pictures from travel books and lifestyle magazines. If your desire is to lose weight, create a picture of what you will look like when you reach your target. A participant in one of my workshops superimposed two photos. She used the body of someone else who had the figure she wanted, and put her own head on it! Visual images are powerful. You can expand on this by creating a picture book of what you want using different categories—health, fun, vacations, hobbies, career, family, financial, relationships, contribution.

> *Dare to dream big dreams based*
> *on your heartfelt desires.*
>
> —Glenna Salsbury

Our good friend Glenna Salsbury, who lives in Arizona, has enjoyed great success in business and traveled extensively throughout her career. Glenna has cultivated the habit of focusing on what she wants through the use of pictures.

For more than twenty-five years she has cut pictures from magazines, catalogs and travel brochures and created picture books. Amazingly, most of the pictures have become reality for her. Here's an example of how this works:

One year Glenna received the Banana Republic catalog.
She said, "The main feature was a new line of safari clothes—the African Queen movie theme, the Katherine Hepburn look, the whole regalia, slouch hat and all. For some reason I was magnetically drawn to these clothes, so I cut out the pictures and put them in my book.

Practically, I knew I would never wear these clothes in my work or socially. I had no plan, just a strong feeling that something was going to happen. Over the years I've learned to respond to things that draw on my heart. It provides clues and direction for my life.

One night I suggested to my husband Jim that maybe we should go to Africa on a safari. He wasn't really enthused and so I didn't pursue it. About six weeks later Jim received a phone call out of the blue from his best friend, who said: 'My wife and I are booking a six-week safari to Africa and we were wondering if you and Glenna would like to come along?' To me this was more than coincidence. Jim agreed. We decided to go, and had a great trip. I got to buy and wear my safari clothes. We even tracked Dianne Fossey's gorillas—an amazing experience that I will never forget."

GLENNA'S CHILDREN ALSO USE PICTURE BOOKS and achieve similar results. The message is clear. Any time you feel a tug on your heart, respond to it. Let your intuition guide you. Interestingly, Glenna does not look at her pictures very often once she puts them in the book. She says: "The pictures just help identify what's important to me—they give me a visual connection." As Glenna has proven, when you constantly present a vivid image to your conscious or subconscious mind, amazing things happen. It's like a strong magnet is pulling you toward your goals. Amazing "coincidences" seem to happen—that perfect car is advertised in the local paper by an owner who has hardly driven it; even better, it's your favorite color and has all the extras that are on your checklist.

I'm not sure how all of this happens. However, I do know that when you focus on what you want and use vivid imagery, the process seems to accelerate. Just go with the flow and be conscious of the doors that start opening up for you.

Focus On What
YOU DO BEST

I believe everyone is blessed with unique talents and skills. An important part of life is discovering what these are. Do you know what you are brilliant at doing? Yes, I said brilliant. That's a word most women shy away from. Look at it this way. What do you do with ease that other people find difficult? What energizes and stimulates you? When does time fly for you? What are your natural talents?

If you are considering a change in your work or career, check outside of your current resumé. Do you have any hobbies, dreams, pastimes or talents that may be seeds for a new vocation? Too often we turn a blind eye to things that come easy to us; we think we always need to be working hard at something. Maybe you are an exceptional organizer, over and above the multi-tasking skills virtually all women need to acquire. Perhaps you're a whiz on the computer, or you have a great eye for color and design. Maybe you are terrific with people, or good at delivering presentations. Your natural talents energize you. When you do what you love, not only will you feel great joy and accomplishment, your energy will flow freely. Doing what you enjoy most is a crucial part of tracking your sources of energy and restoration. This is searching out the truth of who you are.

If you haven't already done so, make a list of your various skills and give each a score between one and ten. The highest numbers are what you do exceptionally well. If you are unsure, get feedback from your closest friends and co-workers. Sometimes they can see your talents better than you can. Ask yourself how much of your time is invested in doing what you do best. At work, are your best talents being utilized, or do you spend most of your day using lesser competencies?

Here's what I've discovered. My energy fluctuates when I'm immersed in the early stages of a major project such as designing a new workshop, preparing a great presentation or writing a story that has emotional impact. For me, this is not easy work. However, I find the creativity is invigorating. It can still be stressful, because I want to create the best value possible for my audience and in the early stages the value is not always evident. I need to keep reminding myself that I'm a recovering perfectionist! The end result, however, usually gives me energy and boosts my confidence.

Start focusing more of your time on what you do best, especially in your work. You will be more energized and create more opportunities for yourself by constantly honing your natural skills.

Patricia Fripp is a unique, dynamic woman who knows what she wants. She loves what she does and is constantly adding value to other people's lives. She is also comfortable with the choices she has made. Here's her story:

Patricia Fripp does not fit the typical female role.

Born in England, she quit school ten days before her fifteenth birthday to work as a hair stylist. A few years later she ventured to the United States on her own, landing in San Francisco with no job, no place to stay, and no contacts. She says her mother gave her the gift of unconditional love while her father's parting advice was, "Always control your own environment."

Eventually she found work in a high-end hair salon for men. In addition to being a good stylist, she was good at listening. The more she listened to the intriguing business deals that her clients willingly discussed, the more she realized that it was up to her to create her own destiny.

Patricia was a hard worker, driven partly to succeed by the need to make her parents proud. She figured out that the best way to earn income was by working only on commission. She began to do better financially.

Boyfriends came and went, some intimidated by the fact that she was making more money than them. Undaunted, she saw herself as a different type of role model for women. Marriage was not in her plans.

A natural salesperson, Patricia was commissioned to train other stylists on how to sell products. Her communication skills were so effective she later started speaking professionally at conferences and sales meetings for other organizations. Through more hard work and a thirst for knowledge, her fledgling career as a speaker became a thriving full-time independent business.

Every year since 1980 Patricia has spoken to more than one hundred groups, including Fortune 100 companies and major international associations. The National Speakers Association, with more than 4,000 members, elected her its first female president in 1984. She has won or been awarded every designation given by the NSA, including the Speaker Hall of Fame (CPAE), and the association's highest honor, the Cavett Award, considered the Oscar of the professional speaking world.

Now in demand as an executive coach who helps CEOs improve their presentation skills, Patricia is at the top of her game, traveling constantly. She says enthusiastically, "I am a small, mobile, intelligent unit. I like the way I am at age fifty-eight. I'm happiest doing something that demonstrates I'm really competent. The trouble for many people is that their everyday reality does not measure up to expectations. In retrospect, I feel grateful that my life has far exceeded my expectations."

QUITE A JOURNEY, from dropping out of school to becoming one of the world's most successful professional speakers. It took intense dedication, inner drive and an overwhelming desire to make her parents proud. Patricia makes a wonderful role model for anyone who wants to carve out a special niche; whether that niche is defined by a high-powered, driven lifestyle or by that of a cherished mother, wife and homemaker. Patricia is proof that anything is possible if you want it badly enough.

What brings you joy and happiness?

Behavioral geneticist Dr. David Lykken conducted a revealing study of the human brain and the effect of happiness on twins. He concluded that 50 percent of our predisposition to happiness is hereditary. He claims that we all have a set point which measures our genetic capacity for happiness.No matter what ups or downs we experience, our happiness level will return to this genetic set point.

Some fortunate women are born with a high set point and enjoy a natural predisposition to be happy; others are born with a low set point. You might find some small comfort in the knowledge that you are not 100 percent responsible for your own happiness. That still leaves 50 percent over which you have control.

Happiness is as a butterfly, which, when pursued,
is always beyond our grasp, but which, if you
will sit quietly, may alight upon you.

—Nathaniel Hawthorne

THE DOORSTEP

I stood on the doorstep
Your chubby two year old hands
Are wrapped tightly around the Popsicle
Which melts a river of orange
Down the front of your dress
My heart is happy as I watch your enjoyment.

I stood on the doorstep
To see you off.
Your six year old hands
Tightly grasp your new school bag
The yellow bus takes you away to a new adventure
Emotion wells up in my eyes, my heart is heavy.

I stood on the doorstep
For a mother daughter pose
You look stunning in your black graduation gown
You hold my hand lightly and stand taller than me now
My heart is full and proud.

I stood on the doorstep
My hand hesitates in a wave
As the white wedding limo whisks you away forever
My arms are empty and my heart aches.

I stood on the doorstep
Alone.

—*Fran Hewitt*

How fleeting life can be; how quickly time slips through our hands. Why is happiness so elusive? I often think back and wonder why I didn't grasp more of the happiness around me. Why was I blind to some of our golden moments? They were there to embrace, and I missed them.

Did I forget to notice, or was I so caught up in the stuff of life that I didn't take the time to slow down and breathe happiness in? I was fairly happy then, but I could have been happier. I think I stood in my own way. I had learned to focus on the negatives, allowing worry and guilt to rob me of positive feelings. Thankfully I know better now. Let me share what I have since learned about happiness.

All of us want to be happy, to lead fulfilling and meaningful lives. This is universal. Happiness can be a temporary, euphoric feeling that lifts us up, or it can be a feeling of contentment and satisfaction—more of an enduring experience.

Different things make people happy. To me, happiness can be enjoying the love of my family or feeling the freedom of a day in the mountains. To someone else, happiness is being totally immersed in the flow of a project. For others, it is as simple as enjoying coffee with a good friend. Happiness is unique to each of us, but most women would like to experience more of it.

> "Happiness is waking to a bright sunny day, or feeling the tight hugs of my children after time away from me," says Anna. "It's a chat with a friend that leaves my sides and cheeks sore from laughing, or a good concert with hundreds of others moved by the same music. It can be the knowing eye contact of someone I love, or the smell of fresh lilies wafting through the house. Relaxing by a crackling fire and sipping an Irish coffee on a cold winter's day makes me feel content. Happiness is knowing that trust is everything, that life is truly abundant as I look inside, not outside, for my source of joy."

Hurdles To
HAPPINESS

Why does happiness seem so elusive? Because many of us are looking for it in the wrong places. Too often we think the answer lies out there, in the pursuit of material possessions. If we buy a bigger home, somehow that will make our pain-filled marriage better. When we get a bonus at work we'll buy a new car—surely that will make us happier. It's true that when we acquire something new, there is an initial surge of pleasure. Our cravings and desires are satisfied for a short while, then the happiness bubble bursts and we are enticed into seeking something more.

Even if we elevate our social status by accumulating more, the happiness usually doesn't last. We quickly adapt to this new level; what was originally "more" becomes normal. We still want to increase our pleasure. Many people compare themselves to others who have what looks like a more successful lifestyle, believing that if they had the same lifestyle they would be happier. Money is often the way we measure our success. If only we had more money, life would be great. "If I could just win the lottery, all my worries would be over and I'd be happy." Research proves this is not true. In fact, the opposite is more often the case. Many lottery winners claim their newly found wealth created more strife and misery, not happiness. Divorce and loss of friends are commonplace after a lottery win. The evidence is indisputable. Money does not buy happiness, yet we have the illusion that it does.

Receiving an unexpected windfall only makes you more of who you already are. If you were a shopaholic before you won the financial bonanza, you will probably just become an even bigger spender. The reason so many lottery winners

"See, isn't this better than being happy?"

are not able to hang on to their winnings is that they haven't yet become the type of person who can successfully manage large amounts of money. They blow it on extravagant living, flashy cars, bad investments and divorce settlements. No wonder they end up unhappy.

Choose to be happy now. Are you in the habit of putting your happiness on hold for some future date? Remember the when-then game?

- **When** I retire, **then** I'll be happy.

- **When** I meet the right man, **then** I'll settle down and be happy.

What if our happiness is not out there? Our thoughts, feelings, attitudes and desires are continually changing. Nothing stays constant. Because of this, we will never find enduring happiness out there. Things that used to give us happiness lose their appeal; people who brought us joy in relationships now disappoint us. The great job we thought would be so fulfilling now leaves us empty. Even the purchases that excited us initially grow old, worn, and are no longer good enough. It all seems so futile. So where do we find happiness?

> "I believed that if I moved to Arizona," says Sonja, "I would find happiness. I wanted to open my own business in Sedona and meet some new people. I thought this would make me content. After having lived there for six years, one evening I was sitting at my computer and I realized I was no happier."

We find happiness in the simple pleasures of life; appreciating the beauty of nature, enjoying the warmth of the sun on our body, or walking on a beach with the water gently lapping at our feet. Maybe it's winning at sports, the feeling of satisfaction for a job well done, or simply holding the hand of someone you love. "It's the little things that keep you bouncing along above your set point," says Dr. Lykken.

There are many ways to find happiness in everyday things. We need to be more aware of them. Sometimes we think happiness means giggling and having fun. That's good, but don't we also feel happy when we do a great job at work? Just remembering a wonderful holiday or a favorite piece of music can make us smile and feel warm inside. Filling our day with what matters to us, and living authentically, are the recipes for happiness.

Are simple pleasures enough? Can we ever sustain this feeling of happiness? Maybe we could if we stopped wrestling with how to change our outside circumstances in order to satisfy our inner cravings; when we slow down enough to find the serenity that comes from just being who we are, not what we do, or relying on what we have.

I remember a holy moment I had many years ago. I call it a holy moment because it was not just a moment of happiness and joy, it was much more. It was a moment in time when my life felt great. For an instant, it felt like the world had stopped and held its breath so I would take notice. It was a beautiful spring morning and I had just finished teaching one of my parenting classes. I knew I had done a great job. I went outside and stood in the warm sunshine and felt it, my holy moment. At that point I didn't know why I felt so overwhelmed with joy, but now I know—I had caught a glimpse of my purpose.

Stop Your Negative
FOCUS

Have you noticed how we tend to hone in on the negative aspect of our lives, instead of the positive? That's a big reason why we don't experience more of the nurturing emotions that happiness provides. We focus on the day-to-day irritations and inconveniences, allowing these to color our whole outlook. Over a period of time this becomes a habit—we do it unconsciously. The news media doesn't help. They provide an overwhelming diet of negative events, from wars, murders, rapes and tragedies to family violence, kidnappings and all manner of disasters. Do you realize that 90 percent of all news is negative? Depressing!

Many people see life as one big burden. They obsess on everything that doesn't work, instead of focusing on what is good and on the possibilities to make it even better. Worry, guilt and resentment fuel this negative cycle. No wonder we find it so difficult to have more joy, happiness and contentment.

A happy person is not a person in a certain
set of circunstances, but rather a person
with a certain set of attitudes.

—Hugh Downs

I know how this feels. When I was growing up, life appeared to be a constant battle. I felt that I always had to have my dukes up, ready for the next fight. Optimism was not part of my thought process. I believed in Murphy's Law—something was bound to go wrong, and it usually did. I looked with skepticism at people who were positive thinkers. When things went their way I just thought they were lucky. Then slowly, with the positive influence of my husband, I started to realize that there was another way to live.

When I was faced with challenges, it was healthier to be optimistic and focus on solutions. In my old way of thinking I would crumble into automatic pessimism, blaming everyone and complaining about my circumstances. Gradually I made a conscious choice to be happier and to have a more positive outlook. This wasn't easy for me. It took a lot of mental discipline and awareness to change my perspective.

One reason we struggle to find happiness is due to our limiting beliefs. Does a part of you believe things are too good to be true? Do you ever say things like this:

- I just knew it wouldn't last.
- I always get the short end of the stick.
- I don't deserve to be happy.

One of my ah-ha moments came after realizing that deep down I believed that I needed to feel the pain of sacrifice and suffering first, before I deserved to be happy. The combination of a negative outlook and my limiting beliefs compounded my inability to be happy. It was personal sabotage. Pause for a moment and think about this question. Do you tend to focus on the negative aspects of life? Do you deserve to be happy?

Develop your optimism muscle. Optimists look at the world and see the same things that pessimists see, yet their response is quite different. The optimist admires the beautiful mountain scenery through her kitchen window, while the pessimist sees the dirty fingerprints on the glass. The optimist looks at the possibilities in a project, while the pessimist announces all the ways it is doomed to fail.

To become happier, the pessimist needs to root out self-defeating patterns. This requires more than positive thinking. Well-worn phrases such as "All will be well," or "Don't worry, be happy," are not enough. Let me emphasize from my own personal experience that it's not easy to change your mode of thinking. It takes commitment and a new attitude. Pessimism is a bad habit, and bad habits die hard. As we've seen, some of the most difficult habits to eliminate are worry, guilt and resentment. If left unchallenged, they will produce a negative downward spiral.

Another bad habit to refrain from is blaming and complaining. Pessimists do a lot of this. It's pointless, because when you focus on whatever is bothering you, the negative energy expands. Blaming and complaining just make it worse. Nobody likes to be around a whiner. Some people have become so practiced at this that they do it unconsciously. When someone pushes one of their buttons, it's like starting up a little whining motor —they go into overdrive. Do you know someone like this?

Become more aware of when you are blaming and com-plaining, and focus on finding constructive solutions instead. By doing so you are taking responsibility for the situation, instead of griping about it.

> Women who feel they have control
> over their lives are more likely to be optimistic,
> and are usually happier.

When you feel your choices are limited because of job restrictions, or you are compelled to report to others at work, your sense of control is diminished. One of the reasons so many women are starting their own businesses is because they want the independence of making their own decisions. Despite the start-up uncertainty, they would rather take the risk than be required to answer to other people.

By taking responsibility for your life and having a proactive approach to challenges, you will become more confident and self-assured. Have you noticed that confident people tend to be happier? It's important to develop a solution-oriented mind. Give yourself the opportunity to turn problems and adversity into something meaningful. Every day, confront any pessimistic thoughts that arise.

I've found that putting things into perspective helps. When something pulls you down, step back and observe it from a much bigger stage. What does this one situation look like compared to your whole life picture? How important is it in the whole scheme of things? Even a critical turning point like a layoff at work, when viewed simply as a single event or a chapter in your life, can be compressed into a less significant role.

Laugh and
BE HAPPY

Have you noticed how serious most people are these days? The pessimists say our world is falling apart, and they complain that it's no laughing matter. Wonderful speaker and comedienne Loretta LaRoche has a different point of view. "We know suffering is part of living and we need help to endure it. Resiliency comes from understanding that there are always times when we can laugh, have fun and be grateful for what we have. We don't have to wait. Laughter is medicine for our souls. Just as we need food to sustain our body, we need laughter to soothe the soul."

Combat dogmatic thinking with a sense of humor. I'm talking about good healthy fun, not making snide comments that deride others. Laugh at your own foibles and let go of your rigidity. Lighten up. Find an excuse to laugh more often, it improves your mood. Go to a funny movie or watch a show that tickles your funny bone. Look for the humor in everyday life. Hanging around people who laugh a lot is infectious.

The older I get, the more I value a good laugh.
Nothing puts life into perspective more effectively
than seeing the absurdity in it!

—Loretta LaRoche

Our good friend Annette Goodheart, a psychotherapist, helps people who are stressed out to heal, simply by getting them to laugh. Her clients include CEOs and go-getters from all walks of life. One of the best demonstrations I have ever seen of the infectious nature of laughter occurred when Annette was introduced as the main speaker at a business conference. Three hundred people were packed into the room. She walked on stage holding a child's teddy bear and surveyed the expectant audience. For thirty seconds she didn't say a word. That's a long time on a platform!

Some people were getting impatient. Unfazed, Annette stood silent. A few moments later she let out a little giggle. This was followed by another, and then another. The giggles turned into a laugh, and her laughter intensified. Someone in the audience started giggling, then a few more. Pretty soon others were laughing along with Annette. In just over a minute she had the whole audience laughing their heads off, and she hadn't said a word!

We need to laugh. It's nourishing and it promotes better health. Laughter strengthens our immune system, and it can lift us out of emotional pain.

You can choose to be happy. Some people believe that happiness isn't a choice. They claim nobody deliberately decides to be unhappy; whatever happens is outside their control. I agree that bad things happen to people, but I disagree about having no choice. Consciously or unconsciously, we decide to be unhappy through our thoughts and our attitude. We may not stand up and announce, "Today I'm choosing to have a miserable day," but the fact is, if we are holding a grudge, resenting someone at work, being angry at our spouse or feeling over-whelmed with too many commitments, we may unconsciously be deciding to have a miserable day. We always have the choice to flip our mental switch from unconscious-reactive mode to conscious-choice mode. Remember the downward spiral? It's a funnel for negative energy. We are only aware of this when we consciously sense the shift in our bodies.

A five-year-old boy was seated beside his Dad in the car. Deep in thought, the man wore a serious expression. The little boy suddenly asked, "Dad, are you happy?"

His father replied, "Yes, of course I am."

"Then why don't you tell your face?"

Maintaining happiness is essentially a state of mind. Do everything you can each day to keep the state of your mind healthy. Why do we wait for tragedy, such as the loss of a loved one or serious illness, to occur before we realize that happiness is about living now, appreciating every moment, every hour and every day? It seems to be part of the human condition.

One of the many gifts I received after my scare with cancer was the gift of appreciation. My eyes were finally opened to the richness of my life. I felt truly blessed, and with a new sense of gratitude I joyfully began to cherish each and every day.

Often we are blind to the joy and happiness around us because we have not been taught or conditioned to see it. We rush through our busy days, yet all around us miracles are unfolding. To recognize and appreciate all of the blessings in our lives, we need to develop eyes that can see them. Cultivating an attitude of gratitude will have the greatest impact on your happiness.

Oprah Winfrey says it well: "I live in the space of thankfulness and I have been rewarded a million times over for it. I started out giving thanks for small things and the more thankful I became, the more my bounty increased. That's because what you focus on expands, and when you focus on the goodness in your life, you create more of it. Opportunities, relationships, even money flowed my way when I learned to be grateful no matter what happened in my life."

We can all learn to refocus on what is good about our lives. It takes effort to do this every day, especially when you experience a setback. A friend of ours had just finished writing his new book. While on a business trip his laptop was stolen from the hotel room. His manuscript was stored in the computer and he lost everything.

Imagine the pain and frustration he must have felt. He decided to rewrite the book and set an almost impossible timeframe to complete it. Happily he made his deadline and now says he was grateful for the loss because the second edition turned out better than the first.

"I can't wait to grow up and be happy."

Research has shown that people who describe themselves as having an attitude of gratefulness have a higher vitality and optimism for living. They are not as materialistic as others, so they suffer less anxiety about lifestyle and status. They describe themselves as happy and satisfied. Grateful people in general are more spiritually aware, and more likely to appreciate the value of others in their lives. Gratitude is the most transforming force in the world, because it's an expression of love. There is a positive shift emerging in the world today, with more people waking up to the fact that gratitude can make a huge difference to their quality of life and level of happiness.

> A mother invited some people to dinner. At the table, she turned to her six-year-old daughter and asked her to say the blessing.
>
> "I don't know what to say," the little girl replied.
>
> "Just say what you hear Mommy say."
>
> The daughter bowed her head. "Lord, why on earth did I invite all these people to dinner?"
>
> —Anonymous

Cultivating Gratitude

It's a good idea to start your day with a grateful heart. When we first awaken in the morning our minds are in a receptive state. This is an ideal time to implant something positive that will influence us throughout the day. As an example of this, have you ever heard a song on the radio first thing in the morning, and hummed it all day?

Think of three things you are grateful for. It may be the fact you have a great job, or that you love your wonderful spouse, or that the sunlight is streaming through the blinds. Think of three new things each morning. You will be amazed at how many things you can be grateful for. Uplift your heart, mind and spirit before you get out of bed.

End your day with gratitude too. No matter how bad your day was or how busy you were, make this a priority. It is especially important to do this if you had a tough day. Mentally shift your focus from the negativity of the day and look back to the good things that you may have missed. This will help clear away the negative cobwebs and let you regain perspective, so you can sleep more peacefully.

Give Positive
ACKNOWLEDGMENT

Acknowledgment is sharing your love with someone else. This not only gives you joy, it uplifts the other person. How do you feel when someone singles you out for a job well done? It feels good. What happens when you acknowledge a child? He or she lights up! Every human being has a need to feel validated and loved. Women on the home front often feel that they are taken for granted. Women in the workforce often do not get the recognition they deserve. Lower salaries are a sign of a lack of validation. Elderly people seek to be validated by a smile or even by just making eye contact. When we get hurt we need to be heard, we want someone to understand our pain—pain that usually comes from a lack of validation.

We forget how wonderful acknowledgment feels, and then we forget to acknowledge others.

When we acknowledge others and don't expect anything in return, they are touched. Their spirit is lifted for a while. This has a ripple effect, in that they often reach out and touch others as well. Are you familiar with the concept "pay it forward"? My friend Anne gave me a great example of this. She was standing in line waiting to pay for her coffee:

Anne was filled with gratitude and felt so lucky to be alive.
However, the woman behind her was visibly unhappy. Anne said, "She looked miserable and I was concerned. As I handed over my $5 to the cashier, I said, 'This is for my coffee and also for the woman behind me.' When the woman heard that, her face brightened with a beautiful smile. 'Thank you!' she said, 'And this is for the person behind me.' Soon others were smiling and laughing. For under a dollar I was able to share my gratitude and happiness by helping others begin their day with a smile."

SOMETIMES WITH ONLY SECONDS to respond we miss the opportunity to acknowledge someone. Become more spontaneous—act when you first get the feeling or thought. The longer you wait, the less chance there is of following through.

Start the wonderful practice of acknowledgement. Before you do, a word of caution: Giving acknowledgement to get something in return is manipulation (I want her friendship, I want their approval), so check your intentions. True acknowledgment is unconditional.

For years our family has used handwritten Post-it notes to acknowledge one another. When Les goes out of town he leaves a love note on my pillow, and I tuck one into his suitcase. Just before our daughter Jennifer walked down the aisle on her wedding day, she presented me with a beautiful poem she had written, *You Gave Me Wings To Fly*, and a lace handkerchief. Boy, did I need that hanky!

One morning Les had an important presentation to deliver for a high-profile new client. As he sat down to breakfast, sitting on his plate was a little note with the words, "Good luck with the presentation Dad. I'm so proud of you! Love, Andrew." Our kids latched on to the habit of writing positive notes at an early age and still do it now as adults.

Start doing this yourself. Tuck a few words of encouragement into your child's lunch bag; attach them to your staff's pay checks. There are a thousand different ways to acknowledge people. See how creative you can be and make it a habit to acknowledge at least one person every day. Acknowledgment and encouragement; there's nothing greater to someone who needs it.

Many women like the idea of writing in a gratitude journal. This is a formal way to record your gratitude. Judging from the phenomenal sales of the bestselling book, *Simple Abundance,* by Sarah Ban Breathnach, many people are catching on and capturing their blessings on paper. The concept is simple and need not take too much time. You write in your journal what you are grateful for and what blessings you noticed in your day. This helps reinforce your positive feelings. It is wonderful to revisit your journal later and see all the blessings you may have forgotten. Memories will come flooding back and you will experience the joy all over again.

I love this topic of gratitude. Here is another point to consider. It's easy to be grateful for all the wonderful gifts we have, but what about being thankful for adversity? Can you be grateful for pain and challenges, too? Character is built in times of adversity. We change and learn from life's painful lessons. Without pain, how could we know joy or happiness? It is only after the sting of the pain has gone that many of us can look back and see the gifts that were hidden in the challenge.

> *When passion and courage join forces,*
> *adversity cannot stop you.*

—Les Hewitt

A story on television one day touched my heart. A couple had lost their twenty-three-year-old daughter in a car accident. She was their only child. Shortly after her death they found her gratitude journal. Through reading it they realized that their daughter had been happy every day of her life and had loved every member of her family. What a wonderful gift, to read about the feelings she had for them. They decided to make bookmarks of gratitude based on the journal, and had given out more than 20,000 of them. They turned a painful situation into a marvelous blessing for others. Giving to others in your own time of pain is healing.

I am grateful for my fight with cancer. The experience was a nightmare at the time. It caused such pain and anguish for all my family, and in the midst of the fear I couldn't see anything good. But now I can look back and see the many blessings for which I am truly grateful.

Faith and Community

For many people happiness is directly related to their spiritual faith, and the feeling of being part of a tight-knit community. Every week churches around the world are filled with passionate believers who express great joy and emotion through song and worship. Having a strong faith builds hope; hope for things to be better tomorrow, hope for ourselves.

A sense of community revives our spirits and keeps us connected. It's amazing the projects that are conceived and achieved when like-minded people band together in the name of a cause. Oprah Winfrey's Angel Network enriches thousands of lives every year. Mother Teresa created a worldwide order that gave dignity to the terminally ill and shelter to the poorest of the poor.

Some religious communities like the Amish and Hutterites choose to live simple lives without the trappings of modern materialism. Research shows they are mostly happy. Curious tourists often visit these farms, many coming away marveling that the people living in these communities appear to be happier than they are. Happiness and excellent relationships go hand in hand. So does service. Do you participate in your community, and enjoy the simple pleasures of serving others? Do you need to make a spiritual connection, or revisit your roots?

Reignite Your
PASSION

Does your passion get you out of bed in the mornings, or is it just the fact that the bills need to be paid? We all need passion in our lives. I have met many women who have suspended their dreams and aspirations to accommodate everyone else. They do what they think they should be doing, what they think is needed and expected of them. There are certainly times in a woman's life when she may choose to sacrifice her dreams and ambitions, or put them on the back burner in order to raise a family or take care of an elderly parent. This might be practical and necessary at the time.

But how long do you wait? As a woman, it is easy to put your life on hold. Many women get to a point where they feel they are not living the life they imagined, or they believe that their life could be more. They put up with a job or a situation they do not enjoy, struggling through each week, dreading the thought of Monday. Many wait too long. They feel that when they lose track of their dreams it's too late to do anything. They tell themselves they're too old to go back to school or make a multitude of excuses why they can't step out of their routine. But mostly it is because they are fearful.

Rosita Perez is a dear friend, and one of the truly wise people I have met. She did not find her passion until she was almost forty, when her kids were still teenagers. It took Rosita a long time to realize that her gift was the ability to impact people with words.

The first step in her new career was to study and earn a degree in social work. Initially this was for practical reasons. Her husband, Ray, wanted her to have a means of support in case he died suddenly. The job involved a lot of paperwork.

This was not to her liking so she started talking more to the people in her care, listening to their pain. She used music to add variety, rearranging a few songs and playing guitar. This led to small presentations and Rosita knew she had found something significant.

It seemed like all the energy in the universe was being sent her way. She had no doubt this was being divinely directed. Rosita created a wonderful award-winning career that spanned more than twenty years, speaking to all types of audiences. Now sixty-seven, recently retired and battling multiple sclerosis, she took a few moments to reflect on happiness and relationships.

Her words carry a very important message for us all.
Rosita says, "Here's a question every woman should ask. 'If you knew you were going to die in a year, would you still be doing what you are doing now?' So many women have unique talents, but sadly they go to the grave with their music still locked inside them. And the world is a poorer place because of it. Don't wait that long.

As far as relationships are concerned, next to a strong connection with God, I have valued a marriage that has given me joy for forty-five years. Ray and I have had fun. Life is so busy for people today that they have largely forgotten what fun is.

If you feel jaded, think back to what used to be the greatest fun for you, and do it again. Do more of it, and laugh more. We get so entrenched in our obligations we become boring. Women focus on a lot of stuff that's not important. Only when you are focused on what is really meaningful to you, will anything significant come of it.

Unfortunately, we usually learn this when we are older. Wouldn't it be great to discover this when we were young? A lot of people would end up with fewer regrets. I think happiness is difficult to sustain. In fact I wouldn't want to be happy all of the time! My greatest lessons were learned when I was unhappy. Be careful though, because misery is sustainable. It can color everything you do.

Relationships are so important. At this stage of my life my grandkids give me such joy. I sit down and read to them, intently looking into their eyes—and they respond magnificently. Children are not appendages; they have so much to give, and yet reading the newspaper becomes more important in some households than reading to the kids. As far as marriage goes, Ray and I vowed on our honeymoon we would never go to bed angry. That has not always worked out, but no matter what is happening, either he or I will kiss the other on the cheek and say good night. Somehow that lets us both know that hope is still alive, and although we may feel like killing each other, getting a divorce, or just disappearing, everything will be okay in the morning.

With other relationships, sometimes it's important to let go. I discovered a newfound freedom when I stopped attempting to save others who did not want to be saved. Learn to express your true feelings about issues, even when others do not agree. Let go of guilt. It's okay to put yourself first now and again. Don't lose yourself along the way by being beholden to everyone else. I did not take time for myself until I was fifty! Another thing I've learned is that a perfect home, like you see in those glossy magazines, is not real life. Also, when you buy something really nice, use it and wear it! Don't save it for special occasions. If you have beautiful chinaware, enjoy it, don't lock it away in some display cabinet.

Regarding retirement, there are no guarantees these days. As a woman you should give this subject some thought. Plan wisely so that when your September Song comes it will be financially feasible for you to retire. Don't allow a sense of prosperity to seduce you, or you will work forever. Unless you want that—I did not.

All of these lessons have contributed greatly to my happiness and well-being. Lastly, stay young by being alert. My speaker friend Allen* gave me a lovely example of this: Every time Allen's mom, who is 92, goes to the doctor, she hires a van service to take her there and back. One late afternoon her ride home didn't show up. Since the doctor had to close the office, he suggested that she wait for the van in the pizza parlor downstairs. After waiting a long time, the van still hadn't shown up, so his Mom went up to the counter and asked, 'Do you deliver?' The man behind the counter replied, 'Of course we do, we're a pizza place.'

'Great,' his Mom said, 'I'd like a pepperoni pizza and I'd like to go with it.'

Isn't that great? I urge you to be passionate about life. Get involved; it will keep your mind forever young long after your body begs to differ."

You don't need an exciting or glamorous career, or to own your own business, to have passion for what you do. Passion comes from you. Work and relationships do not make you passionate, you do. Passion is like a flame inside that needs to be ignited. Some women are passionate about their work, even though most people wouldn't choose to do what they do. They are alive and happy doing it.

Frances worked in a busy cafeteria at the airport. I noticed her right away. She stood out from all the other employees mechanically doing their jobs. Frances was having a party. She laughed and smiled as she cleaned the tables and directed people to the buffet. She chatted to people as they sat down. I felt as if she had welcomed me into her home. I asked her what made her so cheerful. "I have the best job in the whole world. I get to visit with interesting people every day, and they pay me too," she chuckled.

* Allen Klein: http://www.allenklein.com

Women who live with passion savor life. They have a vibrancy and vitality for living, and they lead authentic lives. Ask yourself, what am I passionate about? If your answer is nothing, perhaps apathy and indifference have seeped into your life and it's time to do some spring cleaning. The passion is already inside you, all you need to do is light the fire. It's never too late. How can I convince you it's worth it, despite the fear and the risk? All I can tell you from my own experience, and that of many others, is just go for it. As our cookbook experts Greta and Janet demonstrated, feel the fear and do it anyway. Live a life of no regrets. Be happy so you can enjoy the fullness of who you are.

Don't underestimate yourself.

You are an amazing multi-talented woman, living a busy, complex life that demands an enormous assortment of skills. Respect the talents you have developed over your lifetime, from running a home and parenting children to going to work, organizing schedules and handling finances.

The chances are you already have everything you need to follow your dreams. A plan has already been placed deep in your heart; find it for yourself and reignite your passion for living. Just get started, move into action. A ship at sea can totally change course with only a two degree shift in direction—you, too, can change the outcome of your life by making a few simple adjustments.

No matter what circumstances you find yourself in right now, know one thing for sure: if you want, you can change what you don't like. You can start out on a new journey.

"That sounds wonderful, but it seems overwhelming," you may be saying. "How do I get started?" Here's a simple way to start. Do you remember Jana Stanfield's story at the end of Chapter Four, about how she turned her dream to be a singer-songwriter into reality? I promised I'd share her formula with you, so here it is.

Three Steps
NO FAILURE

Jana acknowledges her uncle, the Rev. Clyde Stanfield, a United Methodist minister and professional counselor, for teaching her this technique. Over a series of weekly lunches he expertly guided and monitored her progress. The great thing about Three Steps No Failure is that you don't need to know exactly where you are going for its magic to work. It's like crossing a bridge; you don't need to see the other side yet. You just look at the first three steps. Those will move you forward enough that you'll be able to see the next three steps. Here's your first assignment:

- Make a list of three things you can do in a week
  that will take you closer to where you want to be.

There is only one guideline for choosing the steps. Each step has to be something you can't possibly fail to complete in a week's time. With each step you build confidence. Just like Jana discovered, you'll soon start believing that you have the ability to make your dreams come true, if you just take it one easy step at a time. Focus on your progress every week, not on the final goal.

If you ask what I came to do in this world
I am here to live out loud.

—Emile Zola

After you start this process you will begin to understand that none of the three steps need to be the perfect thing that makes it all happen. Each step is simply crossing your bridge. Not every step will produce a miracle. Some of your steps will feel like your feet are stuck in mud! However just keep pushing forward, making plodding progress. If you stay focused, a year from now you will be in awe of everything you have accomplished. Get started—and good luck!

Some people have an inner drive to succeed.

Canadian speed skater Catriona LeMay Doan is one of them. From an early age she wanted to be the best. By her own admission she is competitive, stubborn, and a constructive perfectionist. All of these qualities helped her reach the top of her chosen profession of speed skating—an Olympic champion with two gold medals and one bronze, twelve world championship victories, and the world record holder in the 500-meter competition. An impressive career by any standards. When asked how she had managed to become number one in the world, she responded: "I just put my mind to it and focused. I was inspired by other athletes who had won at the Olympics. Nobody pushed me, they knew better! I do my own thing, and I do it 100 percent. I like the feeling of getting better at something, so I'll do whatever it takes. After every race, the first thing I do is reflect on what I could have improved. I can celebrate later.

It's very important to have a great support team; my parents, my husband and all of the coaches. My faith is also a strong foundation for me. To reach the top at anything in life requires drive, intensity and belief in yourself. Confidence was something I had to work on. To focus better, I use certain words at different stages of the race. Just before the starting gun goes off it's, 'Go-powerful!' Coming off the last bend it's, 'Aggressive-power!'

When you have big goals, life is very challenging. Its okay to admit it's hard, instead of denying the reality. My advice to other women is, be proud at the end of every day knowing that you did your best, even if you didn't accomplish everything."

Success or
SIGNIFICANCE

Which is more important to you, success at work or significance in what you do? To me, significance is more important. Success rewards my bank account, but having significant, meaningful work rewards my spirit. I know as I serve others, doing work that I love, that success will follow. You have heard this phrase before, "Do what you love and the money will follow." It's true.

One of the secrets to living a fulfilled life is shifting your focus from acquiring material success to being of service to others. There are many opportunities to do this as a teacher, mother, doctor, entrepreneur, cafeteria worker; you name it. Martin Luther King Jr. said, "Everybody can be great, because anybody can serve. You don't need a college degree to serve. You don't have to know about Plato and Aristotle or Einstein's Theory of Relativity to serve. You only need a heart full of grace and a soul generated by love."

Enjoying a significant, successful life will have you bounding out of bed in the morning excited about going to work. This is work you love and are passionate about. it's capacity is much greater than you are. As you step out in faith, you have the confidence of knowing it will never be more than you can handle.

Life will test your capacity.
"After my breast cancer surgery I was given five years to live. That's if I was lucky. Then I would die. I was thirty-three and I couldn't handle the uncertainty and fear of what was to come. I had never been more afraid. My mother stepped in, so the day-to-day household duties were in her capable hands.

The children were happy to see me come home from the hospital. They were six and three at the time. Everything looked normal to them, but how could anything ever be normal again? Would I ever be able to have fun with my kids again? Or would I hold onto them too tightly and never want to let go? Would I ever again feel the freedom of doing ordinary chores without my every thought being focused on my fear?

My mother took one look at me and told me to go for a rest. I lay down on my bed longing for the oblivion of sleep. But my body shook uncontrollably. I was frozen in fear. It had overwhelmed me. I felt like I was alone in a dark pit, there was no way out, nothing to hold on to, no light to guide my way. I was going to die. The reality hit me—I wasn't going to see my children grow up. I would be saying good-bye to everyone I loved.

My anguished voice pleaded, "God help me." In my torture I cried out again, "Take me now! I cannot bear another minute, I'm so afraid." My heart exploded with pain, and tears soaked my pillow. My whole body shook with fear.

Then it happened.

I felt warmth on my feet. It spread slowly up the length of my entire body, as if someone was pulling a warm blanket over me. My eyes were closed but I knew there was no one else in the room.

An incredible feeling of peace and love permeated me. My shaking stopped. I thought if I opened my eyes I would see a vision beside me. But I was alone. Whatever had happened was not of a physical nature. I am absolutely certain of this. What I had experienced was divine intervention."

THERE ARE PEOPLE OF INCREDIBLE FAITH who believe without needing proof. Perhaps God figured the only way to get the attention of a thick-headed Irish woman was with nothing less than a miracle! That was seventeen years ago. My life *is* a miracle.

Like many others in similar circumstances my illness started me on an amazing journey of healing and seeking answers. One of the people I met along this path was a counselor named Marion Gerries. Marion taught me the importance of having a positive outlook on the future. She asked me to use my imagination to create two pictures. The first was to represent my fears, and the second to represent my future.

In the first picture, I visualized my worst fears in black and white. My cancer had come back. I was lying in a bed, wasted and frail, saying goodbye to my loved ones. Marion had me imagine the picture dissolving and in its place I visualized my future. I was shocked how fast the new picture flashed into my mind. Like a movie production, it was in full color and sound. I was standing in front of a group of women. We were all laughing at something and having fun. I was dressed in a red suit, either teaching a seminar or facilitating a workshop. I felt so great. I was happy at what I was doing.

I didn't know it then, but what I had just visualized would become the purpose for my life. Deep inside, a part of me always knew what my destiny was. But it would be many years before I would recall that picture again. A couple of years later I did get another sign that I was on the right path when I experienced my holy moment. Remember the time I was standing outside in the sunshine after teaching a group of young mothers? This was a confirmation for me, the pure joy of aligning my gifts with what my spirit wanted me to do.

It took two careers and eleven years before I finally actualized the picture I had visualized. Those years were not wasted, they were grooming me for what lay ahead. Finally I tapped into that well of joy again, and I have enjoyed many holy moments since.

YOUR SPIRIT ALREADY KNOWS YOUR PURPOSE AND WANTS YOU TO FULFILL IT

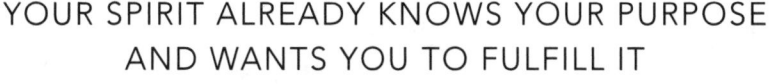

Have you considered what your purpose might be? It is your legacy, the calling of your life, and ultimately why you are here on earth. Take the blueprint of who you are, with your gifts, unique talents and personality, and align them with the passion of your spirit. This is the foundation for your purpose.

Don't panic if you have not yet found the calling for your life. Perhaps you are not ready yet. Either the timing is not right or you have been distracted with other things. Rest assured that a plan is unfolding for your life—you just need to seek it and it will find you.

"How do I find my purpose?" is a question I am often asked. Here's what worked for me. Do you know when the water on a lake is perfectly calm and you can see clearly to the bottom? You need to find that type of clarity within you. Find quietness for yourself. Commit some time for reflection and meditation. This is essential if you are seeking clarity in any area of your life, and more so if you are seeking purpose. Finding your purpose is about seeking your spirit. Pray, and ask for guidance.

Remember the time I prayed when I so was depressed at work? The answer that came to me during that quiet time was, "Call Marie!" Working with Marie gave me the confidence to follow my passion and purpose.

Pay attention. Listen to your intuition and your faith. Your spirit already knows your purpose, and wants you to fulfill it. Watch for coincidences—those phone calls out of nowhere. Journal the answers to these questions: What am I most passionate about? How do I want to be remembered? What legacy do I want to leave behind? Consider writing your own eulogy to clarify your thinking even more. What do you want your friends and family to say about you when you are gone?

Sometimes through the dark nights of our soul we start seeking and sometimes we are inspired at just the right time. I was attending a workshop at Santa Barbara University facilitated by Jack Canfield, the co-creator of the *Chicken Soup for the Soul* series. One of the assignments was to do a five minute, video-taped presentation in front of my peers. A panel of experienced judges was there to critique our performances. I received a standing ovation that brought me to tears, but it was the right words at the right time that had a life-changing impact on me. Barry Spilchuk, one of the judges, took me aside and said to me, "Angels are sent to do God's work on earth, and you, Fran, have been sent to do the hard work."

That was it. Those simple words unlocked what I had kept deep inside. Those words unlocked my courage and passion. Those words were my impetus, my freedom to explore what I had known all along. It was like the heavenly forces got behind me and pushed me through every obstacle in my path. I was driven, my creativity was heightened, and I was never happier.

I will always remember my first workshop.
After a year of study and preparation I was ready to start, and I was petrified. The night before the start of the program I went to bed early, so I would be fresh and ready to go the next morning. Sleep evaded me. Finally, at 2 am in desperation I took half a sleeping pill. My alarm woke me at 5:30 am. I felt terrible. The fear in my gut and the remains of my sedation made me feel nervous and unfocused. I then made the mistake of gulping down two strong cups of coffee. Now I was like a volcano ready to explode. However, when I finally stood in front of my first group it felt like deja-vu. Here I was in my picture, only this time it was for real.

I don't know how I made it through that first day, but I did. I had decided beforehand that no matter what happened, nothing was going to stop me. As I think back I applaud my courage and faith, for facing my fear and doing it anyway.

I had finally come home.

IF AN IRISH GIRL wracked with low self-esteem and uncertain about reaching the age of forty can do it, there's hope for everyone else out there. Including you. I encourage you to find your heart's desire, find your calling in life. There is a well of passion deep inside you, waiting for you to tap into it. Have faith that you already have what you need to move forward; your spirit will guide you when it is the right time.

A Man's Perspective Les Hewitt

Last Valentine's Day I received a card from my beautiful wife. On the front it said, "I thought you should know that if you lost your job and were flat broke, I'd still love you!" Very touching, I thought. Then I opened the card and read, "I'd miss you, but I'd still love you! Happy Valentine's Day."

To me, humor is an important part of life. (I *think* Fran was joking!) Often the business world is devoid of laughter. Urgent deadlines, boardroom meetings, quarterly results and focusing on the bottom line uses up most of our energy. If you notice the man in your life becoming too serious, see if you can induce some laughter. Rent a funny movie, pull some humor from the internet, or share a personal experience. I know it's helped me in the past.

Also, writing those little handwritten notes of love and encouragement will score big points with us every time. I treasure those more than anything, especially when I'm on the road. I don't throw them away either. If I'm having a particularly tough day, I'll read those notes again; it always brings a smile to my face. Happiness is often found in unique moments when it is least expected. Be creative. And encourage your man to do the same for you.

CONCLUSION

Why not live life to the full measure of who you are?

Like Catriona and Patricia, you too can find purpose and happiness. It's never too late to start. Use pictures, like Glenna does, to clarify what you want. As Rosita says, find the music that is inside you no matter what form it takes. Perhaps your music is work-related, maybe it is raising a family, volunteering or pursuing a hobby. Whatever your passion is, do it purposefully with love and enthusiasm. Let your spirit guide you and happiness will follow. Embrace these concepts gratefully every day. Unwrap the gift of who you are, and give yourself away.

Everyone has been made for some particular
work, and the desire for that work has
been put in every heart.

—Rumi

ACTION STEPS

Find True Happiness

Focus On What You Want

Live On Purpose

These Action Steps are in the form of twenty life-changing questions. Give them the time they deserve. Your answers can be a springboard to a new way of life, one filled with clarity, purpose and unlimited joy.

1. What do you do best and love doing the most?

2. What did you like to do as a child?

3. What do you really want, and why?

4. What would you do if money was not a concern?

5. What one thing do you dream about doing that you've never told anyone about?

6. Who is successfully doing something you would love to do? (Ask that person how they did it.)

7. Is the environment you are currently in allowing you to fully express what you do best? (If not, figure out three ways you can improve it.)

8. Do you deserve to be happy? (If unsure, check any negative belief systems and their source)

9. What makes you unhappy?

10. What makes you happy?

11. Who makes you feel unhappy?

12. Who makes you feel happy?

13. What do you need more of that will give you joy and a sense of fulfillment?

14. What do you want to let go of that is no longer acceptable?

15. As a woman, what do you value most that you will not be persuaded to give up?

16. What is the main purpose of your life?

17. What would you do if you knew you couldn't fail?

18. What gives you the most satisfaction?

19. As you consider the future, are you willing to become all you can be? (If you said no, what's holding you back? Be careful to separate practical realities from excuses!)

20. If your life was ending shortly, what would you regret not having done?

*Now use the Three Steps No Failure
technique to start living the life
you really want.*

FINAL WORDS

May the road rise to meet you
May the wind be always be at your back
May the sun shine warm on your face
The rains fall soft upon your fields
And until we meet again...
May God hold you safely in the
palm of His hand.

—Irish Blessing*

Our journey together has come to an end. But is this the end for you, or a new beginning? As you close this book, consider your future. What is your next step? Simply hoping that change will come, merely wishing for something different, isn't good enough. To make change happen, you need clarity, commitment and focused action.

Life can be easily squandered just going through the motions of everyday living, but it has the potential to be much, much more. If you decide to pursue the life you really want, make this book your reference guide. If you haven't already done so, complete the Action Steps at the end of each chapter, starting with the chapters that were most meaningful to you. This will help clarify what you want, what you'd like to change, and where you want to go from here.

This project took commitment and focus on my part. There were times when I felt deep emotion as I wrote about my journey, and there were many times this assignment required a lot more than I wanted to give. It would have been easier to quit and crawl back under my security blanket, that comfort zone which stops me from stretching and taking risks.

Gratefully, my spirit wouldn't let me. Everything you want takes effort. Fulfilling your dreams, enriching your family life, healing relationships. Give up the illusion that life should be comfortable. The truth is, life is difficult. To overcome its challenges you must exercise and strengthen those muscles that produce tenacity, passion and persistence.

Be careful what you pursue or you may end up controlled by your lifestyle, buried under an avalanche of debt. It's much better to live a balanced life, a life based on your most important values. This is the secret to experiencing joy and meaning in every day. Be gentle with yourself. Vanquish the critical voice of judgment. Accept all of who you are with love and compassion, so you can love others too. Recall the child you used to be—she too deserves love and acceptance. Be playful. Remove your masks, liberate the authentic you, and you will feel powerful.

Set personal boundaries that teach people how to treat you with respect and the love you deserve. Start reclaiming your life—learn to say no. This skill takes time and persistence, so be patient. Move forward, measure your progress and keep your gaze fixed firmly on the next three steps.

You cannot move forward if you're always looking back. Unchain yourself from past issues and heal what is broken. For the sake of your health and your relationships, release any anger you have been holding inside. Learn to forgive.

I pray for blessings and holy moments for you as you begin the next chapter of your life. Use the power of focus to become the best you can be, one day at a time. Move forward on your journey with courage and faith.

Above all, start living the life you really want, and in doing so, give the world an incredible gift—the gift of you!

Fran

The Power of Focus for Women
— Workshop —

Experience the Joy of Living
by Design, not by Default

THE POWER OF FOCUS FOR WOMEN program is a highly interactive three-day workshop that will help you implement the strategies you've learned in this book. The group size is small, the environment stimulating and supportive. All participants receive a comprehensive workbook of exercises and practical tools that will anchor the learning long after the program is over.

If you are looking for a breakthrough in your life, are ready to set new boundaries, and want to release yourself from the obstacles of the past, this program will help you do it. And if you want to make the changes you only dare dream about, this unique experience will open your eyes, open your mind and open your heart to make it happen.

"A powerful program that inspired me to let go of my self-sabotaging behaviors. Definitely one of the most rewarding and enlightening gifts I have treated myself to in a long time."

—Marie Wallace, President, Wallace Design and Space Planning Inc.

For more information, call: Toll Free 877-678-0234
E-mail: info@achievers.com
www.achievers.com

Call Today for your FREE copy of The Double Spiral,™ a unique process that will dramatically enrich your most important relationships.
Toll Free 877-678-0234

RESOURCE GUIDE

The following is a list of recommended books, CDs, courses, music and nutritional information that will enhance the eight focusing strategies we have outlined. The references mentioned in *The Power of Focus for Women* are included. (*see asterisks*)

RECOMMENDED READING

Awaken The Giant Within by Anthony Robbins. New York, New York: Summit Books, 1991.

Boundaries: When To Say Yes; When To Say No; To Take Control Of Your Life by Dr. Henry Cloud and Dr. John Townsend. Grand Rapids, Michigan: Zondervan Publishing House, 1992.

Celebrate Your Self: Enhancing Your Own Self-Esteem by Dorothy Corkille Briggs. New York, New York: Doubleday, 1977.

Chicken Soup For The Woman's Soul by Jack Canfield, Mark Victor Hansen, Jennifer Read Hawthorne and Marci Shimoff. Deerfield Beach, Florida: Health Communications, Inc., 1999.

Claiming Your Self-Esteem by Carolyn M. Ball, M.A. Berkley, California: Celestial Arts Publishing, 1990.

Diamonds, Pearls And Stones: Jewels Of Wisdom For Young Women From Extraordinary Women Of The World by Jennifer Read Hawthorne and Barbara Warren Holden. Deerfield Beach, Florida: Health Communications, Inc., 2004.

Emotional Intelligence by Daniel Goleman. New York, New York: Bantam Books, 1995.

Feel The Fear And Do It Anyway by Susan Jeffers, Ph.D. New York, New York: Ballantine Books, 1987.

Feeling Good: The New Mood Therapy by David D. Burns, M.D. New York, New York: Avon Books, 1980.

Follow Your Heart: Finding Purpose In Your Life And Work by Andrew Matthews. New York, New York: Price Stern Sloan, Inc., 1997.

Getting The Love You Want: A Guide For Couples by Harville Hendrix, Ph.D. New York, New York: Henry Holt and Company, 1988.

Glad To Be Me: Building Self-Esteem In Yourself And Others by Dov P. Elkins. New York, New York: Prentice-Hall, 1976.

Guilt Is The Teacher, Love Is The Lesson by Joan Borysenko, Ph.D. New York, New York: Warner Books, 1990.

Healing The Child Within by Charles L. Whitfield, M.D. Deerfield Beach, Florida: Health Communications, Inc., 1987.

Healing The Shame That Binds You by John Bradshaw. Deerfield Beach, Florida: Health Communications, Inc., 1988.

Here I Am: Finding Oneself Through Healing & Letting Go by Mark Linden O'Meara. Blaine, Washington: Soul Care Publishing, 1997.

How To Raise Your Self-Esteem by Nathaniel Branden. New York, New York: Bantam Books, 1987.

*Laughter Therapy: How To Laugh About Everything In Your Life That Isn't Really Funny by Annette Goodheart, Ph.D. Los Angeles, California: Andrew J. Lesser, 1994.

*Life Is Not A Stress Rehearsal by Loretta LaRoche. New York, New York: Broadway Books, 2001.

Make It So You Don't Have To Fake It! by Patricia Fripp. Mechanicsburg, Pennsylvania: Executive Books, 2000.

"No" Is A Complete Sentence by Megan LeBoutillier, New York, New York: Ballantine Books, 1995.

Relationship Rescue by Phillip C. McGraw, Ph.D. New York, New York: Hyperion, 2000.

Seeds Of Greatness by Denis E. Waitley. New York, New York: Pocket Books, 1983.

*Self Matters by Phillip C. McGraw, Ph.D. New York, New York: Simon & Schuster Source, 2001.

*Simple Abundance by Sarah Ban Breathnach. New York, New York: Warner Books, 2000.

Simple Living In A Complex World by David Irvine. Calgary, Alberta: Red Stone Ventures, 1997.

Stand Up For Your Life by Cheryl Richardson. New York, New York: Fireside Publishing, 2003.

Take The Step: The Bridge Will Be There by Grace Cirocco. Toronto, Ontario: Harper Collins, 2001.

*The Art Of The Fresh Start by Glenna Salsbury. Deerfield Beach, Florida: Health Communications Inc., 1995.

*The Confidence Factor by Dr. Judith Briles. New York, New York: Master Media Limited, 1990.

The Dark Side Of The Light Chasers by Debbie Ford. New York, New York: Riverhead Books, 1998.

The Five Love Languages: How To Express Heartfelt Commitment To Your Mate by Gary Chapman. Chicago, Illinois: Northfield Publishing, 1992, 1995.

The Men We Never Knew: How To Deepen Your Relationship With The Man You Love by Daphne Rose Kingma. Emeryville, California: Conari Press, 1993.

The Music Is You: A Guide To Thinking Less And Feeling More by Rosita Perez. Granville, Ohio: Trudy Knox Publisher, 1994.

The One Minute Millionaire by Mark Victor Hansen and Robert G. Allen. Harmony Books, a Division of Random House, 2002.

The Seven Habits Of Highly Effective People by Stephen R. Covey. New York, New York: Simon & Schuster, 1989.

Twelve Powers In You by David Williamson, D.Min., Gay Lynn Williamson, M.A. Psy. and Robert H. Knapp, M.D. Deerfield Beach, Florida: Health Communications, Inc., 2000.

Unstoppable: 45 Powerful Stories Of Perseverance And Triumph From People Just Like You by Cynthia Kersey. Naperville, Illinois: Sourcebooks Trade, 1998.

Upsize Woman In A Downsize World by Deborah Lynn Darling. Garrettsville, Ohio: Radiance Publishing, 1998.

Wake Up, It's Later Than You Think by Carole Collins and Carolyn Christison. Canada: Self Published, 2002.

What Ever Happened To The Real Me? by Neva Coyle. Ann Arbor, Michigan: Servant Publications, 1999.

Work For A Living And Still Be Free To Live by Eileen McDargh. New York, New York: Time Books, A Division Of Random House, 1985.

Why Am I Afraid To Tell You Who I Am? by John Powell, S.J. Valencia, California: Tabor Publishing, 1969.

FINANCIAL BOOKS

10 Smart Money Moves For Women: How To Conquer Your Financial Fears by Dr. Judith Briles. New York, New York: McGraw-Hill, 1999.

Rich Dad, Poor Dad by Robert Kiyosaki with Sharon L. Lechter. Paradise Valley, Arizona: Tech Press Inc., 1997.

The 9 Steps To Financial Freedom by Suze Orman. New York, New York: Random House, 1998.

The Richest Man In Babylon by George S. Clason. New York, New York: Penguin Books, 1998.

The Wealthy Barber by David Chilton. Don Mills, Ontario: Stoddart Publishing, 1989.

AUTOBIOGRAPHY/BIOGRAPHY

Going For Gold: The Struggles And Success Of The Fastest Woman In The World by Catriona LeMay Doan. Toronto, Ontario: McClelland and Stewart Ltd., 2003.

POETRY

For The Mystically Inclined by Charles C. Finn. www.poetrybycharlescfinn.com

HEALTH AND NUTRITION

*Crazy Plates: Low Fat Food So Good, You'll Swear It's Bad For You! by Greta and Janet Podleski. Waterloo, Ontario: Granet Publishing Inc., 1999.

Fit From Within: 101 Simple Secrets To Change Your Body And Your Life —Starting Today And Lasting Forever by Victoria Moran. New York, New York: McGraw-Hill, 2003.

Fit From Within by Victoria Moran. New York, New York: McGraw-Hill, 2003.

*Live It! Lifestyle Coaching by Laura Simonson. Phone: 403-701-1088. Website: www.liveitlean.com.

*Looney Spoons: Low Fat Foods Made Fun by Greta and Janet Podleski. Waterloo, Ontario: Granet Publishing Inc., 1999.

WEBSITES ON HEALTH AND NUTRITION

www.bionutrition.org - Dr. Ray Strand - Author of two bestselling books, most recent *What Your Doctor Does Not Know About Nutritional Medicine May Be Killing You.*

www.colganinstitute.com - Michael Colgan Ph.D. - Bestselling author *The New Nutrition; Optimum Sports Nutrition; The Power Program; Prevent Cancer Now.*

www.comparativeguide.com - How to choose a quality supplement.

www.deniswaitley.com - World-renowned speaker and trainer Dr. Denis Waitley - author, *The Ultimate Fitness And Wellness System* (audio).

www.drnorthrup.com - Dr. Christiane Northrup - Renowned physician and author of *Women's Bodies, Women's Wisdom* and *The Wisdom Of Menopause.*

www.hsph.harvard.edu/nutritionsource/pyramids.html

www.drweil.com - Dr. Andrew Weil - Renowned physician and author *Spontaneous Healing* and *Eight Weeks To Optimum Health.*

www.humannutrition.com - Dr. Laz Bannock - UK renowned Ph.D.

www.kidseatgreat.com - Dr. Christine Wood - Author *How To Get Your Kids To Eat Great And Love It!*

www.laddmcnamara.com - Dr. Ladd McNamara - Specialist in women's hormonal health.

www.paulzanepilzer.com - Paul Zane Pilzer - Author, *The Wellness Revolution.*

www.phpi.ca - Personal Health Planning Institute - Complete preventative screening and testing.

AUDIOTAPES

How To Design And Deliver A Charismatic, Life-Changing Sermon by Patricia Fripp. San Francisco, California. 800-634-3035.

Let's Talk...About Money by Barry Spilchuk and Paul Barton. North Bay, Ontario. 705-497-5940.

Let's Talk...About Relationships by Barry Spilchuk. North Bay, Ontario. 705-497-5940.

Self-Esteem and Peak Performance by Jack Canfield, Boulder, Colorado: Career Track Publications and Fred Pryor Seminars, 1995, 800-237-8336.

The Art Of Exceptional Living by Jim Rohn, Dallas, Texas. 800-929-0434.

POSITIVE MUSIC - CDs

Brave Faith (2 CD Set) by Jana Stanfield.
   Ph: 880-530-5262. www.janastanfield.com

If You Can't Fly by David Roth.
   Ph: 877-365-5372. www.folkera.com/windriver.

In A Moment by Ken Johnston.
   Ph: 530-432-8559.www.heartsoundmusic.com.

Let The Changes Begin (2 CD Set) by Jana Stanfield.
   Ph: 880-530-5262. www.janastanfield.com

Nights At The Chez by David Roth.
   Ph: 877-365-5372. www.folkera.com/windriver.

ORGANIZING

Smart Works! Professional Organizing Solutions by Georgina Forrest.
smartworks@shaw.ca

COURSES

The Achievers Coaching Program by Les Hewitt.
The purpose of this two-year program is to help businesspeople focus on
their strengths so they can maximize their productivity and income while
enjoying an excellent balance between work and family.

Head Office - Canada
Toll Free 877-678-0234
 403-295-0500

USA	Australia
913-498-0164	61-3-9866-5820
United Kingdom	New Zealand
44-7710-881-005	64-3-214-2415

Republic of Ireland
353-65-684-0077

Email: info@achievers.com www.achievers.com.

The Power of Focus for Women Program by Fran Hewitt.
This is a three-day interactive workshop exclusively for women. Conducted
in groups of 15–20 people, the program is tailored to women who want to
experience the joy of living by design instead of by default.

Toll Free 877-678-0234 Canada 403-295-0500.
Email: info@achievers.com www.achievers.com.

PERMISSIONS

We would like to acknowledge these publishers and individuals for permission to reprint the following material.

Anna Jarmics story. Reprinted by permission of Anna Jarmics. © 2003 Anna Jarmics.

Annette Stanwick story. Reprinted by permission of Annette Stanwick. © 2003 Annette Stanwick.

Catriona LeMay Doan story. Reprinted by permission of Catriona LeMay Doan. (c) 2003 Catriona LeMay Doan.

Glenna Salsbury story. Reprinted by permission of Glenna Salsbury. © 2003 Glenna Salsbury.

Jackie Winter story. Reprinted by permission of Jackie Winter. © 2003 Jackie Winter.

Jana Stanfield story. Reprinted by permission of Jana Stanfield. © 2003 Jana Stanfield.

Laura Simonson article. Reprinted by permission of Laura Simonson. © 2003 Laura Simonson.

Patricia Fripp story. Reprinted by permission of Patricia Fripp. © 2003, Patricia Fripp.

Piers Steel article. Reprinted by permission of Christine Johnston. © 2003 Christine Johnston, Maclean's Magazine.

Please Hear What I'm Not Saying excerpt. Reprinted by permission of Charles C. Finn. © 1966, Charles C. Finn.

The Workaholic story. Reprinted by permission of Marie Bliss. © 2003, Marie Bliss.

The Total Truth letter. Reprinted by permission of Jack Canfield. © 2001, Self-Esteem Seminars.

Three Steps No Failure technique. Reprinted by permission of Jana Stanfield. © 2003, Jana Stanfield.

Tips For The Home checklist. Reprinted by permission of Georgina Forrest. © 2003 Georgina Forrest.

ABOUT THE AUTHORS

Fran Hewitt is an international workshop facilitator and speaker who specializes in women's issues. She has invested 25 years into personal development training including more than 500 workshops and seminars.

Fran is the creator and founder of The Inner Circle program, a powerful three-day self-awareness experience designed for women from all walks of life. Fran is a dynamic speaker and challenging facilitator who tells it like it is, and connects with people at a heart level. Her most important values include family, faith, balance, quiet time and meaningful work.

To book speaking engagements and for more information about *The Power of Focus for Women* workshop:

toll free: 877-678-0234 / ph: 403-295-0500 / fax: 403-239-4393
website www.achievers.com / email info@achievers.com

Les Hewitt, originally from Northern Ireland, is one of the top performance coaches in North America, and the co-author and driving force behind the international bestseller, *The Power of Focus*.

He is the founder of the highly successful Achievers Coaching Program currently operating in the United States, Canada, United Kingdom, Republic of Ireland, Australia and New Zealand.

This unique two-year process has been the catalyst for many of his clients' remarkable transformations. Since its inception in 1983, Achievers has conducted training programs for thousands of businesspeople from a wide variety of industries.

Les is a dynamic speaker, business coach, sales trainer, writer and entrepreneur. For the past twenty-five years he has personally coached hundreds of entrepreneurs to achieve exceptional profits and productivity.

To contact Les, or obtain information about The Achievers Coaching Program, licensing partnership opportunities, speeches, seminars and workshops based on *The Power of Focus,* plus additional Achievers' products and services, write or call:

Achievers Canada
5160 Skyline Way NE
Calgary, AB T2E 6V1

toll free: 877-678-0234 / ph: 403-295-0500 / fax: 403-730-4548
website: www.achievers.com / email: info@achievers.com